CERAMICS

Ways of Creation

AN EXPLORATION OF
36 CONTEMPORARY CERAMIC ARTISTS
& THEIR WORK

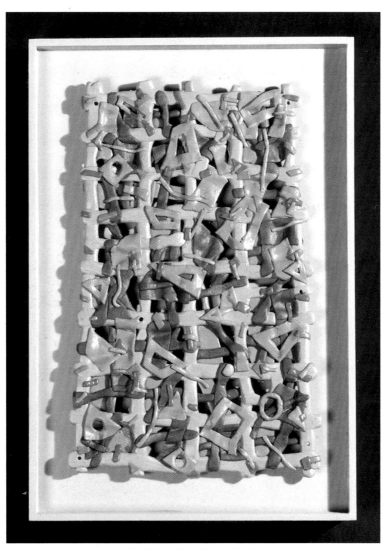

Wall Panel by Richard Zakin

RICHARD ZAKIN

Krause Publications

700 East State St., Iola, WI 54990-0001
Telephone (715) 445-2214
www.krause.com

Please call or write for our free catalog of publications. Our toll-free number to place an order or obtain a free catalog is 800-258-0929 or please use our regular business telephone 715-445-2214 for editorial comment and further information.

Printed in the United States of America

Library of Congress Catalog Number: 99-61448

ISBN: 0-87341-610-4

Front cover photo: **Ruffle Vase** by Sandi Pierantozzi
Back cover photos: top left, **If You Cracked Open a Football While Sleeping** by Aurore Chabot; top right, **Marie's Madonna** by Andrea Gill; bottom right, **Cloud Bank Bay** by Wayne Higby

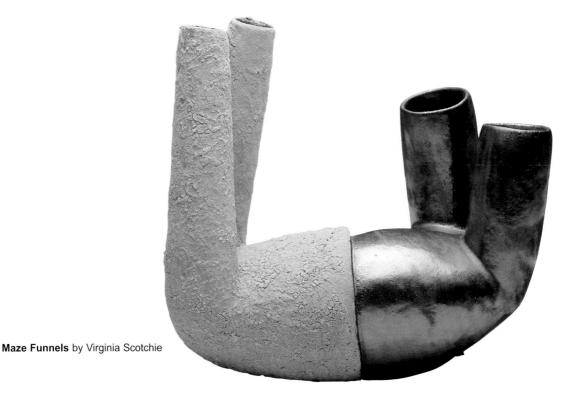

Maze Funnels by Virginia Scotchie

Table of Contents

Chapter 1: Expression - 6
    Ric Hirsch - **7**
    John Gill - **13**
    Roy Strassberg - **21**
    Rimas VisGirda - **27**
    JoAnn Schnabel - **34**
    John Chalke - **41**
    Louis Katz - **48**
    Richard Notkin - **55**
    Victor Spinski - **61**

Chapter 2: A Sense of Order - 68
    Andrea Gill - **69**
    David MacDonald - **77**
    Harris Deller - **84**
    Bruce Cochrane - **91**
    Greg Pitts - **98**
    Wayne Higby - **105**
    Sandi Pierantozzi - **113**
    Neil Patterson - **120**
    Ron Roy - **126**
    Ewa Kwong - **133**

Chapter 3: Idea and Object - 141
    Linda Huey - **142**
    Jim Lawton - **150**
    Sylvia Netzer - **158**
    Mary Barringer - **166**
    Neil Forrest - **173**
    Virginia Scotchie - **180**
    Joanne Hayakawa - **187**
    Kirk Mangus - **194**
    Jamie Walker - **201**

Chapter 4: The Logic of Process - 208
    John Neely - **209**
    Aurore Chabot - **217**
    Jeff Oestreich - **225**
    Angelo di Petta - **232**
    Barbara Tipton - **239**
    Richard Zakin - **246**
    Barbara Frey - **254**
    Peter Pinnell - **260**

Chapter 5: Concepts - 268
    Introduction - **268**
    Technology & Invention - **268**
    Work Strategies - **269**
    Ceramic Form & Volume - **271**
    Form & Surface - **271**
    Education - **272**
    The Art Environment - **273**
    The Sense of Personal Identity - **274**
    A Final Note - **275**

Glossary - **277**
Index - **284**

Ewer
by John Gill

Industrial Landscape by Linda Huey

Introduction

How the Artists in This Book Arrive at Their Work

I have been waiting a long time to write this book. For many years I've wanted to write about the way ceramists invent their imagery and create their work; recently the pieces began to come together. For a long time I thought this book would be a sort of technical book, though I didn't want to use the usual format of such books. I wanted to write a technical book that centered on ceramic work and the way technical matters dictate the look of the piece. This seemed okay; I love the material aspects of ceramics and deal with them daily in my own work with great enjoyment. I see these technical matters as part of the creative tools of the ceramist. I found myself, however, always coming back to the idea that it was arbitrary to separate the intangibles in ceramics from the tangibles - that establishing a sense of unity in the piece is as important as choosing a good clay body, that knowing how the artist came to make this type of work is as important as knowing how a glaze reacts to a kiln atmosphere. I found myself trying to link the tangible and the intangible, exploring the relationship of the material to the creative aspects of the field, asking if creativity can be generated by a new material, a new way of firing, a new work strategy, or a new idea.

Instead of a theoretical discussion, I have chosen to write this book in the form of essays based on a group of ceramic artists. I decided to talk not only about their work but about the way they came to make this work, their ideas, and their aims. I wanted these artists to represent a wide variety of work and ideologies, but at the same time I wanted each essay to cover the material in depth. This meant I had to cover the work of a number of artists but couldn't include too many. I decided to talk with 36 artists. This number seemed a good compromise between exclusivity and inclusiveness and allowed me to give the work of each artist reasonable attention. I then began to choose the artists.

How did I select the participants for this book? I had a number of aims in mind: I wanted to show the work of artists who I saw as successfully wrestling with problems in their work; I wanted to feature people who I felt were either coming to an artistic maturity very quickly or were at the height of their working careers; I wanted to find artists who were involved with the material character of the ceramic medium and took an experimental approach to it; I wanted to use the work of this group of lively, strong, and creative ceramic artists to illustrate the way they use ideas (both technical and aes-

Boomerang:
For Gordon J. Lippencott
by Sylvia Netzer

thetic) to create their pieces. I have included throwers and hand formers, traditionalists and those addicted to the most contemporary imagery. Some tell a story through modeled or painted imagery, some let the clays and glazes tell their own story.

I wanted to show how the work of these artists came to look as it does. I see ceramics as a balance between the tangible and the intangible and wanted to reflect this balance in the book. Because I hoped to provide an accurate view of ceramics, I wanted a book that was far more technical in orientation than any critical text and far more aesthetic in orientation than any technical book.

As I got down to work, I began to ask the artists a series of questions. I came to realize that if I wanted to track the reasons for the way the pieces look, I had to ask the artists about the ideas behind their work, about their background, ideas, and work experiences. I found it very important to ask each artist for a personal history of the evolution of the work. I also asked each for an education history and work history because I know these matters influence the character of the work. If we are going to discuss those things that distinguish one ceramist from another and those things that all ceramists face, then all of these aspects of ceramics - all these tools and strategies and concepts - take on the same importance.

When the artists answered my questions I found their individual responses (many of them very hard won) to be fascinating. I interviewed these artists at some length to find out what they have really done and what they are really thinking when they make their pieces. I decided I would discuss each artist and show their work in separate sections. I would, however, talk about the same group of topics with each artist. These topics serve as a thread, binding together my discussion of the artists and their work, and will, I hope, give the book a feeling of unity. I developed a group of questions I could ask of all these ceramists: What clay body did you use? What glaze? What image-creation strategies? What firing? In this part of the essays I tried to take an approach that was concrete and work-based. This was a descriptive rather than a concept-oriented approach. I also asked other less concrete questions: What influences affected you? How did you develop your way of working? How did your work evolve? Even when dealing with these questions, I wanted to take a descriptive approach. I have arranged this survey into four broad categories: I discuss those artists who seem to center their thinking around expression, those who are concerned with a sense of order, those who are concerned with the ideas behind the work, and those who base their thinking on process.

There was one question I didn't want to ask outright but was implicit in all the other questions: Where do you get your ability to translate your sense of energy into ceramic form and image? It seems to me that these artists are united mainly by this sense of "specialness," urgency, and energy. This transcends starting points, materials, strategies, and even ideas.

So I have written a book that allows me to talk about both the tangible and the intangible aspects of our wonderful field, a book with a lot of material that falls under the definition of the technical and a lot that doesn't fit that definition. This book has allowed me to deal with some of the questions in our field that I find most interesting and I have found the process of coming to grips with this project exciting and revelatory. I have found this search for understanding to be fascinating. I hope you will find it so as well.

Richard Zakin

Above right: Vase, Calabash Series
by David MacDonald

v

Chapter 1

Expression

Ric Hirsch

John Gill

Roy Strassberg

Rimas VisGirda

JoAnn Schnabel

John Chalke

Louis Katz

Richard Notkin

Victor Spinski

Expression is a personal and emotional reaction. I feel that expression is a very important aspect of the work of the artists in this section and may even be said to lie at the core of their work. Clay is a very natural and direct medium and a fine medium for expression.

In the past many conceived of ceramic art as a kind of oasis from strong emotions. Ceramists concentrated on formal and utility issues and the work was free of messages. Ceramic art was seen as useful and not impacted by expression or emotion. It communicated easily and was readily understood by its intended audience. The artists in this chapter have discovered, however, that expression can give the work a feeling of energy, commitment, and relevance. Some of the pieces in this section have strong messages and it is no wonder they are carriers of emotion. Others convey emotion by the way their forms and surfaces have been handled.

In recent years many ceramists have created work that is expressive of their "engaged" and political emotions. The work influenced by these views is imagery centered and message laden. The work of Richard Notkin, Rimas VisGirda, and Roy Strassberg represents this approach. Other contemporary ceramists see ceramic art as an intensely personal expression. This work too is highly expressive, but here the expression seems to be about the ceramist's mental state during the process of creation. The pieces by Louis Katz and John Chalke are examples of this approach. They too make work that is "engaged," but here the engagement is one that faces inward instead of outward.

Ric Hirsch

Ric Hirsch has worked in the vessel form since the beginning of his career in ceramics. In recent years, however, he has been moving much closer to sculpture. Though he still maintains his interest in vessel forms, his pieces have taken on a much more sculptural character and he now feels they fall into the category of sculpture. These pieces are monumen-

Photo credit: Geoff Tesch.

***Altar Bowl with Bone Artifact #2 (Judaean Desert Series)**, 16-3/4" x 19", 1997. Low fire, lacquers. A variation of the knife/bowl and base format often seen in Hirsch's work, here compressed and rock-like.*

tal in size and character. Hirsch is intent on creating powerful images that move the viewer.

Hirsch makes his own clay bodies from dry clay ingredients. His fire clay and spodumene body recipe works well for all his pieces, including work fired to cone 04, cone 1, and for raku. He constructs his pieces in multiple sections, starting with a thrown base. Many of these bases are quite tall and he throws them in parts, then assembles the parts. He constructs other sections using hand-forming methods. He combines hand-formed sections with wheel-formed sections, placing one on top of the other. He paddles his forms to control the contours and models and carves some of the surfaces to create rock-like imagery.

Before applying the surfaces, he disassembles the piece and glazes each section separ-

Photo credit: Geoff Tesch.

Altar Bowl with Weapon Artifact #6 (Judaean Desert Series), low fire, 33-3/4" x 14" x 1/2" x 11". In this piece the focal point is the bowl. Hirsch calls the bowl "the soloist"; it is of primary importance. He sees the knife as the second player. The third player is the base, which serves as the foundation for the piece. Hirsch used a fire clay and spodumene body to make this piece. He threw the base in sections, then assembled the sections. He threw the bowl with a thick wall, then applied thick soft clay to the thrown form. The wall ranges in thickness from 1-1/2" to 3". He then altered the bowl's shape from round to strongly elliptical. He then waited until the clay was leather hard and paddled it.

He made the knife form using slab forming and carved its surface to resemble carved stone. While the base was still in its greenware state, he applied a gritty texture using a slip made with silica sand. He colored part of the slip with yellow ocher and part with rutile. He spray applied a black glaze to the bowl, then spray applied a slip colored with yellow and ocher colored stains. He finished the surface with a light spray of soluble salts which enhanced the slip's color and texture and encouraged translucency. He made a sigillata from Hawthorn fire clay colored with yellow and pink stains and applied it to the dry greenware of the knife blade, then burnished it. He then smoke fired the blade to add texture and color variation. Though he used a sprayer to apply most of the surfaces, he applied the gritty slip on the base section with his hands.

Since each segment was fired separately and in a different way, the firing is difficult to track. For the bowl form, he started with a bisque fire (cone 08). The second firing (cone 04) was dedicated to the black glaze, and the third firing (cone 06) was dedicated to the slip and soluble salts application. He fired the base (a single firing) to cone 1. He fired the knife to cone 06, then fired it in a raku smoke fire. All firings (except the final smoke firing) were in an electric kiln.

ately; in this way he can give each section a different treatment. He employs a wide range of surfaces in finishing these pieces including slips, gritty slips, soluble salts, terra sigillatas, and glazes. He makes gritty surfaces from a slip that contains silica sand (applied on the greenware). He uses such colorants as copper, yellow ocher, and rutile. He also uses brilliantly colored stains from commercial suppliers. He finishes some of his surfaces with a light spray of soluble salts while the piece is still hot. The soluble salts (such as cupric oxide) add color and texture to the surface of the slip. They enable Hirsch to build up in layers of color, creating a sometimes shimmering metallic imagery. They also turn opaque slips and glazes translucent, revealing underlayers of imagery that otherwise would be obscured. The resulting imagery can be very subtle. Most of the application is with the sprayer but he also applies his surfaces with brushes and even with his hands.

He fires each section separately and employs a wide variety of firing treatments. Many of the sections are fired three or four times. These may include a bisque fire (cone 08), a firing to cone 04, and another to cone 06. Other sections may be completed in a single firing. Though many of the firings are in an electric kiln, he also fires in fuel-burning kilns for raku and smoke firings. The results of these multi-layered, multi-material, multi-fired work strategies are complex and painterly surfaces.

Hirsch wants his pieces to convey a sense of age and of the archetypal. He wants to convey a sense of formal presentation and to evoke a feeling of ceremony and ritual. He uses forms that are primal cultural artifacts - the bowl and the knife. For him, the bowl form refers to the idea of containment; the knife form to rites of passage and symbols of power.

Photo credit: Geoff Tesch.

Pedestal Bowl with Weapon Artifact #16, *46" x 21-1/2" x 10". Low fire and raku, 1997. This is a very graceful version of Hirsch's exploration of knife, bowl, and base. Here he dramatizes the knife form, turning it into an object simultaneously cruel and necessary to our existence - a weapon of destruction and a tool for getting our food and insuring the continuation of the human race.*

When making these forms, he thinks often of the bronze vessels and jade knives of China's Shang Dynasty. The base also has meaning for him, referring to altar-like forms. His carved and modeled surfaces refer to rocks, especially those rocks he saw on a trip to the Judean desert. He is looking for forms, surfaces, and imagery that have power to move the viewer.

Hirsch began his serious work in clay with raku and used that method for many years. Though raku is no longer at the central core of his work, he says that he "is imbued with the raku attitude and incorporates the principals of chance and accidentals in this work." He is not a victim of chance, however. His decisions are based on judgments derived from experience. He has a general idea of the changes that will occur during the firing. He even has an idea of where they will happen but can't predict *exactly* where they will happen and doesn't want to.

Originally Hirsch wanted to teach art in public school. In 1962 he was accepted in the art education program at the State University of New York at New Paltz. Ceramics was a requirement of the program and it soon became the most important part of his life in college. He took as many ceramics courses as he could from the two instructors, Ken Green and Robert Sederstrom. He worked in wheel-thrown reduction stoneware fired to cones 9/10. In this work he was aiming for personal expression within the format of pottery. He now feels that he

had only a vague notion of what the contemporary issues in clay really were. He began to experiment with raku firings at this time and raku soon became so important to him that he specialized in it. Even though his experiments were hampered by a lack of any information on raku, he persevered.

After Hirsch graduated from New Paltz with a Bachelor of Science degree in education in 1966, he taught art in the public schools for a few years. Ceramics, however, had taken hold of his imagination. He wanted to explore the medium in depth, in a way not possible as a public school teacher. At this point he decided to prepare to be a ceramist and to teach ceramics in the environment of higher education.

In 1969 Hirsch applied for entry into the graduate program at the School for American Craftsmen at the Rochester Institute of Technology (R.I.T.). He studied with Franz Wildenhain and Hobart Coles and is grateful for the quality of his education. "It was just the right combination of technical information, aesthetic content, and inspiration." His work at R.I.T. was totally dedicated to reinterpreting raku. Wildenhain disapproved of raku (Hirsch says he communicated the feeling that it was a kind of parlor trick) but Hirsch kept on reading, experimenting, working, and developing his own work strategies. He feels now that this formed the basis for what has remained his own approach to ceramics and to creativity. He learned that he

could break the rules of accepted glaze technology and that with effort he could create pieces that were strong and innovative. This was the time when he learned the importance of exploration unfettered by preconceptions, plans, and schedules. This now seems especially important to him. Toward the end of his work at R.I.T. he discovered that he could use glass-blowing lustering techniques in raku. These techniques encouraged brightly colored iridescent lustered surfaces. They were further enriched by the post firing smoke reduction effects associated with raku.

Hirsch graduated from R.I.T. in 1971 with an M.F.A. degree in ceramics. Upon graduation he began teaching at Sault College in Sault Saint Marie, Ontario, Canada, a place of rugged beauty but far from centers of culture. He felt isolated and that he was working very much alone. To build bridges he began to show his work wherever he could and began to write a book on raku with Chris Tyler, a critic and writer on artistic matters. This was a period of intellectual as well as artistic growth. In 1975, having achieved some recognition, Hirsch was invited to teach at the Program in Artisanry at Boston University.

In 1978 Hirsch was invited to represent the Western attitude toward raku at the World Craft Conference in Kyoto, Japan. Hirsch met members of the Raku family, including Raku Kichizaemon 14th. Here were members of a family carrying on a traditional family pottery, interpreting an aesthetic approach to clay that had been laid down in the 16th century. Hirsch participated in the workshop and dialogue with this raku master and was strongly affected by the sense of pride of those carrying on a vital tradition. He admired their carefully worked out system of beliefs and the clay work that reflected the impact of these beliefs. He studied their work strategies and tools, which seemed simple but were superbly designed to help the potters carry out their work. Hirsch saw these potters as less time-bound than most of us, as rooted in the 20th century but connected intimately to the 16th century. Shortly after this profound experience, he saw an exhibition of the work of Peter Voulkos at the Museum of Contemporary Crafts and was very moved by Voulkos' work. These two experiences were in many ways quite different. His experience in Japan was based on a long-standing tradition, while Voulkos' work broke with tradition. Both, however, had great power and led him to seek a way to enhance and deepen the power of his own work.

Out of sheer frustration with his previous ceramic work, he developed the first piece in which he used a tripod form. Though this piece was the result of a kind of artistic accident, he seized upon it and made a conscious decision to intensively explore the format. This form seemed to him to be truly primal in its character and

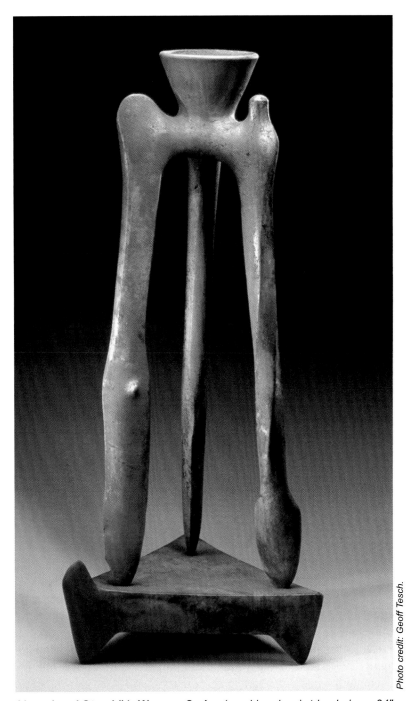

Vessel and Stand #1, Weapon Series *(an older piece), tripod piece, 34" x 15" x 15", 1993. Hirsch made the tripod legs of this piece from solid clay forms. He threw the bowl form and made the base from slabs. To finish the legs and bowl, he applied terra sigillata colored with orange, rust, and green commercially produced stains. He applied a terra sigillata made from a red clay to the base. He bisque fired the piece, then fired it in a raku kiln. When he took the still hot piece from the kiln, he sprayed it with cupric sulphate. He returned the piece to the kiln, removed it again, and post fired it in straw. Hirsch cites the work of Swiss sculptor Alberto Giacommetti, English ceramist Hans Coper, and the forms of archaic weapons as the source of inspiration for this piece.*

this, he felt, gave it the power he was looking for. He wanted to develop a cohesive body of work, dedicated to the exploration of the tripod format. He used Neolithic bronze pieces as models for his work with the tripod form. He worked solely in the tripod format for 15 years. He has come to feel that to develop a strong body of work, one must set limits and boundaries to allow a deep level of focus and study.

In the early 1990s he felt the need to move on to a new area of work and study. He wanted to say similar things, but with totally different means. The tripods are sleek, linear, and stylized; they challenge the nature of clay. He now wanted to make pieces that would do the opposite - pieces that deal with real weight, that appear to be heavy and are. He wanted to handle the material in a much more natural and intuitive way with a wider range of surface texture and color. He wanted an approach that was more emphatic than the tripod format. When he decided to work in a new way, he felt he had to start by figuring out what kind of character he wanted in the work. After this important first step he could work out new forms and from there he could learn how to "support the concept" by developing his ceramic work methods. He did lots of drawing, lots of looking in books and in museums (mostly anthropological museums, especially looking at the work of primal cultures). He wanted this work to convey the sense of a contemporary artist looking at the whole of history, choosing from a wide grouping of cultural artifacts. In his new work, he has been searching for another form with the same primal character as the tripods. He chose bowl and knife forms as primal forms that had resonance for him. Both of these forms are very ancient and have associations with the origins of culture. He also began to use rock-like surfaces in his work. Rocks, for him, are primal and the essence of the planet.

Hirsch prefers to assemble his pieces from disparate parts, then create a strong ensemble feeling. He strives to create a sense of unity so that what could be disparate and disconnected can work together. Always conscious of the audience for his work, most of all he wants to convince and move that audience.

Photo credit: Richard Zakin.

Ric Hirsch.

John Gill

John Gill lives in Alfred, New York, and teaches at the New York State College of Ceramics at Alfred. He is a strong teacher, has a wide ranging and urgent sense of curiosity and an intense involvement with clay.

Photo credit: Mick Castle.

Ewer, height 11", 1996. Fired to cone 9/10 in a fuel-burning kiln. Gill first built a wide cylinder, then cut it to create the top and bottom. The resulting object was like a closed irregularly shaped sphere. He then cut, overlapped, and tucked parts of the wall to make the flat box-like shape facing us in the photograph. He placed a slab across the top of the form and pressed it downward to make a shallow inverted cone. He made the spout with two square tubes made by wrapping a slab around a square stick. He cut the tubes at an angle and joined them together. For the rear spout, he made a tapered cylinder from a truncated cone-shaped form. He added these to the body of the form, dried the piece, and fired to bisque. He masked the surface and painted it with glazes to finish it.

Since 1978 Gill has used a buff-colored cone 9/10 clay body with high percentages of fire clay and ball clay, adding grog only when he works with larger pieces. He says it is a fine body for hand building. Gill starts his pieces by working with soft, highly formable clay. He has a highly developed sense of autonomy and has developed a very personal set of methods for working with clay. This is especially true of his approach to forming - he has strong opinions about the way he wants to work with clay.

Gill doesn't like to use a paddle while forming his slab pieces. He strongly emphasizes that he doesn't smooth the clay, that once he makes the form, he tries to leave it alone. He feels that too much touching can deprive the clay of life. In a forming method he favors, he tucks, folds, and cuts his clay slabs. He scores edges, applies water, and joins the edges together to assemble his pieces. He assembles very complex forms and instinctively knows how to make them come together in an object with a sense of internal consistency. In a favorite strategy, he uses a repoussé method to work on both sides of the clay, moving and shaping it from both directions. He uses this strategy to produce raised and ribbed imagery. He gives his ewers and teapots spouts by wrapping thin slabs around a tapered wooden dowel. When he has formed the spout, he removes it from the dowel and bends it a bit, lets it become firm, then attaches it to his base form.

Gill paints his glazes. He first draws his imagery with a pencil, then lays down masking tape to define the edge of each glaze color. He then uses a sponge or brush to apply the glaze. By using the tape, he can apply a broad sweep of color without having to worry about the edge of the colored field.

Gill's work is high fired. He likes to mix the classical colors of stoneware - ocher, tan, brick red, soft blue, and green - with more unusual colors such as orange and scarlet. Until recently, brilliant orange and scarlet were unavailable to ceramists working in the high fire. It can be quite surprising to see a bright scarlet glaze next to a visually textured stoneware glaze of a very classic type. It is even more surprising to see a glaze that is simultaneously scarlet and has the sort of texture we associate with a stoneware glaze.

Though Gill fires to cone 9/10 in a downdraft kiln fueled with natural gas, he uses no body or glaze reduction. He likens reduction to "burning the clay." He says, "I look at the back of the kiln to see if I can still see the crack between the brick in the back. If it is too foggy back there, I know the atmosphere isn't clean enough." He slows the fire at the end so the glazes have a chance to melt. When he first started firing, he hated the process (he also hated glazing) but has since developed a simple and direct way of firing and really enjoys it. He says he has learned "to be that pot in the kiln."

Gill's life has been strongly influenced by the difficulties he has encountered in reading, writing, and mathematics. He finds the field of the page very hard to follow; his visual field seems to jump around in a way that is difficult for him to control. He had to deal with these problems when he attended school in Seattle, Washington, in the late 1960s. Fortunately, in high school he had a friendly English teacher, Don Bunger, who read to him. Gill made images from these stories. He is very grateful for Bunger's work with him and they recently had a wonderful reunion. Bunger is very proud of Gill and proud of his own contribution.

Gill loved art and did well in it even as he encountered difficulties with most of his other courses. He took as many courses in music, theater, and art as the rules would allow. He was especially interested in figural sculpture and took classes from Phil Levine, a sculptor in Seattle. Gill also took a course in clay at a summer school at a local college. He says with some irony that at that time he didn't like clay. He had been working with sculptor's wax and liked it much more and found it easier to control.

After Gill finished high school in 1968, he attended the Cornish School of Allied Arts, a small art school in Seattle. Though it was a diploma rather than degree granting school, it was an excellent place and its program fit Gill's needs very well. He enjoyed the school and thought his major area would be sculpture. In his sophomore

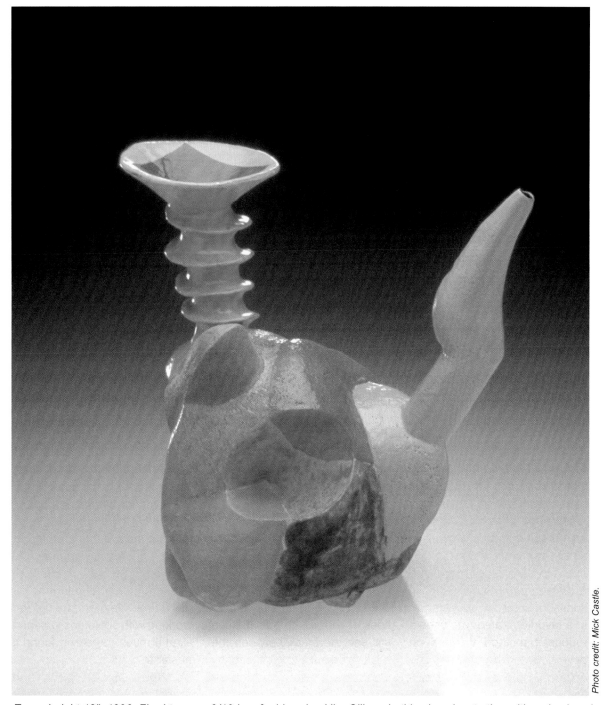

Ewer, *height 12", 1996. Fired to cone 9/10 in a fuel-burning kiln. Gill made this piece by starting with a simple cylinder. He then pushed the walls of this form from both sides, pressing both from the outside to the inside to create lively irregular shapes. He cleaned the form, then employed a cut and overlap strategy and cut again on a 45° angle to reshape the form and close the top and bottom. In this way he was able to turn the cylinder into a ball-shaped form. Once he arrived at this form, he turned the sphere and decided "which way was up." To create the dimple shaped depression, he cut a hole in the wall of the sphere and put in a shallow inverse cone. He now formed the foot and let the piece stiffen. He assembled the spout from two tapered tubular forms and placed them on the pot. For the handle/spout on the back of the piece, he made a narrow cylinder and, pushing out from the inside and pinching on the outside, he made a spiral that went up its length. After the piece dried, he fired to bisque and painted it. He then fired it to cone 9/10 in a fuel-burning kiln.*

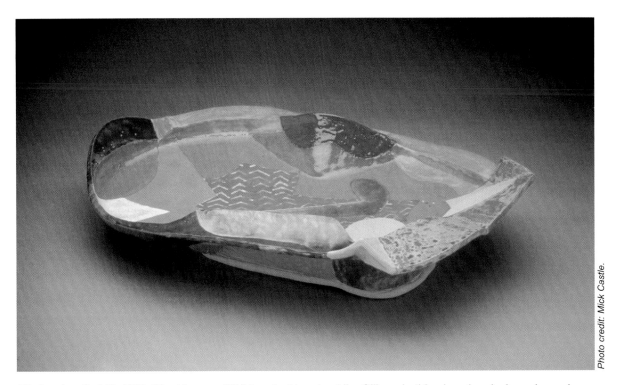

Platter, *length 24", 1996. Fired to cone 9/10 in a fuel-burning kiln. Gill made this piece by placing a large, irregularly shaped clay slab on a mold. As the clay began to stiffen, he lifted it off the mold and placed it on the work table. He then added more slabs to the walls. He adjusted the angle of the slabs so they cantilevered outward. When this structure stiffened, he added more slabs. He let the piece stiffen to a point where he could flip the platter over to build a foot. He rested it on a large pillow shape made from a newspaper "envelope" stuffed with wadded up newspaper. He formed the foot and turned the piece over after the foot had stiffened. After the piece dried, he fired to bisque. He then penciled the design of the painted imagery on the surface of the plate, placed masking tape on the surface, and painted his glaze designs.*

year, Thorne Edwards, a fine potter and teacher, was hired to start a program in ceramics with very little money. Gill took the course and found the clay easier to control than he remembered. He began to concentrate on hand forming, a concentration he still maintains. Edwards left at the end of the semester to start his own studio and was replaced by Patti Warashina. Gill really enjoyed working with Warashina and by the end of that semester was convinced that ceramics was his medium. He tried all sorts of things, "hand building, all kinds of crazy stuff down in the basement [of the school], just working hard and having a great time." He made hand-formed vases, cups, and teapots. He was strongly influenced by Warashina and looked at a lot of work by Jacquelyn Rice and Joyce Moty and generally played with various aspects of the Funk movement. He says that, "Once I had Patti [Warashina], then I was really stuck. I mean you go home and you have dreams about the clay."

The following year Warashina moved to the University of Washington and was replaced by Irv Tepper, who taught Gill how to throw. In his own work Tepper concentrated on slipcasting. Gill took this up as well and made a great many slipcast pieces strongly influenced by Tepper and Robert Arneson. In the eyes of the faculty, Gill had become a very promising student artist.

At the end of his second year at Cornish School for the Arts, Tepper decided that Gill's great promise would best be fulfilled at the Kansas City Art Institute and suggested he apply there. Gill remembers that he sent slides in his portfolio of a Funk-influenced bust of Sir Thomas Lipton and a duck teapot with a sweet potato on its back with a paintbrush handle and a parsnip for the spout. All this work was low fired and Funk inspired. Gill was accepted and that January transferred to Kansas City. He had a very strong art background by then, but had problems with the academic courses. The liberal arts teachers knew that Gill was a promising artist and worked hard to bring him up to speed in the college level academic courses. Like many who have trouble reading, Gill has an unusually accurate memory. His memory for visual information is especially powerful. He says that when he can, he translates information from text to visual format and draws visual outlines, diagrams, and pictographs. He worked hard in the courses and got through them.

At Kansas he studied with Ken Fergusen, Jackie Rice, and Victor Babu. He liked Fergusen's direct approach to pottery and learned from him the idea of structure and order in clay. From Jackie Rice he learned a natural effortless way of hand building. From Babu he learned much about hand building as well. Gill says of Babu, "He had a wonderful way of creating hand-built forms that had a dramatic, almost symphonic life of their own. He told great stories about pots that might not really exist but I have been looking for them ever since."

In Kansas City Gill began making loose forms. He learned to start with very soft clay bodies and to use tucked seams to make his forms more surprising, complex, and sculptural. He was encouraged to try a great many ways of working. He worked in earthenware in the low fire and porcelain and stoneware in the high fire. In 1972 Andrea Gray (later to become Andrea Gill) came to study at Kansas City. Gill graduated from there in 1973 with a B.F.A. degree.

In 1973 Gill went to Alfred where he studied with Bob Turner, Wayne Higby, Val Cushing, Ted Randall, and Betty Woodman. Gill admires Turner very much and thinks of him as a teacher with a great gift for listening. He admired the way Turner could make forms fit together. He found Wayne Higby to be a breath of fresh air and especially valued his critiques. He also worked with Higby on ways of pushing the limits of function in ceramics. He studied technical aspects of ceramics (including glaze calculation) with Val Cushing. In Gill's second year, Betty Woodman came to Alfred as a visiting teacher and he was very impressed by the spontaneity of her work. At Alfred, Gill worked with earthenware, stoneware, and porcelain. He liked to treat these clay bodies in unusual ways, making thick-walled porcelain pieces and thin-walled earthenware. He loved Alfred's simplicity and isolation. He is sensitive to the characteristic architecture of a place and liked Alfred's simple architecture and ambiance. In the fall of 1974 Andrea Gray

came to Alfred and at the end of his second year of graduate school he and Andrea "went away on vacation and came back married." Gill graduated from Alfred in 1975 with an M.F.A. degree.

In 1975 Gill began teaching at the Rhode Island School of Design as part of a program in which talented artists just out of graduate school were invited to teach for two years. Gill taught there from 1975 to 1977. He liked the city and the School of Design. Gill taught with Lucien Pompili and Norman Schulman. He was very impressed with Schulman and learned from his teaching style. Furthermore, he always found Schulman's work challenging and unorthodox. Though he feels he had a lot to learn about teaching, Gill liked teaching and liked the students. He spent a good deal of time on his own work; he hand formed his pieces and used both low- and high-fire strategies to finish them.

Gill taught at Colorado State University in Fort Collins for a year and in 1978 both John and Andrea won awards at the Young Americans exhibition. That year both he and Andrea were awarded grants from the National Endowment of the Arts (N.E.A.) to go to the Archie Bray Foundation in Helena, Montana. In the fall, without a job, they decided to stay at the Bray and make pots for a living. Gill now says of their time at the Bray, "We were on unemployment and learned how to make pots. What was really good about being at the Bray was that it gave me a chance to become believable as a potter, to figure out what it meant to get up every day and go down to the studio and figure out the most economical way to make something. It forced me to really make sense of what I had learned at school." They were there for a year.

The following year Gill got a job teaching at Kent State University in Ohio where he taught for five years. He admired his fellow faculty at Kent State, found them to be very talented, and enjoyed working with them. It was while at Kent that he began to settle on stoneware as the preferred material for his pieces. At this point Gill learned to "turn the kiln on and turn it off." He did not fire in reduction, as he explains "everything is just… I melt it."

Gill has shown his work in a succession of highly respected art galleries in New York City. The Hadler Rodriguez Gallery began to represent Gill in 1979 and he had four exhibitions there before he left the gallery shortly before it closed in 1984. For the next six years he showed with the Grace Borgenecht Gallery. He now shows in the Kraushaar Gallery.

In 1984 the job at Alfred came up. He relates that he did not apply for it but was invited to visit Alfred and they offered him the job. "We drove back home and had some time to think about it. I went to an Indiana Jones movie, *The Temple of Doom*, and said, 'Well you know, if Indiana

Photo credit: Andrea Gill.

Ewer, *fired to cone 9/10 in a fuel-burning kiln. This is an older piece from 1983. Gill built this in much the same way as he built the more recent pieces. He used a brushed glaze application over masking tape. He still uses this glaze application strategy. The glaze color, however, is very different because at that time he did not have access to the brilliant red and orange stain colors he uses now.*

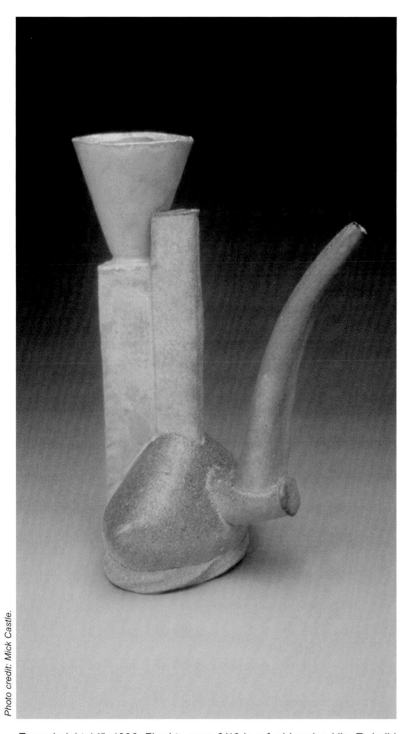

Ewer, height 14", 1996. Fired to cone 9/10 in a fuel-burning kiln. To build its central section, Gill took a vertical cylinder and shaped it so it became triangular (with rounded corners). Its base is a conical shaped form. He added the inverted cone at the top and the spout to complete the form. He used masking tape to paint the relatively simple and reserved imagery.

Jones can do it, I can do it' and so I came here." Teaching at Alfred gave him a chance to work with Tony Hepburn, Val Cushing, Wayne Higby, and Ann Currier, all of whom he very much admires.

At Alfred he expanded his color spectrum, an important change in his work. For many years Gill used two completely different sets of color. He used brilliant color for the low fire and the somewhat more somber colors available to those who work in the high fire. By the 1980s Gill was centering his work around stoneware clay bodies and a group of high-fire glazes with the color spectrum we associate with stoneware. He liked much about the high fire but missed some of the brilliant orange and red colors he could get in the low fire. Providentially, a whole group of brilliant stain colors that could be fired at high temperatures became available. Now Gill could use brilliant orange and scarlet red in his stoneware alongside his classic stoneware glazes. He even began to add these brilliant stains to the classic stoneware glazes such as Shino glazes. He says that after the new stains became available, "Alfred became color."

For Gill, ceramics has been a field that seems to exactly fit his needs and powers. It has been a challenge that he can deal with and learn from. Furthermore, it has given him a structure he can use to anchor his life and his relations with the world. Gill had trouble showing intelligence the way most people show intelligence because he had difficulty learning the way most people learn. In our culture, people learn by reading or writing or solving mathematical problems and Gill had difficulty doing these things. Even so, as a young boy and later as an adolescent, he seems to have known instinctively that he was as smart as his peers. To prove this, he needed to find a field that would require him to use his intelligence, allow him to express it, and to excel in this expression. In his adolescence Gill found art and then a particular branch of art - ceramics. This may be one of the reasons he embraced ceramics with such great intensity. Ceramics had a language that seemed obvious to him and that he could use with great facility. Though Gill was hindered by his learning difficulties, he could flourish as a ceramist and bring special skills to his work in clay. He feels he has a special gift for dealing with spatial problems. He calls it "an intuitive sense of geometry." He seems to "see" what he can do next. This is an extremely useful skill for the ceramist. Learning ceramics seems to have done more for Gill than give him an outlet - it seems to have educated him in a way few other things could have, giving him the highly structured skill training he needed to shape his intelligence. Gill owes a great deal to ceramics. It has brought him more than a decent life, it has brought him the opportunity for intellectual challenge, honors, and respect.

John Gill.

Roy Strassberg

Roy Strassberg lives and works in Mankato, Minnesota. For many years Strassberg worked on a series of low-fire sculptural pieces. Their crisp elegant surfaces and bright decorative color resulted in a body of work with a pleasing but essential-

Photo credit: Roy Strassberg.

Fat JazzHouse *(an older piece), 20" h x 18" w x 20", 1986. In this piece we see the elegant and precise imagery of Strassberg's work during the 1980s. The piece conveys the sense of control and intelligence that Strassberg reacted against in his work of the '90s. He built this piece from slabs 3/8" to 1/2" thick in a way that is similar to the way houses are built. He made it from four outside walls with interior walls for support. He carefully measured and cut out the walls, let them become firm, and assembled the piece. He then used rubber scrapers to smooth the surfaces and clean the edges. He slowly dried the piece under plastic in his moist basement, a process that helped keep the piece free of cracks. He made a series of drawings on his computer for the surface imagery, which he drew on the surface of the piece when it became leather hard. To do the drawing, he used a sharp tool to create a precise hard line. He then fired to a cone 04 bisque. He now needed to apply his color imagery. He made part of this imagery using untextured color but used highly textured surfaces for many of the color areas. For both the textured and untextured surfaces, he used tape to mask areas bordering those he wanted to paint. If working with the textured imagery, he applied underglaze color by loading a bamboo brush and with a snap of his wrist cast it onto the surface of the piece. He applied many layers of color until he built up a rich, textured surface. In those color areas painted with flat color, he painted two or three coats of an underglaze stain color. He periodically dried his imagery with a hair dryer. He also applied glaze surfaces in a few places for contrast. When he felt he had applied enough color, he removed the tape and moved on to another color area. He fired the piece to cone 06 in an electric kiln, then painted the surface with a gel acrylic medium to enrich surface and color.*

ly detached character. After years of working this productive vein and creating a committed audience for his work, Strassberg opted for a radical change in direction. He took as his subject the theme of "Holocaust." He jettisoned the bright color, crisp edges, and most visibly the cool dispassionate character of his work. He began to explore a highly limited color, intertwined, energetic, and twisted forms, and a highly charged emotional tone. He has had plenty of opportunities to study the Holocaust for he has lived in a period when many in the world have tried to come to terms with this appalling event.

Strassberg uses a simple low-fire clay body composed of ball clay, fire clay, and Goldart stoneware clay to make the pieces in the *Train* series. He loads this body with 20% to 40% grog and a small amount of chopped nylon. The grog and chopped nylon encourage workability and discourage cracking and are an important aid to Strassberg as he makes his complex forms. Strassberg characterizes his forming methods as very simple and direct. He starts with long stick-like forms for the base and builds on this foundation.

Strassberg begins by using a slab roller to make several slabs 24" x 36" x 1/2" to 1". He then cuts the slabs in strips and rectangles and starts to fabricate the parts of the piece. Many parts are stick-like (typically 24" x 1-1/2" to 2"). He makes several of these pieces; they are the basic forms for the

structure he is building. He also fabricates irregular shapes by folding a slab over, almost as one would fold a tortilla, to create organic/bone-like forms. After making a wide variety of shapes, he slices big solid chunks of clay with a sharp paint scraper. Then he allows all the parts to stiffen overnight (or even a few days). He

smooths the elements with an elephant ear sponge and begins to assemble the forms on a kiln shelf (the attenuated forms he builds remain very fragile until fired, so the kiln shelf provides support). Strassberg characterizes his actions as very spontaneous, very intuitive, and based on repeated gestures with small

Detail of **Kinderschlech/seite**. Here we see a detail of Strassberg's pieced together structure.

Photo credit: Roy Strassberg.

but significant variations. It takes him two days to make the foundation of one of these pieces.

When he begins to work on the main body of the piece, he switches over to small segments. He places segments alongside and on top of each other. He builds a layer of imagery, allows this to become firm, then makes more segments and uses them to build another layer of imagery. He builds these pieces layer by layer, over a period of several weeks. It is the way he carries out this step by step process that makes his work complex. In the several weeks it takes Strassberg to make one of these pieces, he can create a very crowded and complex imagery. As he builds he makes more small forms as needed, lets them become firm, scores and slips them, and puts the piece together like a puzzle. At intervals he fills in the spaces between forms with soft clay to further strengthen the structure. Once he has made his basic structure, he can fill in the spaces with all sorts of form elements. To keep these pieces moist during the lengthy building process, Strassberg works in a moist basement. To further slow the drying process, he covers the piece with plastic sheeting when he is not working on it.

In Strassberg's crowded pieces we see forms squeezed together. He estimates that

Photo credit: Roy Strassberg.

White Trains with Chimneys #2, *36" x 10" x 23", 1997. In this piece Strassberg has used the image of a train packed with bodies to evoke the Holocaust. This image brings to mind the technological power of those who coolly managed the Holocaust machinery. Strassberg uses forms that suggest body parts and compacted fragments of the victims. The imagery is very dense and knotted.*

60% of the space is taken up with solid clay forms and 40% with negative space (the space between one clay element and the next). Therefore a piece with dimensions of 36" x 28" x 12" might weigh as much as 30 to 40 pounds.

Once the piece is dry, Strassberg is ready to fire it to bisque. Because these pieces are so complex and awkward, he lifts the kiln walls off the kiln floor, then he and his wife (ceramist Barbara Strassberg) carefully carry the piece on the

kiln shelf to the kiln and place it on the kiln base. They lower the wall section of the kiln structure back onto the kiln floor with great care. To begin the firing, Strassberg preheats the kiln overnight then slowly fires to bisque (typically a ten to 12 hour firing).

Strassberg finishes these pieces with terra sigillatas. To make his terra sigillata, he uses a ball mill to make a slurry from a kaolin and ball clay mixture. He adds more water and a deflocculant (sodium silicate) and decants the mixture to separate the fine particles (the terra sigillata) from the coarse. He keeps the fine terra sigillata particles and discards the rest. After letting the mixture thicken, he is ready to apply it to the surface of his pieces.

Using a brush, he applies a white terra sigillata for the first application. He says this application "takes forever because I have to get into every little part of the piece." After he burnishes every part of the piece he can reach, the piece is ready for its second firing. This cone 06 firing is an intermediate firing - he will fire the piece one more time. After this firing he takes the piece from the kiln for the final step in the creation of the surface. He adds water to thin a black stain which he then applies and carefully wipes with a wet rag and a sponge. After this treatment the edges of the forms reveal the white color of the body while the black stain predominates in the center of the forms. This surface reminds him of the look of a black and white photograph. He fires the piece once more to cone 06 to finish it.

Strassberg's imagery is a very powerful evocation of the Holocaust. Strassberg is trying to digest a historical reality and understand it as an artist understands it - through the medium of his work. Because of his awareness of his Jewish ethnicity, he feels very strongly about this monstrous series of events. He communicates deeply felt emotions in this work. He sees it as his job as an artist to use this powerfully affecting subject matter as the engine that gives force to his work. He uses this force to help him create compelling forms. For him, the forms are most important because they define his pieces and his identity as an artist. His subject will work for him if it gets the creative process going. He doesn't want to make a narrative or a propaganda object, he wants to make an art object.

In *White Train* Strassberg has used the image of a train. This image powerfully evokes the Holocaust because transportation was one of the most important parts of the Holocaust machinery. The Nazis packed their victims into trains to deliver them to the

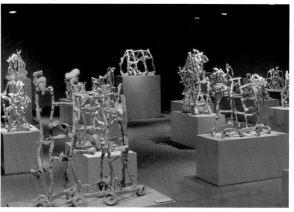

Photo credit: Roy Strassberg.

Installation at Mankato State University, Mankato, Minnesota. These pieces gain a great deal of power when they are exhibited as a group. They remind us at once of bodies and of nettle filled bramble thickets.

camps. The image of freight trains stuffed with humanity enroute to death camps is one of the most powerful images of the period. In Strassberg's train, the forms suggest body parts and compacted fragments of the victims. The train refers to the technological power of those who coolly managed the Holocaust machinery. Strassberg says that when he is working on these pieces, he has feelings of anger. He uses certain instruments to encourage focus, primarily photographs related to the Holocaust, which are especially powerful because they were mostly made by those carrying out the program of death. The victims were not allowed to document their suffering.

Until he attended college, Strassberg had no particular interest in art or in ceramics. From 1968 to 1972 he attended the State University of New York at Oswego. His introduction to ceramics was accidental. As time went on, however, he became highly committed to ceramic work. At Oswego,

Strassberg studied with Richard Zakin and Ron Brown. He attended workshops with William Parry, Bill Stewart, and Don Reitz. During this period he struggled to make sense of ceramics and find a way to create a body of strong and personal work. He made the semi-utilitarian pots that many ceramists made during this period. He was awarded a degree in art from Oswego in 1972. In that same year he was accepted in the graduate program of the University of Michigan at Ann Arbor. Most of his work there was with John Stephenson. He concentrated on sculptural pottery fired in raku. He worked at finding a voice. He says of this period, "There I was, 21 years old, meeting people who knew much more than I did for I had been working in art for only a few years." Graduate school was in many ways a difficult time for Strassberg, but it was during this stressful period that he began to develop as an artist with a strong personal identity. In 1974 he received an M.F.A. degree from the school.

After graduation Strassberg took a position as a ceramist at Memphis State University in Tennessee. He taught there from 1974 to 1976 and continued to work in raku, making sculptural vessels. He concentrated on a group of lidded containers he called *Pyramid Jars*. These were sculptural vessels in which he used brilliant color and geometric forms. He remembers really enjoying himself during this period and feeling that he had finally found his own voice.

In 1976 he joined the faculty at Mankato State University in Minnesota. When he arrived, he was still making the lidded containers he had been working on for the last few years, but he soon started to move away from the idea of pots. He began a new series he called *Walking Bun Monuments*. This work was purely sculptural and its painted imagery highly kinetic. In the early 1980s Strassberg made an installation piece he called *Roll Call at Auschwitz*. This installation was made up of a series of 20 standing X-shaped forms. He drew in the surface of each piece; these were abstract surface markings suggesting prisoners standing in rows. He views this piece as a precursor of his recent work in which he uses the Holocaust as his subject.

During the mid 1980s Strassberg worked on a group of form-oriented pieces he called the *Jazz Series*. With their sharp-edged geometric patterns, they could have been very stiff but Strassberg animated the imagery by using unbalanced patterns and bright color to create a feeling of movement. He learned how to use a drawing program with his computer to design some of his patterns. He made these complex geometric and highly refined images for a long time and really loved making them. When he developed their shape relationships, he felt like an architect.

Photo credit: Roy Strassberg.

Eloquent Gesture, *34-1/2" x 14" x 20", 1995. This piece is more open and active in form than some of the other pieces in this series.*

He employed imagery he thought of as "city imagery." He notes that he has always worked with imagery that reflects a built environment rather than a natural one. These pieces were very successful with the public. He still likes this work and thinks it is among the best he has made. However, as he says, "I am just not going to make it anymore." He has completely lost interest in making this work. For a time he lost interest in almost all the work he had been doing. He didn't know what sort of work he wanted to do next but he knew he wanted something else. For the first time in his life as an artist, he thought that if something good didn't happen he was going to stop working in clay. He now feels that the key lies in his immersion in extraneous details. He became too immersed in surface patterns and in using the computer to design them. In 1990 he found that the design process was taking over the work. Though it was successful, he wasn't sure why he was making his work anymore. He felt he had gone into a blind alley and that he had to start working in a radically new way.

To revitalize his work he tried a number of different directions. Two that seem most important to him now are a group of pieces he called the *House Series* and another he called *JazzMan Meets the Technicians*. In the *House Series* he abandoned the highly controlled slab work he had been using since the 1970s. These new pieces were very loose and unstructured, they were built step by step rather than designed. In the *JazzMan* group he turned again to imagery of the Holocaust. In these pieces, which looked like those of his series of *Jazz* sculptures, he tried to picture the cold technical skill with which the Nazis established

their machinery of death.

When he combined the subject matter of *JazzMan Meets the Technicians* with the looseness of the *House* pieces, he found the way he needed to revive his work. He called this new work *Holocaust Bone Structures*. He applied for a research grant from his school, Mankato State University, to create images of the Holocaust in clay. He still had to make many changes. He found that he needed to change the way he worked - to change almost everything about it. Since his graduate student days, he had always planned his work beforehand; now he had to stop planning and let instinct take over. He had always worked with slab-walled forms with empty space in the interior - the classic ceramic space. Now he needed to develop a whole new way of constructing his work where the interior wasn't empty but rather crowded with fragments and stick-like forms. In his 1970s work he made images with harmonious forms and rich color that pleased his audience. Now he needed to make knotted forms with limited color. He needed to connect to his core beliefs and to his own history. Strassberg feels he experiences as much joy in making this new work as he ever has, but now there is a new dimension - he has been searching for a spiritual core in his work and in these pieces he has found one.

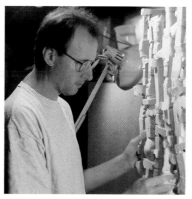

Roy Strassberg.

Rimas VisGirda

Rimas VisGirda is a ceramic artist who is known for his powerful imagery. In recent years, especially, this imagery has become marked by an atmosphere of dark comedy and a threatening sense of dread.

Conversation, *charcoal fire and luster. The turmoil associated with the periods just before, during, and especially just after World War II was a profoundly traumatic experience for many who trace their roots to the Baltic Republics. In this piece we see VisGirda combining a very American Funk-influenced style with ironic comments on life in Eastern Europe in the aftermath of the collapse of the Soviet Union. VisGirda used a firing technique he calls charcoal firing on this piece. His friend Phillip Cornelius developed the firing strategy. To carry it out, he first loaded an updraft kiln with his pieces surrounded by sawdust in a manner similar to a sawdust firing and filled the whole kiln. He then fired the gas-fired kiln in his normal manner to cone 10. He then filled the kiln with charcoal, loading it through holes he placed in the side of the kiln. He also poured charcoal in through the damper at the top of this updraft kiln. He then fired for another hour or so. The charcoal reacted with the clay to flash, reduce, and melt. You can see the smoke patterns on the surface of the two figures.*

Clay body: VisGirda uses a white stoneware clay body.

Six tile kaolin	44
EPK kaolin	22
Ball clay	11
Ground silica (flint)	11
Nephaline syenite	11
Crushed decomposed granite 10 mesh	20
Coarse grog 10/20 mesh	20
Silica sand 30/40 mesh	10

VisGirda makes his clay body from dry materials. This body has good working characteristics both in throwing and hand forming. To this he adds decomposed granite particles. This is a grog-like material; its particle sizes vary from five to 60 mesh. He gathers this material himself, going up into the hills looking for granite rubble. He sieves this material and wedges it into his clay body. During the firing it bleeds out, creating a scattering of small sparkles; the decomposed granite contains feldspar so when it melts it leaves a small glass bubble. This phenomenon is particularly noticeable under a luster glaze.

VisGirda keeps his forms simple because he knows he will draw and paint complex imagery on their surface. He forms many of his pieces on the potter's wheel, then takes them off the wheel head and modifies their shapes. He usually works with soft wet clay,

joining his forms by scoring, then applying a heavy bead of slip (perhaps 1/4" thick), which oozes out of the join. Sometimes he leaves this bead of slip alone, letting the viewer see it, and sometimes he uses a metal rib to refine and smooth the join. When the clay becomes firm, he paddles the pieces to control the form. He creates his pieces very quickly and in a few days will build up a store of unglazed forms which he uses over a period of

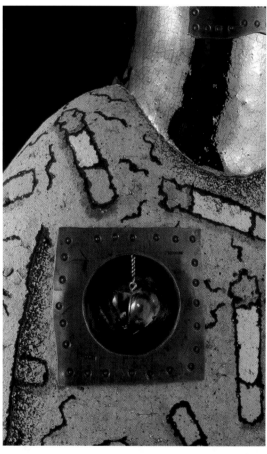

Photo credit: Rimas VisGirda.

*Detail of the torso, **Panevezys**. Here we see depictions of cigarettes and a heart. In this piece we see the combination of a very American image sensibility with ironic comments on life in Eastern Europe in the aftermath of the collapse of the Soviet Union.*

months as canvases for his drawn and painted imagery. He air dries his forms or dries them under a tent made from a shopping bag or stapled newspaper sheets.

After the piece dries (but before the bisque fire) VisGirda applies a liquid wax to the surface. He scratches into the wax to draw his imagery. He uses this method to create a nervous wiry line. He runs a soft brush loaded with a black engobe over the line work. The engobe is drawn by capillarity into the line work and emphasizes the imagery. He fires the piece to bisque (cone 05). After the bisque firing he may apply a clear glaze to the piece and fire it to cone 10 in a reduction atmosphere. The reduction atmosphere makes the white clay look like stone and encourages a dense and granite-like clay body. Because all of his subsequent firings are at very low temperatures, the reduction effects remain. If he uses a metallic luster, he fires that to cone 018.

VisGirda's drawing style is nervous and jagged. His imagery is alternately absurd and threatening, his color, by turns, is acid or overly pretty. The central core of his work lies in the stories he tells in his imagery. VisGirda's imagery is narrative and has its roots in his personal experiences. VisGirda was born in Kaunas, Lithuania, in 1942 in the middle of World War II. It was a very dangerous place. The turmoil associated with the periods just immediately before, during, and especially just after World War II was a profoundly traumatic experience for many who trace their roots to the Baltic Republics. In 1944, when he was two years old, VisGirda's family fled Lithuania to escape the Soviet armies. Though he was not old enough to realize what was happening, he knows he felt his parents' fear and anxiety as they fled from the fighting. In the shambles that was Europe at the end of World War II, VisGirda's family spent five years in a displaced persons camp in Germany, waiting for entry permits to the United States. Once VisGirda arrived, he felt very different from those around him. He had to learn a new language and had to deal with a new place and new standards. He says of that time, "I felt a lot of alienation from my peers, being born in a foreign country, having a strange name, and having to wear non-conforming clothing. My mother, as long as she could, made me wear shorts and sandals where all the other kids had long pants and canvas sneakers. As a consequence, I tried ultra-hard in those days to be accepted and American."

VisGirda wanted to turn his back entirely on any reference to his heritage and completely assimilate. Comic books and science fiction became a big part of this process. He still finds these things fascinating and their imagery compelling. In the late 1960s, during his late adolescence, underground erotic or violent comic books first appeared. These fantasies resonated in his imagination and he identified with their sensibility of wary irony and detachment. He also learned much from such popular culture sources as the movie *The Rocky Horror Picture Show*, city life, punk, and MTV (he still finds MTV visually exciting). All have been important resources for his ceramic imagery.

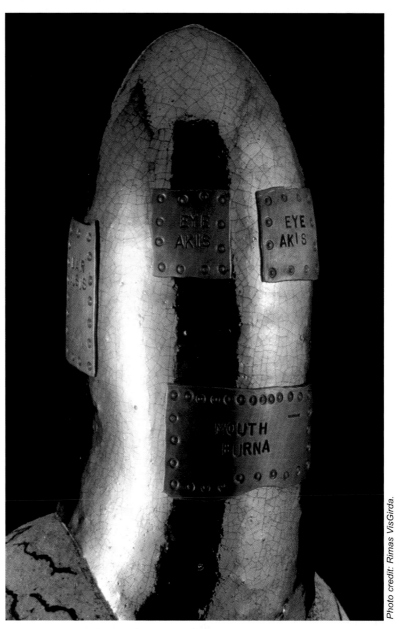

*Detail of the head, **Panevezys**. The silver color is from a low-fire platinum luster. VisGirda made the gray metallic elements from lead sheets. Their dull metallic character gives them a menacing appearance. VisGirda glued these on the helmet form after the firing.*

Though he has never lost his interest in pattern and design, narrative became a central aspect of his work. His stance was that of a removed and cool-eyed observer. In recent years VisGirda has become very conscious of his Lithuanian heritage and has derived much of his imagery from this source.

VisGirda majored in physics as an undergraduate at California State University in Sacramento. He was required to take a fine arts class and stumbled into ceramics. He enjoyed ceramics and took a course in it every semester. His ceramics teacher at Sacramento was Ruth Rippon and he feels she was a great teacher. He took a Bachelor of Arts degree in physics in 1966. After graduating VisGirda worked as a physicist in the aerospace industry in Sacramento. He also taught an adjunct course in physics at the University. He liked teaching and left his job to enroll in the University's education division. He wanted to train as a physics teacher in secondary education, but after his first experience with practice teaching, he saw there was a big difference between secondary and college teaching and began to feel he didn't have the temperament to teach at the secondary level.

He quit the education program and moved to the Sierra Nevada foothills where he started a pottery with a like-minded friend, Richard Hotchkiss. They made thrown, utilitarian pottery. VisGirda specialized in using indigenous materials for these

Photo credit: Rimas VisGirda.

Luster Vase. In most of VisGirda's earlier work the mood is reminiscent of work done by many California ceramists in the 1960s and early '70s. It is satirical and playful. VisGirda's work, over the years, has become much darker in mood.

pieces; he dug his own clay and gathered wood for his firings. He feels his science background and training in deductive logic helped him find interesting and useful ceramic materials and to solve aesthetic problems.

In 1969 he decided to pursue an M.A. degree in ceramics and enrolled at California State to continue work with his former teacher Ruth Rippon. She was particularly interested in sgraffito, sgraffito over engobes, and wax resist techniques. Though he uses very different imagery than Rippon, he has been able to harness these techniques for his own work and they constitute the bedrock of his image making strategy. Another important influence was the ceramic sculptor Robert Arneson, who taught at the University of California at Davis across the river from California State. VisGirda found that he was looking to Rippon for knowledge of the material and design sides of ceramics and Arneson for concepts and ideas about imagery. Arneson befriended VisGirda and had an important influence on his imagery. He encouraged VisGirda to mine his store-house of personal imagery.

VisGirda received an M.A. degree from Sacramento in 1971 and went on to work for an M.F.A. degree at Washington State University in Pullman where he studied with sculptors Jack Dollhausen and Robert Helm. He made sculptural pots and sculpture and as a graduate assistant, taught drawing. He developed his drawing skills along the lines of the comic book derived imagery that had been so compelling to him since his youth. He began to understand that he could use these drawings as imagery for his pots. They became his road for creating a personal approach to ceramics. He received his M.F.A. degree in 1973.

Meanwhile, from 1971 to 1978 while he was in graduate school, he and Hotchkiss ran a ceramic workshop every summer in the Sierra Nevada hills. The area was isolated and beautiful. They constructed a wood-fired, climbing kiln which they fired during the course of the workshop. A number of their students have gone on to make important ceramic work including Kirk Mangus, Eva Kwong, and Arnold Zimmerman.

After graduating VisGirda took a wide variety of teaching positions in the Midwest. These included Millikin University in Decatur, Illinois, where he

developed the practice of firing to cone 10 and then finishing the piece with low-fire lusters. He still uses this work strategy. He moved on to Rochester Community College, then to Bemidji State University, both in Minnesota, then to Drake University in Des Moines, Iowa. By this time he was disillusioned with teaching. There was a new mood on the campuses of most colleges and universities in the U.S. and he was uncomfortable with it. Students were pulling back from their radicalism and freewheeling experimentation.

In 1986 Arneson took a semester leave and asked VisGirda to apply to Davis for the post of visiting lecturer. VisGirda loved teaching there; he felt that Arneson's students had a very unusual sense of commitment. At this time VisGirda was making pots and drawing on them. All of this work was initially high fired, followed by a low temperature luster firing. His imagery had a strong narrative content. In the fall of 1986 and winter of 1987, he had a residency at the Kohler Co. Arts/Industry Program. He enjoyed the challenge of working at Kohler and has come to enjoy the process of setting up shop wherever he is and getting down to work.

While at Kohler, VisGirda found out that a former colleague and friend, Billie Theide, was teaching in Champaign, Illinois. After he was finished working at Kohler, he paid her a visit and they became quite close. They are now married. Theide is a metalsmith and

teaches at the University of Illinois at Champaign/Urbana. VisGirda still travels a great deal but now has a home base. He has fashioned for himself a life in which he punctuates his everyday life at home in Champaign with trips to various workshops and residencies. He tries to stay open to the resources he finds as he travels and to make the best use of them. He feels that in adapting to his changing conditions, he must make adjustments and this leads to progress and evolution. In recent years he has temporarily replaced Paul Soldner at Clairmont College and Phillip Cornelius at Pasadena City College. In 1987 he became head of the ceramics program at Illinois Wesleyan University in Bloomington. This part-time teaching position was perfect for him - it allowed him to take off for a semester if he needed to, gave him time to do his own work, and provided him with a place to fire.

In 1989 VisGirda returned to Lithuania and took part in a five-week symposium at Panevezys (Pah-ne-ve-zhees). He reacted very strongly to returning to Lithuania after it had regained its independence. When he had the opportunity to go back to Lithuania, his outlook started to change. He felt much more that he was "part of the human situation" and that he was more engaged. Though not all participants knew Lithuanian, he feels it was a big help that he did. The facility was in a glass factory and it was excellent. He now visits Eastern Europe on a regular basis.

Panevezys, [pah ne ve zhees]. VisGirda made this piece from two paddled and modified domes, one at the top and one on the bottom. He threw them on the potter's wheel and smoothed their surfaces with a rib. After the forms had dried for a few hours, he took them off the wheel head, cut out their bases, and pressed their walls together to modify their shapes to make them oval (it is much easier for him to do this to the form once it has no base). After he assembled the form and the clay became firm, he paddled the form to shape it. After the piece dried he applied a liquid wax to the bottom half and scratched into the wax to create a wiry linear imagery. He applied a black engobe in the line to emphasize it and fired the piece to bisque. After the bisque firing he applied a clear glaze to the top piece (the hood) and fired the piece to cone 10 in a reduction atmosphere. He then added shading to his linear imagery with an underglaze pencil and fired to cone 05 in an electric kiln. Finally he painted a platinum luster over the top of the piece (the hood form). This luster is very shiny because he applied it over a clear glassy glaze. It is highly crazed; this breaks up the surface. He now needed to

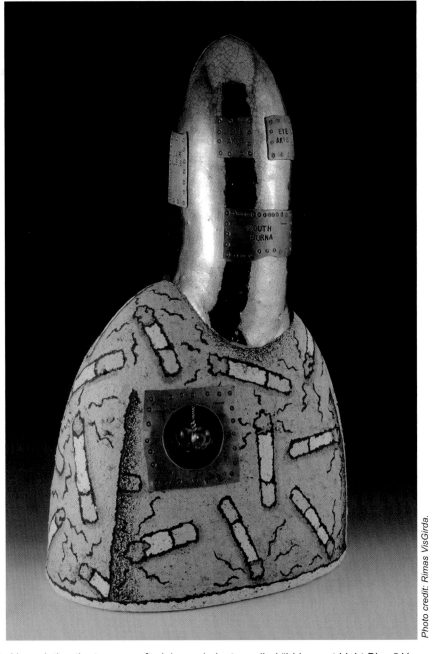

Photo credit: Rimas VisGirda.

add color to the torso. He started by painting the torso a soft pink-purple luster called "Iridescent Light Blue." He then added shading to the cigarettes, using an orange luster for the filters and a red and a gray luster for the burning coals. He fired the lusters to cone 018.

VisGirda next worked on the nonceramic elements that are part of the piece. He began with commercially available lead sheets and ran them through a rolling mill to give them the thickness and smoothness he needed. On the left side of the torso he made a kind of "heart" from a pendant made from Baltic amber. He placed the pendant in a sheet lead panel with a bowl-shaped depression in its center. He shaped the lead panel by making a wooden form and hammering the sheet into the form (lead is very soft and easily shaped). Around the edges of the lead sheet he placed nail marks using a nail setting tool. These make it look as if the lead panel was nailed into the torso, though in truth he attached it with epoxy. He also hammered steel letter stamps into the lead sheets; these spell words in two languages, Lithuanian and English. For example, he hammered the words "Mouth" and "Burna" (Lithuanian for mouth) in the lead sheet placed over the mouth area. He then glued the lead sheets to the clay forms with an industrial epoxy.

He held the position at Illinois Wesleyan University for ten years until 1997. He now works in his studio and participates in symposia and workshops. He also does some technical consulting for industry. VisGirda feels that one of the things that marks his life (in good and bad ways) is a sense of rootlessness. When young, his parents had to take him from his homeland; they traveled from place to place. As a result, VisGirda is interested in the idea of adaptation. It is one of the things that humans do better than other creatures. We are not specialists and therefore we can (and must) adapt to the many situations we find ourselves facing in our lives. In his adulthood he has traveled a good deal in both the U.S. and foreign lands. He travels a good deal still, to workshops and temporary teaching stints. On these travels for work he makes it a point to travel light and to use what he finds in his new environment. He makes it part of his regular practice to study the local materials and work strategies. He then tries to use these for his own purposes. He uses the materials and tools he finds on site and makes them work for him. He saw his own parents do this and he sees these adaptive skills as a significant facet of being human.

Photo credit: Rimas VisGirda.

Rimas VisGirda in his studio with Dorothy.

JoAnn Schnabel

JoAnn Schnabel is a ceramic sculptor who makes pieces that mirror the forms of nature. She builds these pieces from segments that are easy for her to handle and allow her to create large scale pieces in a natural way. Schnabel pays special attention to the surface texture and color of her pieces.

Summer Concoction, 24" x 22" x 27", 1995. Schnabel created this piece using strip coil techniques. She began with a group of segments that allowed her to work in a scale that simplified the process of glazing and firing. To prepare for the firing she took her segmented kiln apart, leaving only the base. She moved a cart constructed level with the kiln base up to the kiln and slid the pieces onto the base kiln. She then reassembled the kiln around the piece and began the firing. Using this method she was able to load her pieces without endangering them. She fired each segment separately and assembled the piece after the final firing to create the segmented arch form shown. She joined the segments using a "cup and saucer" socket reinforced with a slab sleeve. Schnabel is committed to this building method. It allows her to work freely in the large scale and has much in common with the growth pattern of plants. The result is a plant-like form.

Photo credit: JoAnn Schnabel.

Schnabel uses a terra cotta clay body which she likes because it is fairly strong and has a good fired color. This body has a coarse character that results in good workability and excellent strength. In 1991 she switched from cone 04 to cone 3. Schnabel decided on a red body because she uses unglazed surfaces and feels they look best when made with a red body.

Cone 3 Red Body

Red clay	50
Ball clay	10
Fire clay	10
Talc	10
Sand	10
Grog	10
Red iron oxide	1
Bentonite	2

1/2 chopped nylon fiber
Note: Cone 3 red bodies can be marked by scumming (high calcium, white cloudy coating). Many ceramists add a small amount of barium to discourage scumming. Schnabel prefers to avoid using barium in her studio. Since she rarely encounters scumming, she feels no need to add this hazardous material. In his section, Peter Pinnell discusses a way to avoid scumming without using barium that he feels is quite promising.

During the building process Schnabel constantly paddles the clay to compress it and refine the form. She reinforces the clay wall from behind to make sure it will survive the rigors of the fire. Schnabel uses a whole group of hand-forming strategies but emphasizes work with strip coils. In this process the artist creates strips of clay and assembles the form by adding one strip on another.

While building her forms, a line results where she joins one strip to the next. Schnabel wants these lines to be clearly visible after firing. She makes no effort to erase the lines and makes a virtue out of an effect that could be seen as a problem. Schnabel uses these strips as an important part of her imagery. She likes these join marks because they create a rich surface pattern and reveal the construction of the piece. As she builds her pieces she lets the clay bend so that it cracks and tears. She doesn't always try to erase these marks but rather allows them to remain as part of the imagery. At other times, however, she smooths the surface so it doesn't look overworked. She also uses a rasp to refine her forms.

Schnabel builds her pieces in segments and fires each segment separately. She assembles the piece after the final firing to create the overall form. She joins the segments using a "cup and saucer" socket reinforced with a slab sleeve. This segmented character allows her to make, glaze, and fire her large scale pieces freely. Schnabel likes this building method because it has much in common with the growth pattern of plants and the result is a plant-like form.

Schnabel spends a good deal of time and thought on creating rich surfaces. She applies black copper oxide in the interstices of her pieces before glazing to encourage contrasting color and strong visual textures. She uses a great variety of glazes with different surface character and color. She especially likes to use satin mat and waxy surfaces. She also leaves some of the fired surfaces without any glaze. The unglazed fired clay is an effective foil for the glazed surfaces. Schnabel believes it is very important to develop a personal palette of color and a wide variety of textures and rich surfaces when she glazes. She uses commercially made glaze stains to color her glazes. These stains are formulated to have the same color in their unfired state as they have when fired. She likes using these stains because she can rely on their predictability, consistency, and richness of color. She can mix her stained glazes like a painter mixes paint, blending the stains by eye to obtain a rich palette. Usually Schnabel mixes 2,000 grams of a colored glaze at a time. She does not measure the individual components of the mixture and once she has run out of a glaze mixture with its own particular color, it really is gone. She feels this ever changing palette keeps her glazes fresh and interesting and allows her continuous evolution and development while encouraging her to similar development of the form. Schnabel uses a wide variety of glaze types. Most of her glazes are very stable and don't melt down enough to smooth over the surface once they are fired, so the glaze application is very apparent after the firing. She emphasizes the marks, lines, and cuts (interstices) in the surface of her work by forcing a glaze into these marks. She uses either a squeeze syringe or a brush to apply a contrasting color, then sponges it away so it stays only in the interstices. She also often rubs the dry glaze with her finger to smooth and thin the glaze layer before the firing.

Schnabel likes to use one glaze type in combination with another. She doesn't mix them together but rather applies them in layers. This layering enables her to create surfaces with visual depth. For example, she likes to use two or three coats of a mat glaze with one or two coats of a semi-transparent gloss glaze. This gives her a surface with just a bit of a sheen where the gloss glaze is a little thicker. This surface also has a nice range of colors because the two glazes react to each other in varied ways. Sometimes she paints one glaze on top of another with a brush in a thick patterned application; the result is a highly textured glaze imagery. In this way the glaze is integrated with her textured clay surfaces and is not just a layer of color on top of them.

Schnabel fires at cone 3 in an oxidation atmosphere. At one time she worked at cone 04 but changed to cone 3 because she wanted a more durable clay body. She found that when she exhibited, her pieces fired to cone 04 chipped. Aside from the superior durability of cone 3, she likes the glaze colors she

Photo credit: JoAnn Schnabel.

Spring Sonata, 14" x 5" x 7", 1995. Schnabel spends a good deal of time and thought on creating rich surfaces. She applies black copper oxide in the interstices of her pieces before glazing. This encourages contrasting color and strong visual textures.

Spring Sonata, 27" x 39" x 14", 1995. This grouping of work points up the relationship of Schnabel's pieces to each other in terms of form, rhythm, color, and emotional tone.

can get at this temperature. Their color is a little softer and more subtle than glaze colors from cone 04. When she finishes glazing and firing the individual segments for a large piece, she assembles them. This is the first time she gets to see the piece as a total object. At this point she must make her judgment about the character and quality of the piece.

Schnabel had a strong interest in art while still in high school. She spent her first two years of college at the University of Florida. Very shortly after beginning college she chose to major in art. She took ceramics as part of the art program and became very interested in it. During her sophomore year she became interested in the program in ceramics at the New York State College of Ceramics at Alfred. She transferred there in 1978 and spent the next two and a half years there. She worked with Tony Hepburn, Wayne Higby, and Bill Parry. Her experience at Alfred was very positive. She worked in a variety of ways; in her B.F.A. exhibition she showed a group of spiral sculptures made with Egyptian paste. She did a good deal of work at this time with a number of colored clay bodies. She did not see this as lab work or even technical work but rather as a mode of expression. She took an instinctive approach to these materials. This kind of intense and "over the top" sculptural approach was encouraged at Alfred. She received her B.F.A. degree from Alfred in January 1981.

Schnabel heard about a public communal art studio in Atlanta, Georgia, called Callanwould where she might work in clay in return for assisting in the studio one day a week. She was accepted into the Callanwould program and was given a small studio space. She stayed for a year and a half. She liked the program a great deal, though limited space meant she had to work smaller than she had done before. To deal with the size limitations of her work space, she made small scale pieces. During her time at Callanwould she began to exhibit her work.

Schnabel now felt ready to tackle graduate school. From 1983 to 1986 she attended graduate school at Louisiana State University where she worked with Joe Bova, Bob Lyon, and Linda Arbuckle as well as with members of the sculpture faculty. Bova continues to be a mentor even now.

At this time she was firing her work to cone 04. At first in graduate school she used coils to build her pieces, then she began to use strip coils, building her pieces strip by strip. This was a real breakthrough for her, it let her make larger pieces and gave her more control over the contour of her forms. She also learned to create large pieces by assembling small modules after firing. She liked using this work strategy and continues to use it when making large pieces. Soon she decided to see what would happen if she let the seams between her strip slabs

Photo credit: JoAnn Schnabel.

*A detail of **Winter Dream**, 1995. Note the breakup of the glaze, revealing the red color of the clay body.*

show. This too made a big difference in the way the work looked. She felt this change helped the viewer understand the forms more clearly. These were real turning points in her work.

Also at this time she began to intensify her references to organic forms which she is very fond of, both in her work and her life. She is very serious about gardening and is certified as a master gardener. In 1986 Schnabel had her graduate thesis show. The pieces in this show were segmented, fairly large, and fired to cone 04. She still referred to the vessel format in these pieces and titled the show "Vessels Beyond Time." She says this title indicates her wish to evoke a feel-

ing of timelessness. She wanted her work to look at once archaic and futuristic. She had begun to make purely sculptural objects and though she continues to make vessels, most of her work is now in the sculpture format. She had also begun to work in a larger scale and feels this significantly altered the character of the work, enhancing its power and presence.

In the summer of 1986 she worked at the Haystack Mountain School of Crafts in Maine. She spent the winter in Atlanta and returned to the Haystack in 1987. She then went to Penland School of Crafts in North Carolina for a two-year stint (1987 to 1989) as an artist in residence. She was quite involved with Penland and intensively carried on her work. In the 1989/90 school year she taught at Tulane University in New Orleans. Then in 1990 she went on to teach at the University of Northern Iowa in Cedar Falls. She likes the University, though she wishes there was a stronger support system for art and her work in the local area. This is a common complaint among ceramists who teach in schools located away from large cities; they love being in a rural area but feel isolated.

In 1991 Schnabel spent the

Tempest, *(an older piece), 26" x 18" x 20", 1989. In 1989 Schnabel was finishing up a stint at the Penland School of Crafts as a "Core Student." She benefited greatly from the opportunity to spend a good deal of time free from distractions and was able to create a group of pieces that had a strong internal consistency. The work she is doing now stems directly from these pieces. Here we see an example of this work. At the time she was working in the vessel form.*

summer at the Banff Centre for the Arts in Alberta, Canada. It was at Banff that she began to fire at cone 3. She liked the look of her previous work but felt the need to increase the durability of her pieces. She also liked the look of the work fired to cone 3. She tried to duplicate the look of her low-fire work at this new temperature and feels that she was successful in this. Her cone 3 surfaces combined more intimately with her forms than her low-fire surfaces had. Colors that had been a bit brash became just a bit more harmonious and surfaces that seemed to cover the surface of the clay now seemed to become a more integral part of it.

Schnabel's forms refer to the natural world but they are not realistic depictions of natural forms. Like many contemporary ceramists who refer to nature in their imagery, Schnabel is most interested in reflecting the process of nature rather than making a mirror image of it. Her images are meant to remind us of such natural forms as branches and buds, symbolizing growth.

Branches and buds, of course, are quite small and Schnabel enlarges their scale many times over. By doing this she gives the feeling that the viewer is in an *Alice in Wonderland* world. This kind of fantasy interests her a great deal. She finds it in the work of the Spanish architect Antonio Gaudi and is very fond of the playful way he handled materials. She is fascinated by the unique and inspired structures that came from this personal vision.

Schnabel wants to push herself beyond a cognitive understanding of what she is doing as she works. She strives for a very intuitive approach and avoids preconceived ideas. Only when the piece is finished can she really see it. It is at this point that her cognitive faculties come into play. Then she can sit back and study the work and try to understand its nature.

JoAnne Schnabel. "A Portrait of the Artist Glazing a Piece."

John Chalke

John Chalke lives in Calgary, Alberta, where he and his wife Barbara Tipton (see page 239) share a studio. His pieces speak of the core nature of clay and glazes. Chalke is especially known for his richly colored, highly textured glaze surfaces.

Photo credit: Barbara Tipton.

Covered Form with Finial, 4" x 12-1/2", 1997. For this piece Chalke used a stoneware body. He did not fire the body to maturity but rather to cone 05. As a result, the body is very open and absorbent. Chalke hand formed this piece from a single slab of moderate thickness (approximately 1/8"). He used a mixture of vinegar and water to bind the slab ends together at the seam. The form of this piece is reminiscent of a covered jar but the base and the top are attached. This piece is completely nonfunctional. Chalke left the marks of a string tourniquet on the surface of the piece. He carefully placed the tourniquet and then tightened it with a wooden handle. He also manipulated the clay wall, pushing out from the inside and in from the outside to create the irregular, rumpled form.

To create the surface Chalke used a glaze containing bone ash, silicon carbide, and magnesium carbonate. He applied a bright, high temperature orange stain in the grooves. He first painted the grooves with water, then lightly touched a stain-loaded brush in the groove. The water drew the stain into the length of the groove. Chalke used a copper saturated glaze to create the black color. He carefully brushed on the glaze in repeated layers. This heavy application encouraged a highly cracked and textured glaze surface. Chalke bisque fired to cone 05 in a top-loading electric kiln to prepare the piece for glazing. After he applied glaze, he again fired it to cone 05. He fired it twice more (for a total of three glaze firings) to get the active surface he desired. He did not soak the kiln and used quick, ten to 12 hour firings.

Chalke fires a stoneware clay body for his work. He doesn't use talc in his clay bodies because he doesn't like the way talc works and feels his stoneware body is far more workable. Since he works in the low fire, the clay body does not mature and is very open and absorbent.

Chalke makes the clay bodies in the studio from dry materials. He first mixes water and dry materials in equal amounts in a large plastic trash can. He pours the resultant slurry into a device that acts as a large sieve (made from a screen tacked on a heavy wooden frame and covered with a canvas sheet). As the wet clay sits on the canvas, its water slowly seeps through and the clay becomes firm. Chalke then mixes the clay body in a pug mill to ensure a homogenous consistency.

Chalke makes his pieces from slabs. He likes to keep his forms quite simple and irregular in contour. He creates irregular forms by pushing the form outward from the inside and inward from the outside. These forms are simple but effective as carriers of his complex surfaces. His form strategies are marked by great reserve and in this way contrast strongly with his approach to glazing which is marked by an energetic excess.

Chalke likes to use very active glazes that foam and bubble. He doesn't divulge his recipes but does reveal that they include materials such as bone ash, magnesium, silicon carbide, and barium to encourage strong textures and colors.

Photo credit: Barbara Tipton.

Detail of **Covered Form with Finial**. In this close-up view we see the way Chalke was able to create a very rough and highly textured glaze surface. Both the recipe and his thick application of it were chosen with an eye to creating the highly textured effect on this piece.

Chalke is fond of using brilliant, highly saturated, "unceramic" colors. Glaze color is derived from colorants or stains. He applies his glazes with a brush in multiple layers, often very heavily, which encourages glaze surface cracking. Chalke likes to explore the way the clay and glazes react to each other and to his application strategies. His work is an expressive exploration of the material character of the medium.

At one point Chalke fired at cone 6. More recently he has been working in the low fire. This has influenced his glaze color, making it much more brilliant. He says of this decision,

"I've dropped my cone 6 glazes all down to cone 05. Those that would come, anyway. At first I partially regretted the change, seeing all those years spent as some kind of waste, but it's no different from living in another place for a while. You might go back. You might not. Perfectly good, and even intriguing glazes gather dust; diaries of a particular time."

In recent years Chalke has fired his pieces to cone 05. He doesn't use a special kiln or any special firing methods. He fires in a top-loading electric kiln. He doesn't soak the kiln and uses a fairly quick, ten to 12 hour firing. What is special about his

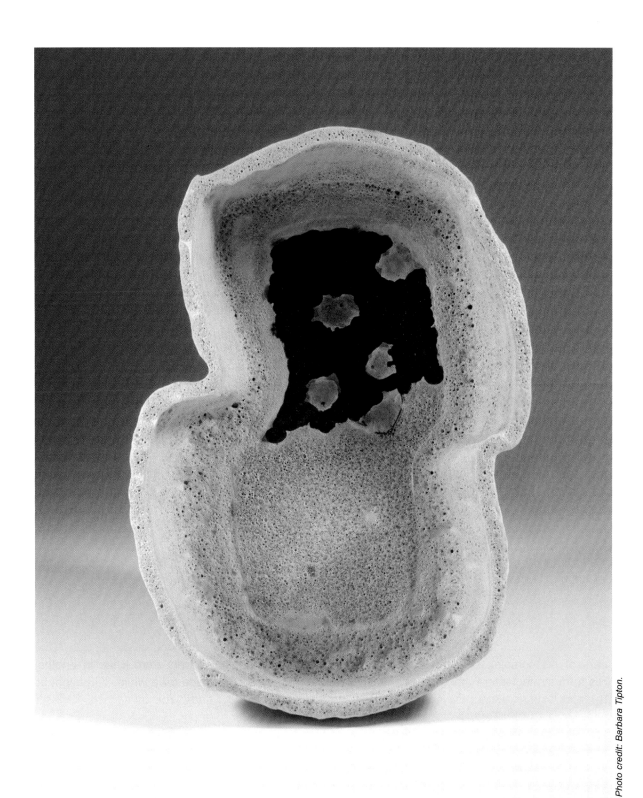

Walled Plate, *13-1/2" x 6-1/2", 1996. Chalke fired this to cone 05 in an oxidation atmosphere. The brilliant colors are derived from barium glazes. This piece is strongly related to highly painted Oribe work from Japan. Chalke has written about his great love for Oribe work. He admires the simple and loose forms and the complex painted imagery of this type of ware. Furthermore, the work often has an audacious character that Chalke responds to very strongly.*

Photo credit: Barbara Tipton.

Green Net and Grey Link, *12-1/2" x 7-1/2", 1996. On one side of this piece we see chrome lead reds and greens and on the other, a highly active glaze containing cryolite and bone ash. Chalke fired it to cone 05 in an oxidation atmosphere. He glazed and fired this piece many times to get the active surfaces and the color and texture he desired.*

firing is the way he uses refire strategies. He fires a piece many times to get the active surfaces he desires. Refiring also improves their color.

Chalke has said he feels he is more in touch with the act of glazing than any other part of the ceramic process and it gets as much attention as anything he does. He considers glazing to be one of the most creative parts of his work. He knows ceramists who think of glazing only as making a covering for the form. His attitude is very different. He is fascinated by the many varieties of glazes - shiny or mat, rough or smooth, colorful or dull, personal or generic.

Glazes are useful in many ways: they have appealing surfaces, they may be used to imitate other materials, they encourage impermeability, and enable the ceramist to create pieces with cleanable and durable surfaces. At one point it was even thought they had protective powers. Chalke reminds us that the Chinese claimed that celedon vessels would break if they contained poisoned food. Glaze may be simple or complex, ranging from one or two ingredients to complex 12 ingredient combinations and these ingredients may come from many different lands. He likes to call glazes of this sort

the "International Melt Meet." Just as important to him is the application of his glazes. They can be applied in thick or thin layers (some of his glaze layers stand as high as 2") they can be splashed, poured, brushed, or sprayed. Glazes can be fired in many ways - in a bonfire, in all sorts of kilns - and cooled for weeks or in 20 minutes. He wants as many choices as possible, for all of them leave their mark on the nature of the piece.

Chalke has worked very hard to create his complex, highly textured glaze surfaces. Until recently most ceramists avoided such surfaces; they looked too much like the dried up muddy surfaces adults were supposed to avoid. Even 20 years ago most ceramists were trying for more finished and polished imagery. In recent years, however, we have come to value these highly textured surfaces. They are surprising and novel. They speak of the nature of clay and of the fire.

Chalke was born in England and attended Worcester Cathedral, Kings School. In the U.S. the school would be called a private or prep school. Founded in 1089, the school is steeped in tradition. Chalke "liked its age and its oddness" but feels in hindsight that it was harsh and eccentric. Those who know him best think it encouraged him to be wary of authority. He was able to take courses in studio art at Worcester and art was his best subject. He attended the school from age seven to 18. In 1958, after graduating from Worcester, he went on to art school at the Bath Academy of Art where he studied painting and sculpture. At the end of his second year at Bath he says, "I got thrown out - I was too visible." He has never been able to ingratiate himself to those who have power.

He spent a year as an "unqualified teacher" (uncertified) outside the city of Stoke on Trent. Stoke on Trent was the most important center of pottery making in the world in Victorian England. When Chalke was there in the early 1960s, he could still see the remains of many old kilns and factories. There was even some barely surviving ceramic production and he could see smoke coming from a few of the kilns. He walked into Stoke on weekends (his pay was low and he couldn't afford a car or even a motorbike). He explored some of these old and deserted potteries. These relics of the Victorian age were fascinating and beautiful, full of dusty machines, bags, and buckets of discarded ceramic materials and silent banding wheels. He was only 20 years old and knew almost nothing of ceramics, but knew he was witnessing something very important.

Chalke returned to the Bath Academy of Art much more confident about himself and very interested in ceramics. Bath had no formal courses in ceramics but one of the teachers there, James Tower (a ceramic sculptor), did work in the medium. Chalke was very much ready for ceramics. He learned to throw a bit, learned a little about glazing, and built kilns. In 1962 he completed his schooling. He then tried to get a job teaching art in a school. Because his recommendations were "not glowing," the jobs he got were not well paid nor were the conditions of work very pleasant and he was required to obey certain rules. He sounds quite aggrieved now when he remembers that he had to wear a tie, shave, keep his shoes clean, and most of all, control the urge to speak his mind; he didn't really succeed in keeping either himself or his supervisors happy. He says he does not crave notoriety or strife and he is not sure why he can be controversial. Most peo-

ple have a mediating persona they use as a kind of diplomat between themselves and others. Chalke does not. He deals with others with a quiet candor which many find threatening. Furthermore, he is completely uninterested in the paper work required to maintain and further the aims of an institution. Much of the work of a teacher is centered not on teaching but on these tasks. He held four different teaching positions in as many years and made pottery in the evenings. At this time he had no fixed identity as a potter, he used both hand-forming and throwing methods to make his pieces and worked with a wide variety of forms. Though he felt he was struggling, he had some successes and his work was slowly accepted into shows. In 1965 he obtained part-time teaching positions at both the Farnam School of Art and the Harrow School of Art, where he taught for four years. At Farnam he met John Reeve, a visiting Canadian potter. Reeve had apprenticed with the English potter and author Bernard Leach, and was very knowledgeable and helpful to Chalke.

In the summer of 1968 Chalke left England to teach at the University of Calgary in Alberta, Canada. Chalke believes Reeve helped him get this job. He thought he might stay for a year, but he so liked the country and its people that he remains in Canada to this day. His work at the time was becoming more sculptural and he was exploring materials new to him. He was gaining knowledge and becoming more dar-

Photo credit: Barbara Tipton.

Platter *(an older piece), 14", 1980. Chalke fired this piece to cone 6 in an oxidation atmosphere. He used glazes containing barium, cryolite, and bone ash to encourage highly textured surfaces. Though Chalke fired this piece in the high fire, it has much in common visually with his more recent work in the low fire. The strong purple color at the center of the piece comes from potassium bichromate, which he applied by sprinkling it over the surface. (Potassium bichromate is a dangerous material. If you use this strategy, wear a good dust mask and a pair of rubber gloves.)*

ing in his work. At the end of the school year at the University, he was not invited to return; once again he had become too visible (and he fell asleep during faculty meetings). Chalke then began to teach at the Alberta College of Art. They too, after a year, failed to renew his position. In 1970, soured by his experiences with educational institutions, he left Alberta to work on construction in Vancouver. He thought he would never teach or make pots again. This experience was numbing. The work was deadening and he became mindless. During the free time the job allowed, he had no energy for the creation of art work. After a year he went back to Alberta, this time to the University of Alberta, Edmonton, about three hours north of Calgary. He taught drawing in Edmonton for five years. He liked Edmonton a great deal and his fellow faculty had more tolerance for his foibles. They had no ceramics program but Chalke took up his own ceramic work again. His new work was mostly in the sculptural vessel format, particularly large plates. He maintained his program of intensive glaze experiments and began to be known for his personal style, his gritty surfaces, and torn abstract forms influenced by the Abstract Expressionist painting movement. He particularly liked the work of the painter Robert Motherwell, the ceramist Peter Voulkos, and the Italian sculptors Arnaldo Pomodoro and Lucio Fontana.

Finally, it was time for him to leave Edmonton and return to Calgary. He rebuilt his studio and built a gas kiln. In the 1970s he became known for his unique surface textures, many created with the unstable material, cryolite. In 1983 he attended a symposium of Canadian and American ceramists organized by the ceramist and writer Barbara Tipton. Over the next year or two they cemented their relationship and in 1985 Tipton and Chalke married. Chalke temporarily moved to Ohio where he did a great deal of glaze experimentation and made pieces, a number of which he entered in exhibitions. In 1986 he and Tipton moved to Calgary. Upon his return to Canada, he built a wood kiln and carried out a great deal of glaze experimentation with soda firing. He received a Canada Council Grant to carry out research on soda firing and, over the years, has been awarded several grants including further awards from the Canada Council and various prizes, both national and international. He continues his work with highly textured imagery in ceramics. He has had numerous exhibitions and his work is in great demand in Canada, the U.S., England, and Europe. He has given numerous workshops and guest teaching stints. He says, however, that he feels a bit like a fish out of water in the very public atmosphere of such events.

All this describes a person who is a classic example of the inner-directed artist. Chalke seems less inclined to pay attention to the opinions of others than most people. This seems to come not because he rejects the ideas of others, but because he seems to feel things very directly and deeply. This gives his work a character that is authentic and self-contained and is his recipe for being uniquely himself.

Photo credit: Barbara Tipton.

John Chalke.

Louis Katz

Louis Katz throws pots with surfaces that speak of unglazed, highly textured clay bodies and of the wood fire. He is a strong advocate of the vessel form and an avid explorer of ceramic surfaces.

Photo credit: Louis Katz.

Recumbent Bowl, *14" x 16" x 10", 1998. Fired to cone 10 in a reduction kiln. Katz flattened the base while the piece was still quite moist. The flattened base has great appeal and allows the viewer to easily view the inside of the piece.*

Clay bodies are very important to Katz. He doesn't cover them with glazes, he gives them the chance to play a major role in establishing the identity of his pots. He works with many different clay bodies. Most of his recent bodies are simple and require only a few materials. Katz loads these bodies with aggregates that allow him to create his highly textured clay bodies. These additions make the bodies difficult to work - in his word, highly "finicky." They don't throw well, are unworkable, and often crack. He uses them because he values their fired texture and color.

He makes his pieces with body recipes such as Dark Anagama Body: 34 red clay; 33 kaolin; 33 ball clay. Katz enjoys working with bodies such as this because he feels that it creates a very pure experience. Rather than making his clay bodies behave, he wants the material to have as much influence on the final look of the piece as he himself does. He likes it best when he can bring his clays to the verge of collapse in firing. He has worked with heavily contaminated clays such as brick clay and says, "Brick clay has taught me to appreciate lime blows as just another decorative element."

It is very important for him to alter his clay bodies with non-clay additions. He adds poly-propylene fibers for strength; they help keep the pot rims from tearing while he is throwing the piece. He adds aggregates to encourage texture. At first he added "Granite Chicken Grit" and "Sanisorb Kitty Litter." Chicken grit is fed to chickens to provide stones for their gizzards and Sanisorb is a "Calcined Fuller's Earth." In 1997 he began to wedge rice in his clay bodies. He wanted to impregnate his pieces with a material that would burn away, leaving voids and pock marks on the surface and throughout the clay wall. He joked that bisque worms were eating his students' projects because the pots looked termite eaten. "My department chair offered to call the exterminators. I should have let him and videotaped the exterminators." He did not do this, however, and his relations with his department chair remain good. After going through several other grains, he has settled on two particulate organic materials - cow corn and wheat berries. He wedges as much of these materials as he can get in and still keep the body workable. When these materials burn away in the fire, the result is a porous and perforated clay body. He also adds sand for texture and strength. The resulting clay body, with its high aggregate content, is very hard to throw. Rims split, sides tear, and it requires considerable strength to throw. At the end of the day his shoulders ache from squeezing. He says he feels the process does not take much special skill, but acknowl-

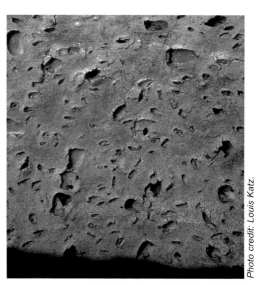

Close-up detail of **Holy Fire Bucket**. This illustrates the richness of Katz's loaded clay body.

Photo credit: Louis Katz.

edges that it is difficult to work with these highly loaded clay bodies. He loves the surfaces he gets, however, and is reminded of termite eaten peachwood in his back yard. He loses a lot of these pieces. When leather hard they are strong - when dry they can break apart easily. They often crack during firing and he has to slow the firing between 410° and 420°, the point at which the organic materials react to the heat and begin to expand; this can crack the piece. He spends a day slowly moving through this dangerous zone. He feels these bodies are worth the trouble and sees this slow firing as a necessary part of the process.

Katz loves the wheel forming process. It gives him great visceral pleasure. He does not aim for finished looking pieces but rather for a feeling of spontaneity and a look of joy taken in the action of throwing. He

7 Salmons, length 5', cone 11, gas/wood soda fired, 1997. Katz considers this to be one piece composed of seven bowls on a ware board.

says, "I throw pots fast. I have heard people say, 'you have to make 100 pots to know a form.' I have found that 100 is nice but a few thousand is nicer. This is true especially if they are thrown in large lots spread over a few years. Your hands lose the need of a directing consciousness during the throwing. More time can be spent on what and why, and less on how. Your hands get water instinctually, move up the clay instinctually, and at the same time take on a dance that expresses your mood, thoughts, and history." Yet behind all this there is also a sense of discipline. Katz set out to see if the writer Michael Cardew was right when he said that one could throw 1,000 pots a day. He decided he could if someone was around to deliver the clay and take away the finished product. For this exercise Katz has chosen to throw bowls 3" in diameter. He estimates that over a period of years he has thrown more than 10,000 of these 3" bowls.

Katz throws on a kick-wheel, though he sometimes thinks he would prefer to throw his pots on a treadle wheel because of the control it offers. When he is working on large forms, he often uses an electric wheel set on a very slow speed. After he finishes centering, he never varies the speed.

Katz has spent a great deal of time studying village potteries in rural Thailand and has been strongly influenced by many of the attitudes he found there. As a result, he is very sensitive to the nature of work processes and his throwing tools. He tries to use work strategies and tools he thinks are appropriate to the results he wants. He prefers not to use a work strategy he sees as overly complex or tools that are overly sophisticated for his very direct work. As a consequence of these attitudes, his approach to technology is quite simple. He is very interested in the techniques and attitudes that prevail in pre-industrial cultures and in the early potteries of the Industrial Revolution. He believes that intent has impact on the product. He feels his work is not about modern industrial materials or processes and that such tools as glaze calculation for the most part play no part in his day to day studio life.

He is very conscious of his tools. He makes some of his own tools and uses tools he obtained in village potteries in Thailand. He avoids all tools he thinks are too "mass production." He feels a rib is no less a functional art object than a pot. It is no less expressive. He asks, "Why make a handmade object with a mass-produced tool?" He prefers a tool marked by a sense of individuality and free from what he sees as a depersonalized, mass-produced character.

Katz makes very little use of slips or glazes. The complex textures created by the materials he wedges into the clay account for most of the surface energy of his pieces. He may use a very thin wash to finish a piece. He makes these washes from a single clay, such as a red clay or kaolin, or from simple mixtures of two or three clays suspended in water.

Katz fires a very difficult kiln; with a combination of pride and frustration he calls it "The Beast." His fuel is natural gas and he fires the kiln to cone 11 but part of the kiln is always four or five cones behind. At the end of the firing he sprays a small amount of soda ash (1,000 grams) dissolved in water in the kiln. This lets him create a slight and irregular sheen over his surfaces. He occasionally supplements the natural gas with wood, bamboo, or palm fronds. He does not fret over the kiln atmosphere when he fires. There is no point in fretting, because The Beast, with its uneven fire and poor quality burners, will not let him control the kiln atmosphere very well. He welcomes the very mixed results he gets - oxidation, reduction, and carbon trapping. He makes decisions about damper settings and final firing temperature based on the way the pots look in the kiln during the firing. He looks at the way the flame passes across the work through several spy holes he has placed in the kiln walls. He doesn't keep a firing log; he wants the work to convey a feeling of spontaneity and engagement. He never loads or fires or adds soda the same

Holy Fire Bucket, soda fired stoneware, cone 10, 7" x 12" x 9", 1998. Katz says it takes days to burn out the organics he has wedged into the clay body. If he fires the piece too quickly, it may crack. The piece has a very loose form and a highly textured surface. Katz wants his work to convey a feeling of spontaneity and engagement.

way, for the same reason. He is devoted to chance and is happy to wait until he unbricks the door to find what has taken place during the firing.

One of Katz's favorite ceramic pieces is known to him only from a photograph of a vessel from Japan that served years ago as a fire bucket. This piece and others like it are plain, totally functional pots. Katz feels these wholly functional pieces have an integrity and honesty that are quite wonderful. They serve as icons for him and this work from Japan has had a profound impact on his thinking.

Katz is very concerned with pots and the ideas we have of the pot form. He talks of representation and presentation. Contemporary potters must ask themselves: Am I presenting a pot or an image of a pot? Katz feels he is exploring the image of a pot. The play between representation and presentation, or put another way, image and object, is extremely important to many contemporary ceramists.

Katz first encountered clay in 1972 while attending high school in a Detroit suburb. He was in the 11th grade and was considering a career as an architect. That year one of the courses he had planned to take was closed so he took ceramics instead. He immediately responded to the clay and took it up with great energy. The next summer (and for the following eight summers) he taught ceramics at a summer camp. He read every book he could find on ceramics. He continued to take ceramic courses and

tried his hand at all sorts of ceramic work. In his last year of high school in 1973, he built a raku kiln in his back yard. In 1974 he entered the School of Engineering at the University of Michigan at Ann Arbor. Katz has never had an easy time with the organized character of most educational institutions and he soon was dissatisfied with the engineering program. It became obvious to him that his professors' ideas of the way beginning engineering students should be taught had nothing to do with creativity. The following semester Katz transferred to the School of Fine Arts to study ceramics. His first teacher there was Kurt Weiser, who remains a strong influence for Katz. He also worked with John Stephenson and Georgette Zirbes. In 1976, after two years at Ann Arbor, Katz transferred to the Kansas City Art Institute. There he studied with George Timmock, Victor Babu, and Ken Fergusen. Katz enjoyed the Art Institute and feels that one of its best points was a strong student body. He feels he learned a great deal from his fellow students. In 1978/79 he needed a break from school and sold wholesale produce in San Francisco. In 1979 he returned to Kansas City and graduated in 1981. He married Gail Busch, a fellow student at the Art Institute, then moved to Rhode Island to set up a studio with his wife. He stayed there for a year. He thought he wanted to make utilitarian pots but instead found himself making 9' high water towers out of plaster, lath, and ceramic shards. It became

clear to him during that year that he didn't want to make utilitarian pottery for a living.

Katz went to graduate school at Montana State University in Bozeman, where he studied with Mike Peed and Ric Pope. Here he mainly constructed kilns that he thought of as art objects. Although their aesthetics were important, they also were working kilns. He fitted them with wheels, which allowed a limited portability so he could exhibit them and remembers rolling them into galleries. Instead of firing them in a kiln with flame around their outside surfaces, he fired them as kilns with the fire inside the firing chamber. Therefore, their firing chambers were fired to maturity while their outer surfaces were unfired. This approach seems inside out, but it makes sense given the nature of these objects. Katz needed to make pots to fill these kilns and made them in great numbers. He also became interested in bricks and made many, which he showed with his pots. He received an M.F.A. degree from Montana State in 1987.

He and his wife then went to the Archie Bray Foundation in Helena, Montana, where they worked for about two years. After the Bray they spent a year in Thailand - a destination Katz reached by a circuitous route. In college he had a Thai classmate who showed him slides of a village pottery with anagama fired unglazed pots. Katz liked the work very much and resolved to go there someday. Intrigued, he learned a few words of the Thai language.

Salt Kiln *(an older piece), scrap clays and straw, 4' x 2' x 2' , 1984. Katz made this piece by throwing it in sections. He then assembled it and coated it with a mixture of floor sweepings and straw. He then fired it, filled with pots, to cone 10 using a salt fire strategy. When the kiln cooled he moved it into an art gallery. Each day of the exhibition he unloaded a few bowls and placed them around the kiln.*

Five years later a woman from Thailand came to visit the Bray Foundation and Katz was able to dredge up from his memory the Thai word for hello. They struck up a conversation and he asked if she knew of Dankwean village. It turned out that she owned a pottery there. He started saving money and applied for a Fullbright grant to Thailand, which he was awarded at the last minute. He spent much of that year in Dankwean village and the rest traveling around the country looking for other village potteries. He documented these potteries by taking video movies and slides. He came back with a collapsed lung and chronic diarrhea, but he had a wonderful time and learned a great deal.

After his return to the U.S. he did visiting artist stints at Arizona State University and Memphis State University. Then he went to the University of Missouri at Columbia and taught art appreciation while his wife taught ceramics. After this he went back to the Bray Foundation where he worked for their retail clay business. Since 1994 he has been teaching ceramics at Texas A & M at Corpus Christi. It was at this time that he started using his "worm eaten" clay bodies. He has had a very positive response to this work.

Katz sees himself as a synthesizer, taking various strands of his work and twining them together to create new work. He sees himself as very spontaneous and sensitive to signals from the materials he uses and the firing. He is afraid of over-planning and of taking rigid positions. He feels those who do may end up with work with no breath of life. He doesn't mind loose ends and he wants his work to be animated and breathing with the spirit of life.

Louis Katz.

Richard Notkin

Richard Notkin's work is strongly image oriented. In the past he worked almost entirely in clay, but in his recent work he has been experimenting with combinations of clay and nonclay materials such as bronze and clay. He often works with molds and in the past used slipcasting to create his complex imagery. Recently he has been working with press mold forming and hand forming as well. In the work he made in the 1980s and early '90s, he used a tan or brown stoneware casting slip. For many years Notkin left the clay unglazed and

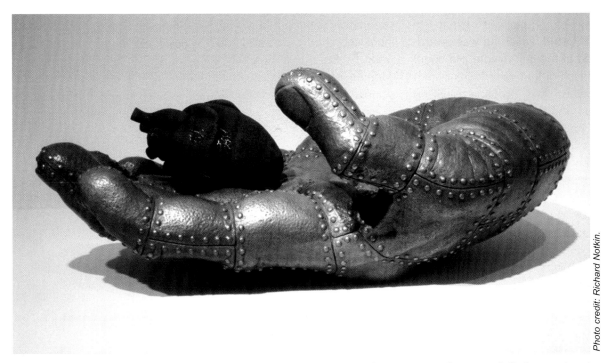

Photo credit: Richard Notkin.

Offering, *bronze and clay, 6-3/4" x 17-1/2" x 11", 1996-97. This piece is an essay on human evil. It shows a heart held in an armor-plated hand studded with rivets. For Notkin the armor plate speaks of militarism and in the image of the hand, Notkin shows us a hand that is used for manipulation and evil. The charred heart speaks of victimization and the death of the soul. Notkin wants it to be an image of both spiritual and physical death. This piece consists of two parts, a heart made of clay and a hand made of cast bronze. We see here the results of an integration of bronze casting and clay. Notkin used a coarse, red colored cone 6 clay body with added grog to make the clay form.*

The hand: Notkin has worked with clay casting slips for many years. The mold making process for metal is similar to that for clay and Notkin is quite comfortable with metal casting. He made the hand minus its thumb by pressing clay sheets into a two-piece press mold, then made the thumb using the same process. He then joined the body of the hand and the thumb. After he assembled the hand, he used soft clay to add a lot of detail such as the plate and rivet imagery. He then refined the imagery and readied it for casting. After he completed the clay form, he had it cast in a foundry known for its to custom work. Once it was cast and cleaned, Notkin worked very closely with the "patineur" (the artisan in charge of creating the surface character of the piece). Notkin would request a particular effect and the patineur would try to achieve it. They looked at the results and when both agreed that the results were good, they knew the piece was finished.

The heart: Notkin made the heart form and the added details such as arteries and veins using hand-forming methods. He used a glaze rich in magnesium carbonate to finish the heart. He applied the glaze by dipping the piece in the glaze. As the glaze dried, it shrank and cracked. The glaze is very stiff and nonflowing and the cracks don't heal in the firing. The result is a highly broken texture that Notkin used to suggest a burnt and charred surface. Notkin fired this form to cone 6 in an oxidation atmosphere. He used a slow firing and cooling procedure to avoid cracking.

fired to cone 6 in an oxidation atmosphere. In the last year or so, however, he has been working with press mold forming using a coarse clay loaded with fire clay and grog. This clay body is strong, has a pleasing surface, and is easily freed from the mold. In this work he is again using glazes. He has been experimenting with very dry surfaced and highly unstable glazes that work well with his imagery. He fires the clay segments of these pieces to cone 10 in a gas-fired reduction atmosphere in a 28-cubic-foot downdraft, soft brick kiln he built.

In his imagery Notkin often deals with human failings, war, and evil. He speaks of victimization, the death of the soul, of spiritual and physical death. He gives us images of militarism, mushroom clouds, death masks, mace-like forms, chains, camouflage, armor plate, and organs such as brains and hearts. Notkin has often used the image of a skull that also speaks of death, reminding us of the Totenkopfverbände (Death's-Head Battalions), special sections of the elite Nazi SS dedicated to the elimination of Jews

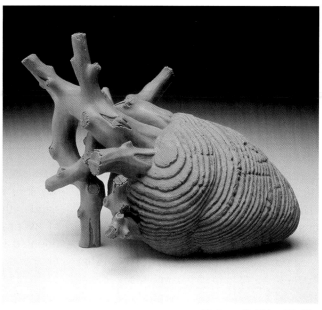

Photo credit: Richard Notkin.

Interior Landscape I. *Stoneware clay body, 6-5/8" x 9" x 6-3/8", 1997. In this piece Notkin fools the observer by showing an imagery that at first appears as a human heart. When looked at more closely, it is revealed as that of grained wood with twigs growing out of it. Here Notkin evoked a feeling rather than trying to tell a particular story or communicate a specific message. Notkin made this piece from a group of press molds. He used one press mold for the large form, the body of the heart. He made seven small press molds for the various branch-like veins and arteries. After he made the forms, he carved the large form with a sharp knife, then assembled the pieces and smoothed the joins to create the finished work. He fired this piece to cone 6 in an oxidation atmosphere.*

in Eastern Europe in World War II. They wore a patch with an image of a skull on their black uniforms.

Notkin gets much of his imagery from his background. He inherited strong social and political values from his father, an immigration lawyer, and his mother, a nurse. Both came out of the idealistic, urban, socially conscious Jewish community of the 1930s and '40s. Notkin became a draft resister during the Vietnam conflict. Many of the students who spoke for the Vietnam peace movement came from this background, including activists Jerry Rubin and Abbie

Hoffman and protest singers Bob Dylan and Phil Ochs.

Notkin's image oriented work started out, in his words, as "three-dimensional political cartoons." Notkin believes these pieces served a real purpose and his remark is not self demeaning. As time went on, however, his themes became less topical, less like a page from the newspaper. He shifted to timeless themes and a more universal view of the human situation.

Notkin was strongly influenced by his teacher Robert Arneson, who was one of the most visible members of the Funk movement in ceramics - a very powerful movement, especially on the West Coast. Notkin was fascinated by many of its ideas but wanted to make work that was precise and intellectual - very different in this way from Funk. This is the source of Notkin's great love of Yixing teapots: they are reserved and thoughtful.

For many years Notkin worked with very small, very precisely carved pieces. Here too, we see a relationship with Yixing teapots. He made small precious objects. He has said of this, "I have always believed that the aesthetic impact of a work of art is not proportional to its size alone, but also to its content." Recently, however, he has been working in a larger scale and enjoys the challenge of this change in his work. These larger pieces are usually press mold formed.

In 1979 the Three Mile Island nuclear power plant in eastern Pennsylvania almost went into meltdown. Notkin made a group of pieces he called *The Cooling Tower Series*. Their imagery came from his distrust of nuclear technology. These featured threatening images of nuclear cooling towers. He also made a group of pieces using imagery of city streets, sewers, dogs, garbage cans, pipes, and wires - the underpinnings of his youth on the south side of Chicago.

Notkin first studied art at the Laboratory School of the University of Chicago, an experimental high school. He did well in his art classes and his teacher, Robert Erickson, a wonderful mentor, encouraged him to think about becoming an artist. Notkin began his studies as a painting student in 1964 at the Kansas City Art Institute. He soon switched to sculpture. At first he was wary of clay but after a friend showed him what could be done with the medium, Notkin became interested in it. In his junior year he decided to major in ceramics. He studied with Victor Babu and Ken Fergusen. He sees Fergusen as one of the most charismatic teachers he has ever met. Like all Fergusen students, he has

tales of the man. He remembers Fergusen at his dramatic best, telling his students a tale with the punch line, "Develop an infallible technique, then place yourself at the mercy of inspiration." Notkin has always tried to do this. He began his work in ceramics with hand forming, moved on to try his hand at the wheel (the program at Kansas City was highly oriented to wheel forming). He discovered that he really wanted to form pieces using slipcast techniques and began to explore that kind of work. In 1970 he received his B.F.A. from the Kansas City Art Institute.

This was the height of the Vietnam conflict and as he was finishing up his undergraduate

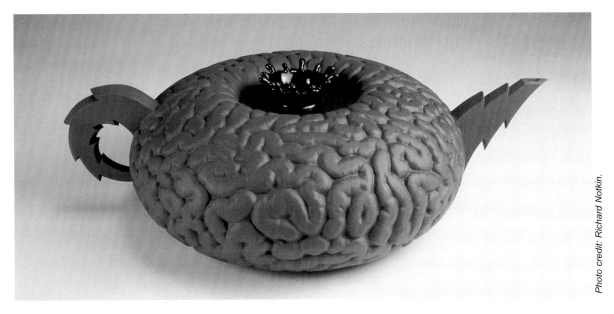

Photo credit: Richard Notkin.

Ellipsoidal Brain Teapot: Primordial I, terra cotta body with glazed sections, 3-1/2" x 11-1/2" x 8", 1993. In this piece Notkin worked with a number of images he liked to use in the 1990s. These include the tangled image of a naked brain, the imagery of splashed water seen in a stroboscopic photograph, and the threatening, spiked lightning imagery on the handle and spout. Notkin used a slipcasting forming strategy and an unusually complex six-piece mold to create the main body of the teapot. He created the handle and spout using slipcast methods in two-piece molds. He made the lid on the wheel and gave it its "splash" imagery by carving the form after it had become leather hard. He glazed the lid to create contrast with the mat surfaced unglazed body of the piece.

Hexagonal Curbside Teapot - Variation #17 *(an older piece), 5" x 7-7/8" x 4", 1988. In this piece from the 1980s we see a strongly pictorial, storytelling imagery, with great attention to illustrative detail. This is the city landscape of Notkin's youth. This piece, one of Notkin's most striking, was very difficult from a technical standpoint. He cast it in sections in 11 different molds, many of which were multi-part. Notkin first made carved positive forms for each of the molds, then made molds from each of these positive forms. The body of the teapot required an eight-piece mold and the Irish Setter forming the top part of the handle required a seven-piece mold. Where necessary, Notkin carved the cast surfaces to create a more detailed imagery and finished undercut areas (these cannot be formed in molds). He detailed and cleaned all the surfaces and built up and smoothed all the joins to remove any vestiges of the slipcast process.*

work, Notkin sent his draft board a letter declaring that he would not serve in this war that he deemed wrong in every way. He was classified 1A - Delinquent. He did report for the medical exam and was declared unfit for war. He was now free to go on to graduate school.

In his senior year at Kansas City, on a trip to New York, Notkin saw a piece by Robert Arneson at the Museum of Modern Art. It was in an exhibition called "Dada, Surrealism and Their Heritage." The 1965 piece was titled *Typewriter*. Notkin describes it as in the form of a ceramic typewriter with female fingers and long red fingernails instead of keys. He remembers saying to himself, "This is the guy I have got to study with." He immediately was convinced that if he wanted to go to graduate school, the University of California at Davis where Arneson taught would be the place to go. He applied and began his studies at Davis in 1971. At this time he was mak-

ing ceramic work with highly political, antiwar imagery. In one project he made hundreds of clay tiles upon which he wrote antiwar messages. He scattered these throughout the campus and even used epoxy to glue a few to campus buildings. He stamped each one at the bottom of the tile "Davis Clay Conspiracy."

Notkin became a teaching assistant for Robert Arneson and got to know him very well. At first he found the atmosphere frustrating. Arneson's style was the opposite of the "hands-on" teaching style he had experienced at Kansas City. When he came to Davis, Notkin didn't know how independent he would be. The graduate studio was in no way a classroom situation. The students worked in an old Quonset hut left over from World War II that nobody else wanted. Arneson had his studio there along with his students. Notkin says of this time, "We simply worked. We worked very hard and we worked all the time, stopping only for sleep or occasional breaks. We were infected with the spirit of the work." Arneson was not easy on the students; he had a way of needling them, testing their resolve, their strength and commitment. It took Notkin a while to see what Arneson did and how he did it. At first Notkin was frustrated with Arneson's way of teaching but then came to appreciate it. "Bob taught us to be artists, not students anymore. We learned as Arneson learned. Furthermore, his work had high visibility and he attracted really strong students." Those students who couldn't deal with Arneson's way of teaching left the program. Notkin stayed and continued to work with his antiwar, socially conscious imagery. In 1973 he graduated with an M.F.A. degree from Davis.

Notkin had been able to sell work for some time, mostly inexpensive items aimed at the student market. This brought in a little money and he also earned some income from teaching adult education class-

Photo credit: Richard Notkin.

*Close-up detail, **Hexagonal Curbside Teapot - Variation #17**. Notkin carved the dogs' fur coats. He could not have achieved this level of detail without going back over the mold-formed imagery with carving tools. The imagery is so complete and accurate that this piece has affinities with that kind of painting termed "Magic Realism."*

es. His income was just large enough to allow him to get by living in Davis, which was an inexpensive place to live and a good town for artists. He decided not to apply for a permanent teaching job when he graduated, but rather keep his days free for the creation of ceramic work. He rented a small house with a garage and set up a studio.

Things changed radically for Notkin in the summer of 1973. He was a half year out of graduate school and working in his studio. Gallery owner Allan Frumkin had come to Davis to see Arneson's work and asked Arneson if there were any other area ceramists making interesting pieces. Arneson offered to take him to Notkin's studio. Notkin was working on a group of cast pieces finished with brilliantly colored low-fire glazes. On this particular very hot day, Notkin was working in his garage/studio wearing only his undershorts. Arneson and Frumkin came into the studio

unannounced and Notkin, a bit embarrassed, started opening cabinets and showing Frumkin his work. He had been working very hard and had a large number of pieces. Frumkin asked Notkin about his pricing and when he replied, Frumkin laughed and said that he would have to double the prices to show them in New York. Notkin's career was launched. Soon he was regularly showing his work in New York galleries and it was selling well. He was introduced to a high powered, high profile art scene he had known little about. He now was making a modest living from his work. He says of this period, "I was very fortunate to be in the right place at the right time with the right stuff."

After a year or so he felt he could afford to stop teaching adult education classes. He moved to a place where he could live quietly and cheaply. It was the remote logging community of Myrtle Point, Oregon. He built an inexpensive house and studio (mostly from recycled materials) in the woods. He sent work across the country by UPS and had a one man show in Chicago with the Frumkin Gallery in 1975. He also took on guest teaching stints over the next few years. In 1975 he began to feel the bright colors and thick layers of the low fire glazes were not compatible with his detailed imagery. He switched from low-fire clay bodies and shiny glazes to porcelain. He finished this work with thin layers of sponge applied stains and fired it in the range of cones 6 to 10.

In 1982 Notkin spent four months at the Archie Bray Foundation. At the urging of Kurt Weiser he sent slides of sculptural pieces to the Garth Clark Gallery. He was just beginning to experiment with the teapot form and had not yet shown this new work. At that time Clark had only seen Notkin's sculpture and wasn't sure the work would be right for his gallery. That same year, Clark traveled to the Bray Foundation and saw Notkin's new teapots and decided they were just what he wanted.

This was the start of Notkin's *Yixing* series, inspired by the teapots of Yixing, China. Notkin had been studying these pots for many years and admired them a great deal. He was moved by the Yixing work, by its small scale, unglazed surfaces, naturalistic imagery, clay colors and textures. His work was already similar to Yixing and he began to make it even more like this work he admired so much. Notkin, however, did not use the bucolic imagery of Yixing ware in his imagery - instead he spoke of atomic technology and the arms race. In 1983 he began work on a series of pieces he called *Cooling Towers Teapots*. He became known for this work and concentrated entirely on teapots. Because of his strong interest in China, he decided to visit and learn more about Chinese pottery. Unfortunately it was very difficult and expensive to get to China at that time. Finally, he was able to visit in the winter of 1991/92 and has visited three times since, always finding the rapid changes in the society fascinating.

In 1994 Notkin decided he would no longer limit himself to teapots. He says of this, "I could make this work almost effortlessly. It lost its challenge and it was time to move on." In 1996 he built a gas kiln and struggled to master the reduction firing process. At present he is focusing on sculptures two or three times the size of his previous pieces (still not large, but larger than what he has done before). After concentrating on slipcasting for many years, he is now using press mold and hand-forming work strategies and is beginning to integrate bronze casting in his work. This has turned out to be a good combination of media - the bronze pieces start out in clay, then he casts them so they have a similar form sense and are quite compatible.

Notkin's pieces communicate a very strong sense of unity in color, sense of proportion, and controlled variety of forms. His work has a strong sense of continuity which he maintains through his regard for a pictorial, human centered imagery, his love of detail, his sensitivity to the surface of his pieces, and his ability to involve us in his obsessive vision.

Photo credit: Phoebe Toland.

Richard Notkin.

Victor Spinski

In his ceramic work *Victor Spinski* imitates objects of everyday life. He very carefully chooses subjects that will work in clay and imitates their form and surface to create artworks with an uncanny resemblance to the real thing.

Breaking Into a Fruit Box, *17" x 11-1/2" x 11". Spinski fired this piece a number of times and used a number of different firing temperatures ranging from cone 04 to cone 018. In his pieces Spinsky documents the ephemeral objects that create the texture of our daily lives. He limits himself to replicating objects at life size (or nearly so). Here we see him replicating objects in a container. He has concentrated on this form concept since taking up his trompe l'oeil work in the early 1970s.*

Spinski uses low-fire clay bodies to make his pieces. He doesn't buy premixed clay bodies but makes his clay casting slips and clay bodies from raw materials in his studio in order to maintain the highest quality. Furthermore, some of his work processes require an open, cork-like clay body. The body is high talc, white in color, and fairly plastic. Spinski adds .025% magnesium hydroxide to the clay body to encourage plasticity and a good working consistency (smooth and a bit sticky). This body is quite absorbent and porous. His pieces are sculptural and will rarely be moved, so there is no real advantage in making a highly durable, dense body. Since Spinski wants to mirror forms made in other materials,

Birthday Party, 8" x 6", multiple firings. This piece is a bit unusual for Spinski in that he has replicated objects on a plate rather than in a container.

he must replicate such forms as wooden boxes and hammer handles. These nonceramic forms would warp and sag if made with a mature clay body. During the firing, a dense mature clay body is prone to warping where an immature body is not. Because Spinski needs to replicate many different colors and textures - wood, paint, metal - he must carry out multiple firings at various firing temperatures. Dense clay bodies cannot withstand the stress of refiring as easily as open,

absorbent clay bodies. Spinski's absorbent clay body allows him to use techniques that call for multiple firings. He also adds a small amount of paper pulp (approximately 8%) to open up the body and make it easier to work with. Paper pulp is acidic and a somewhat acidic clay body is more workable than one that is alkaline. Another advantage is that a clay body that contains paper pulp can be repaired easily. Some of Spinski's students have even used it to patch bisque-fired work.

Most of Spinski's work is hand built, but he also forms his pieces using a wide variety of strategies including slipcasting, wheel forming, press molding, and hydraulic pressing. Many of his pieces have fairly thick walls strong enough to allow the carving and shaping he needs. Once he forms the pieces, he fires the body to a low temperature bisque (cone 018) to prepare it for carving. He then uses a dental drill or small grinding tool to pierce, carve, and finish the bisque-fired clay body. The

Trash Can *(an older piece), 22-1/2" x 17-1/2", 1977. Spinski made this piece using slipcasting methods. He first made the trash can, then the objects inside it. To make the cola and the beer cans, he made the cans, then made labels using decals and applied them to these forms. Spinski fired this piece a number of times at various temperatures, starting with cone 04 and proceeding to a group of firings at lower temperatures. This is part of a series of pieces Spinski made based on the theme of a garbage can filled with trash. He began using this image in the early 1970s. In this piece (and others in this series), Spinski placed clay replicas of discarded, everyday objects in a trash container.*

Chapter 2: A Sense of Order

Many ceramists concentrate on formal issues. Such characteristics as space, form, and surface take precedence over messages and emotions. This is a classic standpoint taken by many ceramists and the history of our craft is full of examples of work that comes from this point of view. The timeless porcelain wares out of China are excellent examples of this. The Chinese artists concentrated on creating the form, color, and surface of their pieces. Their goal was a sense of balance, of perfection, and for the arrival at a place that was free of the stresses of normal life.

In the hands of an accomplished ceramic artist this approach can communicate a sense of order and have a timeless appeal. Such work serves as a kind of oasis in the midst of our lives, lives that we often see as somewhat disorganized. At its best this work is serene, mature, sinewy, and totally unsentimental.

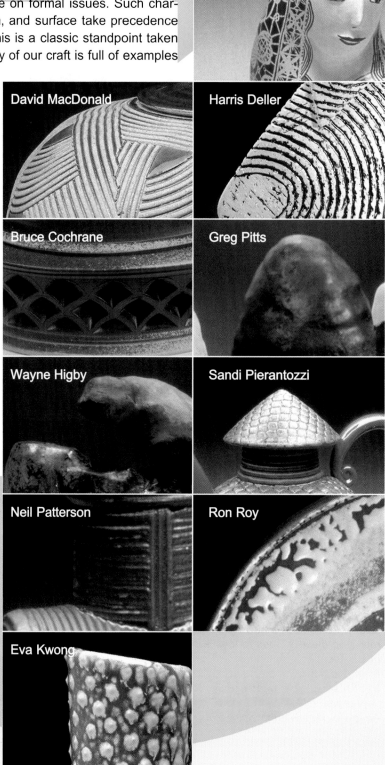

Andrea Gill

David MacDonald

Harris Deller

Bruce Cochrane

Greg Pitts

Wayne Higby

Sandi Pierantozzi

Neil Patterson

Ron Roy

Eva Kwong

Andrea Gill

Photo credit: Brian Oglesbee.

Andrea Gill is a teacher and artist who works at the New York State College of Ceramics in Alfred, New York. She centers her work around the complex, highly painted surfaces she applies to her forms. Gill originally prepared to be a painter. She now paints imagery on the surface of her pieces, combining strong clay forms with very painterly work strategies. These work strategies encourage rich color and precise control of her images.

Ripe Pods, terra cotta with slip and glaze, 44" x 27" x 12", 1996. In this piece Andrea Gill has painted the surface with repeated motifs centering on stylized seed pods. Gill has surrounded these seed pods with abstract imagery.

Gill used a terra cotta body to make this piece. Due to its high percentage of fire clay, this is not a very plastic body. Gill doesn't need a very plastic clay body and wants the strength the fire clay gives. She made this piece from rolled out slabs, some of which she left flat and others she pressed into molds to create a complex form. She allowed the slabs to stiffen, then constructed the piece. After she created the form she smoothed its surfaces to ready it for painting. She first applied her imagery to a test tile to see a preview of what the piece would look like after she fired it, then she was ready to use the application strategy on her bisque-fired vessel. Gill used highly tinted slips to decorate this piece. She began by painting large areas of slip color to create a base for her imagery. She painted large areas of color until the entire piece was covered with five or six large color fields. She was now ready to paint motifs on these color fields. She applied the slip imagery with a brush, repeating these shapes to form a complex image. In some areas she applied five or six colors on top of each other. The slip is fairly thick and creates a subtle relief effect. She used various brushes to get different effects. Finally, to finish the piece she applied a small amount of a commercially produced low-fire glaze to the surface by spattering it with a toothbrush. This created a speckled pattern of enriched color over the surface.

Gill fired this piece to cone 03 in a gas kiln. After the firing she applied a water-based, penetrating sealer called Aqua Mix. It makes the clay waterproof and protects the imagery.

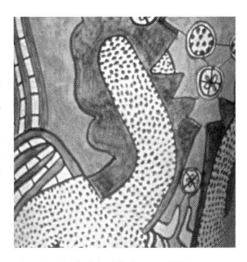

Left: Marie's Madonna, vase, height 33", 1991. Gill used a majolica technique to depict the figure we see here. She flattened the pictorial space and simplified the imagery and generally stylized it. At this time she was beginning to question her color palette. After seeing a wonderful show of Italian majolica at the Metropolitan Museum in New York, she felt the colors she had been using were too dependent on contemporary stains. She took up the use of a more traditional palette similar to that of Renaissance majolica. She feels that contemporary, commercially prepared stain colors have a consistent pastel character that is not always useful to the ceramist. She decided to alter the stain colors by mixing oxides with them and also looked for obscure stains that might be more appropriate for use in her work.

*Detail of **Marie's Madonna**. This detail is useful because it reveals the crisp linear imagery of the majolica medium.*

Gill uses a terra cotta body because she likes its soft red color, the way it handles, and its durability in the fire.

Red clay body - Andrea Gill

Redart clay	60
Fire clay	20
Ball clay	10
Talc	10
Fine grog	10

She adds about 1/4 cup barium to every 100 pounds of the dry clay mixture to prevent scumming. Though this is a small amount of barium, there are those who do not want to work with barium in its powdered form because the material is toxic. It may be possible to avoid scumming and still avoid using barium (see the essay on Peter Pinnell for more on scumming). Due to its high percentage of fire clay, this is not a very plastic body, which works well for Gill because she doesn't need a very plastic body and wants the strength the fire clay gives.

Gill makes her pieces from slabs. She leaves some of these slabs in their flat state and presses others into press molds. Using the molds, she can make curved and billowing wall segments which she uses in constructing her pieces along with the flat slabs. She allows the slabs to stiffen, then constructs the piece from these parts. She uses only a few molds but uses them in many ways, combining the curved segments with each other and with flat slabs to create a wide variety of shapes. After she has created the basic shape, she smooths its surfaces to ready it for painting.

Gill has chosen to center her work on the decorative possibilities of painted images. She works in two ways, with majolica and with slips. In the majolica glaze painting technique, she applies an opaque white glaze which serves as a base and over this she paints imagery using colored stains. In the slip painted work, she paints a layer of slip over the surface of the piece, fires to bisque, and uses this as a base for further slip painting.

Gill started using majolica in graduate school. She says of it, "I call the glaze "majolica" even though it is chemically different from (but visually similar to) 16th century Italian majolica

(my-yoli-ca) and has no technical relation at all to 19th century English majolica (ma-jol-i-ca). My glaze is thick and does not move in the firing, which I try to keep at a cold cone 05." Gill uses the following majolica glaze.

AG 3

Frit 3124	66.0
Frit 3292	8.0
Whiting	5.6
F-4	9.4
EPK	11.0
Zircopax	14.0

She sprays the majolica glaze, then paints a mixture (60/40) of stain and lead bisilicate. The lead bisilicate serves as a binder and a flux.

Over the years Gill has worked with a number of different color strategies for her work with majolica. Recently she has worked with a group of very stable, brilliant orange and red stains afforded by new technologies. A number of companies create them from cadmium/zirconium combinations.

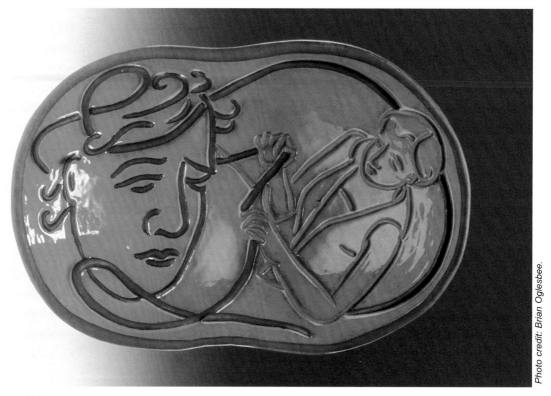

Penelope and Ulysses, 18" x 13" x 5", 1997. Gill's work strategy is different here than in her other pieces. She made the form using a slump mold. When the form became firm, she created the relief imagery. She first made a drawing on the bowl (working from live models). Then she laid the coils on top of the drawing. She wanted to join the coils to the body of the bowl form in a seamless manner so the raised lines would be crisp with well-formed contours. She let the piece dry, then brushed terra sigillatas on the coils. She fired the piece to bisque, then applied a low-fire copper glaze. She had to use a very careful brush application to ensure that the edges were well defined and the various colors remained separate.

Gill's strategy for working with slips is straightforward. She uses a slip recipe with a low clay content. It is very strong at the firing temperature she uses and its color is highly saturated.

Slip (for leather-hard application) cone 05 to 03

Nonplastic kaolin	10
Plastic kaolin	5
Calcined kaolin	15
Talc	10
Frit 3124	15
Lead bisilicate	10
Flint	20
Zircopax	10

She dry mixes and sieves this recipe, then adds stain*: 70 slip, 15-30 stain (depending on its strength).

*Wear a dust mask when mixing and sieving dry ceramic materials.

Through experimentation she has found that this 70/30 combination of her slip with stains works well in most cases (she will vary the percentage of stain if necessary).

Gill's slips are often highly tinted and brilliant in color. She applies them in thick applications. The resulting imagery is raised slightly, creating a subtle relief effect. The slips are mat in surface. She wants to complement the complex shapes she creates with a surface that doesn't reflect light. Multiple reflections make the interaction between the form and surface confusing.

Gill usually begins by applying the slips she wishes to use to a test tile to see a preview of what the piece will look like. When she is satisfied with the test tile, she goes ahead with the decorative process on the piece. She fires the piece to bisque, then applies a layer of slip to create a base for her imagery. Gill paints large areas of color until the entire piece is covered with five or six large color fields. She does this to create a visual structure analogous to her form structure. To paint the repeated motifs, she uses stencils she has made by drawing the motifs and cutting them out of waxed stencil paper. She uses various brushes to get different effects, including stencil brushes, painters bristle brushes, house painters brushes, Japanese brushes, and fan brushes. She says of this, "I collect brushes the way other ceramists collect throwing tools." She uses geometric, overlapping, and contrasting imagery. Some of her motifs are stylized from nature, others are abstract and decorative in character and composed of repeated motifs.

Gill uses both prepared stains and colorants in her slip work. Prepared stains are calcined compounds of kaolin and ceramic colorants which have been modified by additions of oxides which effect their color. These colors are rich, their effects are predictable in use, and they are very reliable. She says she is always looking for colors that will complement each other, though they may not necessarily work well on their own. At one time she could only find stains with a pastel character. The primary customers for these stains are bathroom tile manufacturers and a few tableware companies. The resulting limited palette may be appropriate for interior decoration but Gill found it unsatisfactory. She now can supplement pastel stains

with stains of brilliant color and thus has significantly widened her palette. She has started to mix oxides with stains for stronger color and has searched for unusual stains. She also uses ceramic colorants - minerals or mineral compounds suitable for use in ceramics. The most common colorants are iron oxide, cobalt oxide or carbonate, copper carbonate, chrome oxide, rutile (a compound of titanium and iron), and manganese dioxide. All of these additions, taken together, allow Gill to use a much more intense and varied color palette than she could in the past. In much of her recent work we see the results of her use of an expanded color palette.

Finally, Gill uses a commercially produced, low-fire transparent glaze to finish her slip ornamented pieces. She uses only a small amount of glaze and applies it by spattering it with a toothbrush. This creates a speckled pattern of enriched color over the surface. Gill fires her pieces to cone 03 in a gas kiln. She likes to fire her slip-painted pieces in a gas kiln because she feels the colors are richer and more saturated. After the firing Gill applies a water-based penetrating sealer called Aqua Mix to make the clay waterproof and to protect the painted surfaces.

Gill makes three types of pieces: large abstract vases, vases in the shape of a female figure, and bowls. Each type has its own problems and has led her to different solutions. She needs to make all three because each one encourages

a different kind of imagery. The large vases are non-narrative; they are about formal issues of color and shape. The vases in the form of female figures suggest a more narrative and autobiographical stance. Gill still deals with formal issues in these vases, but the narrative impulse is very important in them. Finally, in her bowls the narrative is at the core of the pieces. Some of their imagery alludes to the wonderful mythic stories from Greek mythology while in others she deals with narratives from her own experience. She emphasizes this narrative character by using linear, storytelling imagery and by placing the image within a simple bowl form. This form creates an intimate space.

Gill feels her painting should be limited, shallow in space, and decorative, not realistic. She likes to call her painting "stylized." For many, the word stylized has bad connotations, but she believes that genius in pottery decoration depends on an ability to stylize. In stylization she sees a way to harmonize image and form. She believes that a decorative flat imagery works best on an object that has form as one of its components. She feels that naturalistic space is incompatible with the surface of the pot because this kind of spatial imagery is inconsistent with the three-dimensional character of her forms.

Gill uses her painted motifs to dramatize the character of the form. She has thought a great deal about the scale and density of her motifs. She sometimes uses very bold, very large scale motifs; at other times she uses extremely small scale motifs that she likens to snow. She exaggerates the scale differences in order to surprise the viewer and create an exciting surface. The motifs float on top of the background and on top of each other, creating a layered decorative space. In some areas she applies five or six motifs on top of each other, enabling her to build up a number of layers of imagery. She controls the density of the painting, placing large elements over small ones and small over large. Lines spiral and whip under and over other shapes. She superimposes asymmetrical images on symmetrical objects. She does this to alternately camouflage and reinforce the form. One of her favorite strategies is to use two different patterns and combine them to produce interwoven, almost musical images. In all these ways she attempts to alter our understanding of the relationship between form and surface, as well as create a complex and punning imagery over the surfaces of her pieces and enhance their feeling of animation.

Gill often studies historical references as resources for her imagery. One of her most valued resources is a book from Victorian England, *A History of Ornament* by Owen Jones. She has often adapted images from this book, simplifying and modifying their scale and mood. Gill is very interested in the nature of decoration and has said of it: "Like the problem I face with color, I have found that imagery on pottery benefits by limitation, in this case the limitation being the way the image is abstracted. Like 'decoration,' the word 'stylized' has had some bad press in the art world. But I believe that genius in pottery decoration depends on an ability to stylize, so that the image meets the demands of the object it rests upon."

Gill is a great fan of a book by the late ceramist and painter Henry Varnum Poor titled *A Book of Pottery*. In a comment that is very important to her, Poor says, "Since the beginning of man, objects from clay have invited surface enrichment. On pots, plates, urns, tiles, and all manner of other ceramic things, men have put many of their richest and most fresh and inventive images and have arrived at simplifications and symbols which have enriched all the arts. The techniques used in this decoration are endless and varied. They all partake of the miracle of the fire, of the transformation from swift fluid movement, which registers every certainty and every hesitation into the permanent and eternal certainty accomplished through the white glow of heat."

Another comment that she values is from the book *The Art of the Potter* by W.B. Honey: "It may well be argued that the most satisfying results [of painting on pottery] are produced when a primitive lack of facility or a deliberate restraint has allowed the color and substance of the piece itself to play a part...[and] to grow out of the very substance of the pot."

Gill took her first class in ceramics in high school in Bethesda, Maryland. After the class was over, she sent a piece she made there to a competition for high school students. She won one of the prizes - a scholarship to a summer program in ceramics at the Corcoran School of Art in Washington, D.C. She took further courses at Corcoran while she was in high school. Gill finished high school in 1967, then went to college at the Rhode Island of Design where she was a painting major. In 1970 she went to Italy to study art and ended up in the hill town of Urbino in northern Italy. There she studied lithography in a technical school that operated under the sponsorship of the Italian government. She felt this was a wonderful school, with a dedicated faculty. In the afternoons after classes, she went out into the landscape around the city and made drawings.

A year later she returned to the U.S. She graduated with a B.F.A. in painting from Rhode Island in 1971. That autumn she was hired as an apprentice by Roger Harvey, a potter working on Cape Cod. He worked in salt glaze and had been a student of Victor Babu in Texas. The year she spent working for Harvey convinced her she wanted to be a potter. In the fall of 1972 she went to the Kansas City Art Institute where she studied with Jacqueline Rice, Ken Ferguson, Victor Babu, and Mark Pharris. She attended Kansas City for three semesters and left in 1973. She worked with hand-formed ves-

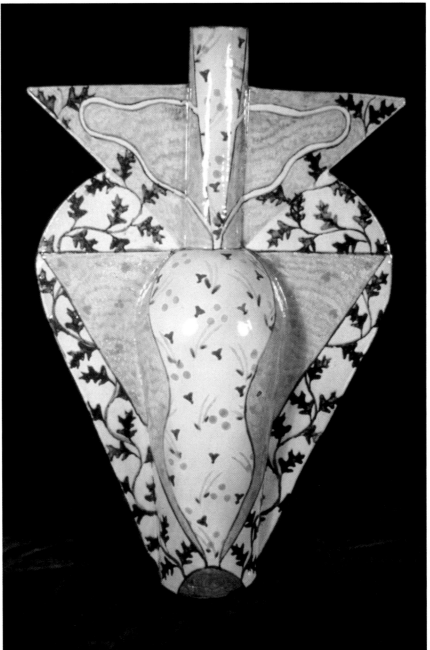

Large Leaf Vase (an older piece), height 30", 1983. In this piece Gill used a majol-ica glaze strategy. She formed the piece from slabs. She left some as flat slabs and gave others a volumetric form by pressing them into molds. She allowed the shaped slabs to stiffen, then constructed the piece. She made the form from a vol-umetric "trunk" with flat, wing-like areas. After she created the form, she smoothed its surfaces to ready it for painting. She first sprayed the piece with an opaque white glaze, then applied her motifs using majolica stains. Gill characterizes the theme she used here as "vase - on vase - on vase." She began with a vase-like central core and ended with the outermost contour, also a vase. She used flattened and stylized neck, foot, shoulder, and handle details. She used a stencil based on an oak leaf to paint the leafy imagery at the rim and shoulder of the piece.

sels and tried all sorts of firing methods, especially raku, stoneware, and porcelain. It was also in Kansas City that she met fellow student, John Gill.

In January of 1974 she went to Alfred as a special student. John was already there as a graduate student. She officially entered Alfred's graduate program in the fall of 1974. She worked with Ted Randall, Val Cushing, Wayne Higby, and Betty Woodman. Andrea and John were married in the fall of 1974. During her second year at Alfred she worked with the low fire. At that time few potters, as opposed to sculptors, had taken up work in the low fire. Gill wanted to make a colorful decorative kind of work that fully exploited the special character of the low fire. She says she thought she would reform ceramics by using the low fire to make pottery and not sculpture. While looking for new low fire recipes, she found majolica. She tried it and it worked. She was also interested in slip-decorated ware, especially early American slipware. Betty Woodman and Wayne Higby strongly influenced her work. At Alfred she started working with the forms and shaping techniques she still uses to form and shape her pieces. Gill did her thesis work in majolica and colored slip imagery. She received her M.F.A. degree from Alfred in the spring of 1976.

John was offered a job at the Rhode Island School of Design and Andrea took an adjunct position at Southeastern Massachusetts University (now the University of Massachusetts at Dartmouth). She was making low-fire studio pottery, mostly ware for the table, but little one-of-a-kind work. She thought she was going to make strongly utilitarian pottery for the rest of her life. In 1977 the Gills traveled to Fort Collins, Colorado, where John taught for a year. After Colorado they went to the Archie Bray Foundation in 1978 for a year where they worked with Kurt Weiser.

In the fall of 1979 the Gills moved to Ohio, where John taught at Kent State University till the spring of 1984. Andrea spent her time in the studio. She had moved on to nonutilitarian vessel forms. In the late 1970s she was in the "Young Americans Show at the American Crafts Museum" and was awarded an NEA grant. After this, her career started to flourish. At this time she was making decorative hand-built vessels including a group of portrait vases that attracted a good deal of attention. She showed her work (all low fire) in the U.S. and Europe. In the fall of 1984 the Gills returned to Alfred, but now in the role of teachers. The demands of teaching at Alfred are great and she no longer makes as much work as she did before she came to Alfred, but she has managed to keep up a very demanding work and exhibition schedule. Though she would like to have more time to work, she feels that in recent years she has gained a better understanding of her work and this is a more than adequate compensation for a lessened level of production.

Andrea Gill.

Photo credit: Richard Zakin.

David MacDonald

David MacDonald teaches ceramics at Syracuse University in New York. He maintains a studio at home where he makes his ceramic work. For many years he has been creating work that in one way or another reflects his African ancestry. In recent years this has taken the form of thrown pieces ornamented with a rhythmic imagery.

Ceremonial Bowl, saw-dust-fired earthenware, height 29", 1989. This piece was a departure for MacDonald. He had not worked in earthenware before. He chose earthenware for this piece because he wanted a look that reminded the viewer of wood and "looked as if it had been around for a while." He first bisque fired the piece in an electric kiln, then sawdust fired it in an above ground brick enclosure.

MacDonald uses the following stoneware recipe to make his clay body.

Fire clay	43
Ball clay	43
Potash feldspar	12
Red clay	2
Medium grog	17

This is the main clay body used in the ceramics department at Syracuse University. MacDonald likes it for both throwing and for hand forming. He adds a small percentage of red clay to improve the fired color of the body. MacDonald throws most of his pieces on the potter's wheel.

In his pieces ornamented with furrowed imagery, MacDonald uses a tool he developed as a device to round and trim the edges of his pieces. His former teacher, Robert Stull, noticed it and suggested that MacDonald could use it to create a pattern of parallel lines. MacDonald has been using this tool for this purpose ever since. MacDonald pushes the tool into the clay and draws it to himself, repeating the process until he has created the parallel furrows that constitute the imagery. This work requires a level of concentration that is physically demanding. It can take him about three hours to create the imagery on a medium size piece and he must take breaks to relax during the process. It is MacDonald's habit to work in three-week cycles. He spends a few days throwing a body of work, a few days cleaning and trimming the pieces, and a week to 10 days carving them. He spends more time

Vase, Calabash Series, height 20", 1983. A calabash is a bottle gourd. It is often dried and used to create containers in Africa.

building the imagery than making the piece.

In his pieces ornamented with this furrowed imagery, MacDonald applies a dark glaze, then wipes it away so it stays only at the bottom of the furrows. He generally contrasts these partially glazed areas with fully glazed sections. He may dip these areas in a glaze or apply the glaze with a brush. If he is using a brush, he keeps the glaze in a very fluid state and loads the brush with glaze so the glaze flows off the brush's tip without leaving brush marks. He applies three to four coats of glaze and alternates the direction of the brush strokes. MacDonald fires his pieces to cone 10 in a gas kiln.

Photo credit: Brantley Carroll.

Stoneware Covered Jar, *14-1/2" tall, 1997. David MacDonald has used a plowed furrow imagery on the surface of this piece. This African-American imagery has its origins in the pottery of Sub-Saharan Africa.*

MacDonald used a stoneware body to create this piece. He threw the piece in two conical shaped sections, then placed them under plastic and let them become firm. MacDonald next joined the two sections together lip to lip. He placed the piece back on the wheel and continued to shape it until it took on a bulbous shape. He trimmed and shaped the lip, then covered the piece and allowed it to sit overnight to stiffen. In the morning he refined its contour. Finally, he made the opening and measured and threw the lid. MacDonald began the drying process by covering the piece with a plastic bag. Every day for a week or so he turned the bag inside out to eliminate the water that had condensed inside the bag. This allowed the piece to dry slowly and evenly. When the piece was leather hard, he flipped it over and tooled the foot. He then tooled the lid to finish the form.

While the piece was still leather hard, MacDonald began the process of creating his surface imagery. He started by dividing the form into equal sections using a compass, a flexible metal straight edge, and a needle tool. These grid lines served as his guides for the imagery, which takes the form of furrows carved into the surface of the clay. He used a tool he made for the purpose to create the furrows. He pushed the tool into the clay and drew it to himself. He made one furrow at a time and repeated the process until he had created the parallel furrows that constitute the imagery. He used water to lubricate the surface of the piece and smooth the furrowed ridges. MacDonald originally developed his furrowing tool as a device to round and trim the edges of his pieces. His former teacher, Robert Stull, noticed it and suggested that MacDonald could use it to create a pattern of parallel lines. MacDonald has been using this tool for this purpose ever since. It took him about three hours to create the imagery we see on this piece.

MacDonald began the glazing process by pouring a simple white colored liner glaze on the inside of the piece. He then brushed a dark brown iron saturate glaze over the outside surface of the piece. He cleaned off the brown glaze with a sponge so that it stayed only in the bottom of the furrows. He painted a brown glaze in those areas of the surface with no clay imagery. He kept the glaze in a very fluid state and kept the brush loaded with glaze to eliminate brush marks. He applied three to four coats of glaze and alternated the direction of the brush strokes. Finally, he dipped the lid into the dark brown glaze. MacDonald fired this piece to cone 10 in a gas kiln in a moderate reduction atmosphere.

79

He feels that he is not romantic about the firing process; while firing is important to him it is not of central importance. He fires in a moderate reduction atmosphere. He is very relaxed about the amount of reduction he achieves in the firing. He deliberately selects glazes that are not overly sensitive to the amount of reduction in the kiln.

MacDonald associates the imagery on the surface of these pieces with the look of a plowed furrow. This imagery has its origins in the pottery of Sub-Saharan Africa. MacDonald has always enjoyed the way African potters carve on their ceramic surfaces to create an elegant, abstract imagery. This imagery is fascinating because it is simple and direct yet very rhythmic and orderly. It is this strong sense of order that is especially appealing to MacDonald. The imagery works well with the form and helps it convey a sense of richness while allowing him to leave the clay almost entirely unglazed. Furthermore, as a kind of bonus, MacDonald very much likes the process of carving. While he admits it can be tedious and is always demanding, it is highly pleasurable as well. He sets up a sense of rhythm while he carves the furrows and loses himself in the carving process. It is a kind of meditation.

MacDonald was brought up and went to high school in Hackensack, New Jersey. He liked the school, it was good academically and had a very diverse student body. He was interested in art and took many courses in painting and drawing. Unfortunately, there were no facilities for ceramics or any other three-dimensional work at the school. The program was limited, but within these limita-

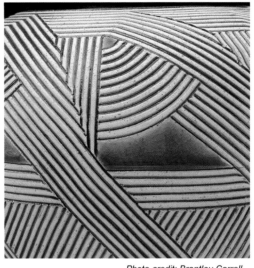

Photo credit: Brantley Carroll.

Detail of **Stoneware Covered Jar**.

tions, very effective. He took courses in music as well and played the clarinet in the high school band. He also excelled in track and field and was captain of the track team. Despite these marks of success, MacDonald enrolled in a program called the "general curriculum." This choice meant that he was not aiming for college attendance. Most important in this calculation was money - his family could not afford to send him to a college away from home and he did not believe he would be awarded financial aid. MacDonald thought he might go to a two-year program at a local art school or in nearby New York City. Then a friend of the family suggested that MacDonald might be able to get an athletic scholarship to help with some of the expenses. She suggested that he talk to his track coach. MacDonald wound up getting a full scholarship in track and field to Hampton Institute (now Hampton University) in Hampton, Virginia. MacDonald graduated with honors from high school in the spring of 1963. That fall he went to Hampton to prepare for a Bachelor of Science degree in art education with a specialization in painting.

The prospect of attending a college in Virginia, far from home, was quite daunting at first. Furthermore, this was the first predominantly black environment he had ever encountered. He came to love the school, however, and now goes back every year. In his sophomore year he took ceramics; it was a required course for students in art education. He was surprised to find that he liked ceramics a great deal - even more than painting. He took to throwing in a natural way and he liked the work. It was very important to him that ceramics allowed him to make things that people could use. A side benefit was that he didn't have to explain the meaning of his pieces to his parents. He studied ceramics with Joseph Gillard, whom liked and respected and still visits every year on his trips to Hampton. As he began to commit to clay in his junior year, he became the studio assistant in ceramics. He held this position until he graduated. MacDonald feels that he received a very strong understanding of the technical basics of ceramics at Hampton. Though he did not realize it at that time, he was taking his first steps to becoming a serious ceramist. His work was in the mode of standard Japanese/Chinese inspired pottery. He says now that when he began, he wasn't sure what he wanted from clay. Then he began to see it as a chance to be really "good at something." Finally, in his senior year he saw that he could use his new skills in a much more personal way and started using the clay to create social commentary. There were many artists at this time who became interested in protest art. As a black American, MacDonald certainly saw aspects of life in the U.S. that were worthy of protest. It was an exciting but very difficult time. It was the time of student protests, riots in the ghettos, and assassinations. The imagery of frustration and protest took on great importance in his work.

During the time MacDonald was becoming deeply involved with clay, he was also training to become a high school art teacher. In his senior year, he did a semester of student teaching and discovered that the lure of the ceramic studio was much more powerful than that of teaching in the public schools. He felt he wanted to make his contribution as an artist. At this point he asked Gillard what he should do and Gillard said, "Go to graduate school, get a Master of Fine Arts degree, and prepare to teach in a ceramics program in a college or university." At first he wasn't sure this would be possible. He was already married with one child and money, as always, was a real problem. If he decided to become a teacher he would be able to go to work as soon as he graduated. The prospect of teaching ceramics in college was too appealing to resist, however, and he applied to a number of graduate schools for admittance to an M.F.A. program. In 1969 he was accepted at the University of Massachusetts at Amherst. He received a teaching fellowship from the school. He stayed there for a semester. Then Robert Stull of the faculty of the University of Michigan at Ann Arbor called MacDonald. Stull told MacDonald that they had accepted him at Ann Arbor and had awarded him a fellowship. MacDonald went to Michigan, was very impressed with Stull and with the campus, and decided to take up work at Ann Arbor. During his two years at Ann Arbor, MacDonald studied with Stull, Bill Lau, and John Stephenson. He continued to make work marked by a strong sense of social commentary, protest, and questions of black identity. This work was mostly hand formed and finished in brilliant low-fire glazes in the oxidizing atmosphere of an electric kiln. In 1971 MacDonald was awarded a Master of Fine Arts degree in ceramics from the University of Michigan.

From 1971 to the present MacDonald has taught at Syracuse University. He began teaching with some trepidation. Most people find the transition from student to teacher to be difficult and MacDonald was no exception. He had to learn how to teach, how to help run a complicated ceramics program, and how to work with his fellow faculty in the art department. In these tasks he was greatly aided by the director of the ceramics program, Henry Gernhardt. Though MacDonald was appointed while Gernhardt was on sabbatical and without his knowledge, Gernhardt welcomed him and a feeling of great trust developed between the two. Though they were different in many ways, they shared a fondness for direct and plain speaking.

MacDonald had been encouraged in graduate school to develop a pace of intense and constant work. He kept this up at Syracuse and began to exhibit the results. He found that this work had very good acceptance throughout the whole art community. People liked the work, admired the skill, and were sympathetic with the political aspect of his pieces. MacDonald's life, however, had changed radically and the imagery of protest no longer had the same meaning for him. His position at the University was by this time firming up. He realized that he liked teaching and was quite good at it. He liked the students, he liked the school, and enjoyed working with his fellow faculty. He was seeing his life in a more positive

Violence is as American as Mom's Apple Pie (an older piece), height 26", 1973. MacDonald made this piece using slab-forming methods. He then threw a plate form on the wheel and joined this to the slab-formed piece. He covered the piece with an opaque white glaze and fired it to cone 6. He used this glaze as a base and on top of it applied low-fire brightly colored glazes, which he fired to cone 06. He then applied lusters and a photo-ceramic decal and fired these to cone 018. The photo image of the grandmother holding a pie refers to a quotation by Stokely Carmichael on violence in the United States. He finished the piece, after he fired it, by spraying a layer of flocking on sections of the surface.

light. This change happened somewhere around 1978. At first the change was subtle and he was not entirely aware of it. Then one evening it was brought to his attention. He was at a reception for an exhibition opening at the Community Folk Art Gallery of Syracuse. A sympathetic stranger asked in a casual conversation, "Is there anything positive about being a black, or is life as a black a succession of humiliations and frustrations?" MacDonald realized that there were many things in his life that were very positive. He came to realize that the work he made based on social protest required a negative mindset and was based on a sense of victimization. Growing away from this, he wanted to base his work on positive aspects of his life. He wanted to celebrate the things he loved. He started to try to figure out how he could use his work to express positive aspects of his background. He had been looking at art objects that came from Africa and more fully appreciated his rich visual heritage. He started to use these themes and images consciously in his work. The strong African influence we see in his work has this feeling as its source. In the spring of 1995

Henry Gernhardt retired from his teaching position and MacDonald, along with Margie Hughto (well known for her tile work), are now the senior faculty in ceramics.

Very recently MacDonald has begun to focus on the "middle passage," the journey from Africa to the New World. His ancestors and the ancestors of all American blacks were forced to make this voyage. He wants this imagery to be positive, not finger pointing, not "look what you've done to us." He wants it to be more a "celebration of what we African Americans have done and how much we were able to build from so little." He feels this is a continuation of a direction in his work that started many years ago. His work started with images of protest in the U.S., he then looked to Africa for a more positive imagery; now he says he looks to this new focus to tie all of his imagery together.

David MacDonald.

Harris Deller

Harris Deller has chosen to work on the frontier between the vessel and sculpture formats and between two- and three-dimensional imagery. He wants aspects of his pieces to seem askew. He wants elegance but he wants tension as well. He is aware of these contradictory aims and feels that in a sense his work derives energy from them.

T-Pot, 13-1/2" x 10" x 3". Porcelain clay body with a 10% addition of molochite. Deller constructed this piece from altered wheel-thrown shapes, then added coils, slabs, and extruded and molded forms. He cut and assembled these pieces and cut and altered them again to achieve the fragmented and flattened imagery he wanted. His final firing was to cone 10 in a reduction atmosphere.

Deller uses a porcelain clay body with a 10% addition of molochite (porcelain grog). He adds the molochite for texture and durability.

Deller's Porcelain Clay Body

Grolleg kaolin	55
Silica	18
Pyrophillite	10
Potash feldspar	22
Bentonite	2
Molochite	10

The pieces are constructed from altered wheel-thrown shapes, coils, slabs, and extruded and molded forms. Deller cuts and assembles these pieces and sometimes cuts and alters them again to achieve the imagery he wants. He uses both additive and subtractive methods. He also makes tiles from slabs.

If he has added molochite to the body, Deller scrapes the clay surface with a rib. The scraping brings the molochite to the surface where it leaves grooved trails. He incises imagery into the greenware clay body. Here the molochite encourages irregular and blurred lines and surfaces. Deller enjoys this textured imagery and feels that it has an interesting character. Deller bisque fires to cone 010, then uses sandpaper to smooth the surface of his pieces. The low bisque temperature keeps the clay soft enough to make sanding easy. After the bisque firing he fills the incised areas with a black satin mat glaze and wipes off the excess glaze with a damp sponge. He then goes over the surface with fine sand-

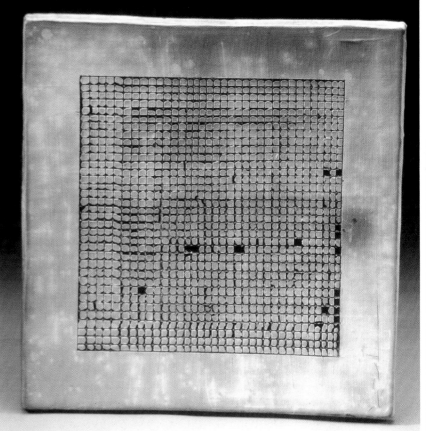

Plate with Grid, 13" x 13" x 3/4", 1996. Porcelain clay body and fused terra sigillata. To create the image of a grid, Deller first applied a black terra sigillata followed by a white terra sigillata. As the two layers dried, he scored lines in the white sigillata. This top layer broke away in an irregular fashion, creating the regular grid lines with irregular edges that we see here. He fired to cone10 in a reduction atmosphere.

Detail of Plate with Grid, 1996. This close-up photograph clearly shows the combination of regularity and irregularity in the imagery that Deller uses in his work.

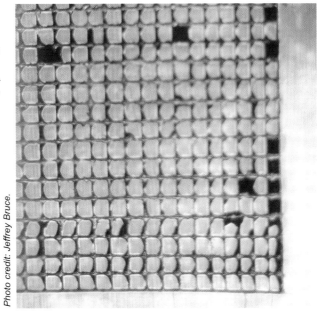

Vase with Nose and Concentric Arcs, porcelain, 13" x 7" x 6", 1998. Deller used a porcelain clay body with a 10% addition of molochite (porcelain grog) to make this piece. He added the molochite for texture and durability. He constructed this piece from altered wheel-thrown shapes, plus coils and slabs. Deller cut and assembled these pieces and cut and altered them again to achieve the imagery he wanted. He used both additive and subtractive methods to create the imagery. Deller scraped the surface of this piece with a metal rib. The scraping brought the molochite to the surface where it left grooved trails. He incised imagery with a stylus and carved the surface with a loop tool. The molochite encouraged an irregular and blurred line and gave the surface an appealing abraded character.

Deller bisque fired this piece to cone 010. He chose this very low temperature bisque firing because after the firing he sanded the surface and the low temperature kept the clay soft enough to make sanding easy. After this he filled the incised areas with a black satin mat glaze. In this piece (as in most of his work in recent years) he

limited his color to black on the white clay body. He wiped off the excess glaze with a damp sponge and allowed the piece to dry. The black glaze left a residue, which he sanded off with fine sandpaper. He then painted a black glaze on the inside of the piece. The final firing was to cone10 in a reduction atmosphere.

Cup (an older piece), 5" x 6" x 5", porcelain, 1974. Deller threw this piece on the wheel. He used an extruder to create the handle. He glazed the piece using a clear Chun glaze. He then painted iron oxide, copper, and rutile stains over the glaze to create the green, ocher, and copper red accents. He glazed the interior with a copper red glaze. Deller says he wanted to create the illusion that the extruded handle was penetrating the interior volume of the piece.

paper. This allows him to remove the glaze residue. He finishes with a brush application of glaze on the inside of the piece. He glaze fires at cone 10 in a reduction atmosphere. He values the hardness and whiteness of porcelain achieved when he fires his clay body close to vitrification.

Deller uses form and pattern as significant generators of imagery. He works with classi-cal form types - vases, teapots, and tiles. He uses imagery that refers to the figure or the land-scape. He creates patterns in his surfaces by incising marks in the surface of the clay body. As he cuts incised lines into the surface of the piece, the molochite in the clay body encourages a rough broken line. The line appears to sub-merge and emerge in a natural way as the moving stylus scrapes off pieces of molochite. This alters the surface and the shape and pattern of the image-ry. He waits for this and many of his responses are reactions to the way the line looks on the surface of the piece. As he creates his imagery he is con-stantly reacting to his materials and processes. He likes to cre-ate a surprising and ironical space by making objects flat where they have depth and highly sculpted where they are flat. In recent years he has limited color in his work. Though he likes this limited color, he is loath to say that he has abandoned color, nor is he prepared to say that he will never use it. He keeps looking for possibilities and imagines that he may surprise himself with a new color scheme.

Deller sees himself as an object maker. He is interested in making sculptural forms from wheel-thrown pottery parts and shapes. He works hard to refine the proportions and contours of these parts and shapes. He has favorite shapes and is especially interested in the trapezoid. He works in series or groups in a way familiar to most potters. Each piece is a response to his feelings about the piece that came before. His work is a record of the creation process.

Deller first attended college at California State University at Northridge in the mid 1960s. At that time he was a liberal arts major without much direction or insight. He first majored in political science though he felt little vocation for this area of study. One night at dinner with a friend he noticed the plate from which he was eating. It was thick, irregular, and definitely not a product of the mass production system. He asked his friend where the piece came from and his friend said that he had made it himself in a class in ceramics. Deller had no idea that there was such a thing as handmade ceramics and the concept strongly appealed to him. Furthermore, he had no idea that such a course was

offered in any college, much less on his own campus. As soon as he could, he enrolled in his first ceramics course. This was a general ceramics course and it was very organized in its approach. His teachers, Bill Hardesty and Howard Tollefson, asked the students to start by making a hand-formed piece. They then moved on to an introduction to the potter's wheel where they were asked to do a lot of throwing. Their form models were quite traditional. The course was intense and the faculty encouraged a great deal of commitment. As time went on and Deller's commitment deepened, he was encouraged to go a bit further afield and test his skills. Skill was a very important issue at Northridge and Deller enjoyed the challenge. He made pieces reflecting the popularity of Funk pottery. He worked with low fire and high fire, including salt firing. Much of the work was in the vessel format, though he also attempted the occasional ceramic sculpture. He stayed at Northridge from 1965 until he graduated in 1971.

In the fall of 1971 he went on to Cranbrook to pursue a master's degree. There he worked with Richard Devore. Deller's first year was very difficult. Devore criticized him for paying too much attention to skill issues and not enough attention to developing a personal aesthetic vision. He clearly remembers Devore asking, "What specific personal identity are you trying to manifest through clay?" At the time Deller was working on a series

of sculptural lidded jars. He placed these on stands in the form of a three-foot tall palm tree. He now characterizes this work as marked by excellent technology but as not consistent in its vision. These pieces didn't meet with a favorable critique. Deller spent the summer between his first and second year of graduate school trying to understand what he would have to do to assert a personal identity and a consistent vision in his work.

His response was to change his clay body and the type of pottery he was making. He began to work in porcelain. He felt a real affinity for this material. Furthermore, he began to feel a strong urge to make functional pottery. He wanted to engage the user in a rich tactile experience. In the beginning of his second year he made a group of cups with tubular handles that seemed to penetrate the wall of the volume, an illusion that had great appeal for him. He feels that these pieces were pivotal to his development. He felt that they were a kind of breakthrough and that this was the first time he was able to make a truly personal statement in his work. He found too that he was able to commit himself more deeply to the work process and became consumed by its demands. In that second year at Cranbrook, Deller was much more comfortable dealing with the demands of the program. His graduate experience completely turned around during this second year. Where he had felt beleaguered and anxious, he now felt positive and optimistic. Deller graduated with an M.F.A. degree in 1973

After graduation Deller taught for a summer at the Art Institute of Chicago and that fall began teaching at Georgia Southern College where he stayed from 1973 to 1975. He liked the school a great deal, enjoyed the students, and received great support from the administration. He taught ceramics and two-dimensional design. In 1975 he moved to Southern Illinois University where he continues to teach today. He was attracted to the high visibility of its programs (including a healthy graduate program). During his early years at Southern Illinois, he worked with one-of-a-kind utilitarian pottery. Its reception was mixed, it won respect but in its elegance and reserve it was seen to be somehow not current. It did not fit in the Funk category but neither did it please the traditionalists. The traditionalists were committed to an aesthetic that Deller respected but did not share. He began to feel that the preconceptions of those who championed utilitarian pottery were getting in the way of exploration. He felt that if he wanted to please the traditionalists, he would have to force his work to live up to the color and form expectations of others. He wanted utility, which was of little interest to those interested in Funk. He also wanted the brilliant, sensuous, unconventional color that offended traditionalists. Like the traditionalists, he wanted people to touch and

interact physically with his pots. Like many contemporary ceramists, he wanted work with new imagery that had not been seen before. He was caught between two oversimplified arguments. In 1981 Deller went to Korea on a one year Fullbright grant for teaching and research. He spent the time looking at a lot of celadon-glazed pieces and studying traditional Korean pottery. Curiously, his mood upon his return was one of disillusion. He liked utilitarian ceramics but wanted to make his own personal version of utilitarian pottery and he couldn't find the audience he wanted for these pieces. The level of his disillusionment was great enough to make him stop all work in ceramics for a year. Then climbing out of this valley, he began to make ceramic work again - mostly platters.

In 1984 he made his first flattened teapots. He sees this as saying, "You don't want your modernist ceramics to be utilitarian? Okay here it is, totally useless, nonromantic, and nonfunctional!" He now saw that he had made a choice to explore a kind of sculptural view of the vessel. He had found a spirit of openness and encouragement from those committed to a sculptural approach to the vessel and this influenced his choice. Now that he had decided to take a sculptural approach, he was able to deal with certain contradictions in his work. He had been glazing his pieces with copper red and celadon glazes. He began to think that these glazes were too

seductive and ingratiating. It began to seem too easy to impress people with rich colorful surfaces. He felt that he was focusing more attention on the surfaces of his pieces than on the form and contour. He decided to abandon color and rich surfaces and to concentrate on form. He began to revisit familiar vessel forms such as teapots and vases. He used these forms that he knew and liked so well and altered them by pushing, pinching, squeezing, and flattening. In doing this he was not reacting against utility, he felt that he was focusing the viewer's attention on those things that really interested him: contour, shape, proportion, and surface manipulation. He began to let contour dominate the volume. He felt that his surfaces were still too refined so he attacked the surface of his pieces with the teeth of a saw blade. He had for a long time admired the work of Hans Coper, a potter active in England in the 1950s and '60s. Coper emphasized rich monochromatic surfaces on his pieces and Deller decided to try this approach as well. He felt that his new, more monochromatic surfaces were much more direct and expressive than those he had used before.

The perfectionist Deller has now reached a point where he has learned to accept contradiction. He still wants to make an object in which everything fits together, where there is a sense of harmony and yes, even beauty. Yet he wants aspects of his pieces to seem askew. This is an interesting idea - something that is askew is not completely and crazily wrong, it is a bit off and somewhat unsettling. He feels that too much harmony, too much unity, too much order and finish can diminish the power of the piece. He wants elegance but he wants to balance it with tension. His teacher, Richard Devore, once said to him that being insecure was one of his best assets and he still ponders this statement.

Photo credit: Jeff Bruce.

Harris Deller.

Bruce Cochrane

Bruce Cochrane makes pottery in which he combines utilitarian and decorative characteristics. He starts his pieces by forming a number of wheel-thrown parts, alters them, and adds hand-formed additions. He is very interested in developing strategies for ornamenting the surface of his forms. Though Cochrane uses a great variety of forming and decorating strategies, his work is always identifiable as his own.

Photo credit: Peter Hogan.

Ewer, *5" x 5" x 6", porcelain fired in reduction, 1998. Here Cochrane combines a celadon glaze strongly reminiscent of Chinese pottery with a form reminiscent of European pottery work.*

Cochrane's Porcelain Clay Body

Grolleg	20
6 tile kaolin	20
Ball clay	10
G200 potash feldspar	27
Silica powder (flint)	23

Cochrane's clay body is oyster white in color and has the fine smooth texture we associate with porcelain. Traditionally ceramists take a great deal of trouble in mixing their porcelain clay bodies. Cochrane is a good example of this tendency. He first uses a dough mixer to prepare his clay. He then uses a de-airing pug mill to finish the process. After putting the clay in 50-pound bags, he stores it. He mixes his porcelain clay body a year in advance. This practice is the one recommended by all the experts but few ceramists get around to actually doing this - Cochrane is an exception. The aging process works because of the natural process of mold growth. Clay bodies are composed of clay and nonclay materials suspended in water. During the aging process molds grow in the water. These molds transform the water into a slippery, viscous liquid that acts as a lubricant and holds the clay body together. This allows Cochrane to create forms that he otherwise could not make.

Cochrane's basic forms are not that difficult to make but he alters his forms a great deal and in this way demands a great deal from the body. Because Cochrane mixes the body carefully then lets it age, it has a superlative working char-acter and throws well. Cochrane does not aim for translucency. He is looking for a body that throws well and takes marks readily. He estimates that the wheel forming takes from 10% to 20% of his time while the construction and alter-ing of the parts takes from 80% to 90% of the building time. Cochrane uses an extremely careful drying process. He has constructed a well-sealed damp cupboard for this process. He places the piece inside the damp cupboard and maintains a high humidity level by placing containers of water in the cup-board. He is quite patient and allows the drying process to take about a month.

After firing the piece to bisque Cochrane applies a thin layer of clear glaze on the inside wall of the piece. He applies no glaze to the outside of the pot and relies almost entirely on the natural wood ash glaze that is deposited on the vessel surface during the wood firing. He will, however, some-times apply a thin coating of terra sigillata to the piece to modify surface color. Cochrane then fires his pieces to cone 10/11 in a wood firing. The effects of the wood ash are especially strong toward the top of these pieces. Cochrane fires in a hard brick wood kiln of his own design - a 50-cubic-foot, single chamber, cross draft kiln with a sprung arch roof. There is no separate fire box, every-thing is contained in one main chamber. There is a checkered bag wall separating the fire box and ash pit from the ware chamber. This is the only struc-ture separating the pots from fire box. Cochrane designed the kiln with stoking and firing in the same chamber in order to encourage very strong wood ash effects. He aims for a 15-hour firing. He uses a full cord of wood for each firing. He feels that for a kiln of this size, this is

Photo credit: Peter Hogan.

Covered Serving Dish, 10" x 6" x 7", wood-fired earthenware with terra sigillata. Fired in a reduction atmosphere to cone 04, 1993. The terra sigil-lata reacts strongly and beautifully to reduced and flashed effects from the reduction fire.

an efficient use of wood. He uses cut up slab ends made from both hard and soft wood that he gets from a nearby wood mill.

Cochrane is very interested in the way his pieces are used and in their ergonomics. He designs and forms his pieces so they are comfortable and encourage thoughtful use. Cochrane wants the user to have to think about the way the piece works and about the way he has formed it. He adds many small ergonomic touches. For example, he often adds twists and textures to handles, knobs, and rims. These help the user grip the piece and give it a pleasing tactile quality.

As a youth Cochrane never expected to become a ceramist. He had no interest in clay or in any kind of art before he went to college. He enrolled in a general liberal arts program at John Abbott Junior College in Montreal, Quebec, in 1970. He did not know what he was going to do with his life. In his second semester, on the recommendation of a fellow student, he took ceramics. The college had a one-person art department run by Julia Manitius, who was fascinated with ceramics. At the time she had not yet begun to specialize in clay. She took this as her opportunity and since then she has become a studio potter. Cochrane was strongly affected by her interest in the medium. The excitement in the studio was electrifying. He found he loved ceramics and three weeks after he began, he found himself in the ceramics studio 12 hours a day.

Cochrane began to learn how to throw on the wheel. The book *Ceramics - A Potters Handbook* by Glenn Nelson became their "bible." Cochrane transferred to the department of fine arts at that point. In his two remaining semesters at John Abbott College he focused on the potter's wheel. Though his pieces were not very personal, they reflected the fact that he was learning a great deal. In the fall of 1971 Walter Ostrom came to Montreal to give a workshop. Ostrom, one of Canada's best known ceramists, teaches at the Nova Scotia School of Art and Design, one of the foremost schools of art in Canada. Ostrom's presentation was intelligent, lively, and energetic and made a big impression on Cochrane. Cochrane decided to apply to Nova Scotia for a B.F.A. degree and was accepted for the following fall. He graduated from John Abbot in the spring of 1972.

During the next four years at Nova Scotia, Cochrane had the opportunity to work intensively with Ostrom. He still is grateful for Ostrom's intense commitment to ceramics and to ceramic education. Another major influence was Don Reitz's muscular and florid salt-fired work. Cochrane took up work with salt firing and pursued this for a few years. Initially the work looked very much like Reitz's. In time, however, Cochrane began to deal with function and this helped him to develop his own, more personal approach. Cochrane spent his last two years at Nova Scotia working on functional pieces. He

became very interested in Japanese stoneware of the Momoyama Period, especially work from the Iga, Shino, Shigaraki, and Bizen kilns. Using the Japanese work as his model, Cochrane worked to make his pieces more fluid and lively. He adopted a slower throwing speed and as a result, created more animated forms. It became important to him to pay more attention to the feel of the clay during the throwing process and to observe and enjoy the process more. He made it a practice when throwing to put the pot back on the wheel after it had lost its initial soft character and push the form outwards from the inside, thus articulating the shape and making it less predictable. Inevitably, a pot treated in this way takes on a subtle asymmetry and he feels that this makes the piece more complex and interesting. Cochrane graduated from Nova Scotia with a B.F.A. degree in the spring of 1976.

In 1976 Cochrane was accepted at the New York State College of Ceramics at Alfred. He studied with Bob Turner, Val Cushing, and Wayne Higby. His fellow students included Akio Takamori, Judy Moonelis, Chris Gustin, and Arnie Zimmerman. At this time sculptural work was very much in the ascendance and as one of two potters in his class, he felt intimidated. He began to feel that he should try to make sculptural vessels. He was not comfortable with this work and feels now that he took it up out of a sense of duty rather than as an expression of per-

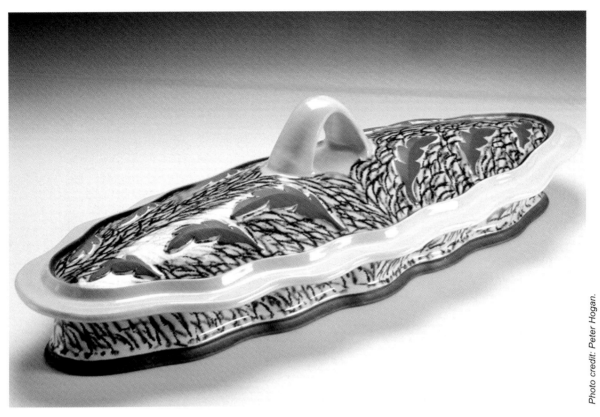

Covered Serving Dish, 20" x 6" x 5", 1992. Majolica and terra sigillata. In this piece we see how Cochrane used majolica glazes. We also see his use of a low-fire terra cotta red clay and extended oval and wavy forms. The surface is marked by painted, stylized patterns colored with iron and copper oxides over a majolica glaze. Though this form is very similar to the reduction fired serving dish shown previously, the two pieces are very different in mood.

Photo credit: Peter Hogan.

sonal need. The faculty observed this for a few months, then Wayne Higby had a talk with him. Higby had a collection of utilitarian pots made by a great number of contemporary potters. He maintained that useful pottery could be expressive and reveal the artist's personality while fulfilling a utilitarian role. They sat in Higby's kitchen and he examined and analyzed each piece. Cochrane says that this was a great collection, that Higby's insights were most revealing, and that this was an intense educational experience. He came away with a feeling that he had permission to make useful pottery and from then on he stayed with this work. He began to collect folk pottery from the 19th century such as salt-glazed crocks and earthenware jugs. It was easy for Cochrane to find these old ceramic pieces around Alfred and they were very inexpensive. He liked these pieces for their natural and gutsy simplicity. He relished their big chunky rims and their substantial handles. These were pots designed to be used every day. Their virtues started to wear off on him and Cochrane began to integrate the lessons from this work into his own. He feels that these pots helped him to make his own pots bolder and more direct. In his graduate exhibition Cochrane showed a great deal of wheel-thrown stoneware and salt-fired ware. His work was taking shape and beginning to take on the look it has now. Cochrane graduated from Alfred in the spring of 1978.

In the fall of 1978 Cochrane began teaching at the School of Craft and Design at Sheridan College in a suburb of Toronto, Canada. He continued to work in the way he had at Alfred. When he first began teaching, he met the potter Ruth McKinley (her husband, Don

94

Photo credit: Peter Hogan.

Ewer and Stand, *8" x 4" x 10", porcelain, wood fired, 1998. This piece is made up of a ewer resting on a stand. Cochrane made the ewer from a number of separate parts, some thrown and others slab formed. To create the domed oval form of the body of the ewer, he brought the sides of the cylinder together at the top of the piece. He pinched the seam closed and used a brayer to seal and smooth the seam. He then allowed all the parts to reach a cheese hard state. To create the large bail handle, he flattened a strap-like form on the table, then gave it its arc-like shape. He let it become firm lying on the table. He made the spout, the lid, and the opening for the lid. Once these pieces were leather hard, he joined them to the basic form.*

For the base he made a stand from a cylinder, a top slab for the stand, and a rim to hold the ewer in place. To create the basic form he pressed the sides of a thrown cylinder into an oval shape. He then added the slab top and created a step-down rim to ensure that the ewer would fit into the top of the stand. Finally, he cut into the walls of the stand with a thin bladed knife.

He estimates that the wheel forming took from 10% to 20% of his time while the construction and altering of the parts took from 80% to 90% of the building time. He wrapped the newly constructed piece tightly in plastic for the first week of drying and placed it in a damp cupboard. Then he removed the plastic and left the piece in the damp cupboard until it no longer was losing moisture. He removed it from the cupboard and let it dry completely.

*Cochrane then applied a thin coating of terra sigillata to the piece. He sprayed the terra sigillata using an airbrush held close to the clay form. He applied the sigillata in such a way as to emphasize the three-dimensional character of the piece. Cochrane applied a thin layer of clear glaze to the inside of the ewer. Apart from this he relied only on the natural wood ash glaze that is deposited on the surface of the piece during the firing. Its effects are especially strong toward the top of the piece. Cochrane fired this piece to cone 10/11 in a wood fire. It is interesting to compare this with his other 1998 **Ewer** (page 91). Compare its strongly textured darker, warmer color with the smooth surfaces and light, high key color of the first piece.*

McKinley taught there). She was well known for her wood-fired work and they did a couple of firings together. McKinley had strong feelings for the wood fire and Cochrane found the experience very special. As he took up his work at Sheridan, he found that he liked teaching a great deal. He feels that the critical process helps him to understand his own work as well as that of his students. He likes the students, enjoys getting to know them, and is glad that this is a natural thing in a ceramic studio. He follows their progress with great interest.

Cochrane has been interested in pottery traditions since his studies with Ostrom in Nova Scotia. He has learned much from majolica work from Italy. His awareness of our ceramic inheritance has strongly shaped the look of his work. In 1985 Cochrane became interested in majolica and decided to try working with it. He felt he should first visit the classic centers of majolica pottery in northern Italy. He applied for and was awarded an Ontario Arts grant and visited the pottery cities of Faenza, Deruta, Gubbio, and Florence. He thought that upon his return he would paint on pots with colored stains in the classic manner of majolica. He found, instead, that he wanted to place more emphasis on decorative form rather than on painted imagery. His study of European pottery with its emphasis on formal invention encouraged him to change his own forms. He enjoyed working with the low-fire terra cotta red

Photo credit: Hugh Douglas-Murray.

*Detail of **Ewer and Stand**. Here we see the rich pattern of wood ash over the terra sigillata. Where there is an especially strong deposit of wood ash, we see a pattern of ocher colored spots at the shoulder of the piece.*

clay and began to use it to make florid forms and rhythmic clay relief detailing. He also started to use stands to elevate the pots. He began to use fluted forms, pierced walls, carved handles, sprigged ornament, and dramatic feet and rim details. He stopped trying to use contemporary stain colors. He knew that these stain colors could do wonderful things but they were not for him. He began to use iron, cobalt, and copper oxides over the majolica glaze and apply them with a sponge to get textured surfaces. Instead of trying to paint in the realistic manner of the classic majolica, he applied stylized plant-like patterns. He felt this

work was more his own, much stronger, more immediate, and less controlled than the work he had set out to make.

Cochrane began to use terra sigillata surfaces with his majolica work. At first he used only a little terra sigillata, then he began to use more. Eventually the majolica glaze disappeared and he began to concentrate on terra sigillata surfaces. He was firing in oxidation, mostly in electric kilns. Then during a bisque firing in a fuel-burning kiln he accidentally created a reduction atmosphere. The resulting pieces were flashed and darkened. The terra sigillata reacted strongly and beautifully to this atmosphere. Cochrane began to think he should reduce and flash all of his pieces. He began to throw some wood into the kiln to create a long flame that moved up and worked its way around the pots. He liked these new surfaces. He did have some problems with this work, however. He found that he had to control the atmosphere very carefully. If he had too little reduction, the work looked raw and under-fired, if too much, it looked dark and was too brittle. Furthermore, he wanted his utilitarian pieces to be durable and the low fire is not noted for durable clay bodies.

Cochrane began to feel that it was time for another change in his work. He wanted to return to the high fire. He had never worked for any length of time with porcelain and wanted to. He strongly admired the great wood-fired Chinese and Japanese porcelains. He also admired the early examples of European porcelain from Meissen in Germany. Cochrane switched to porcelain fired in the wood kiln in 1993. He has worked solely in wood-fired porcelain in recent years and has enjoyed it a great deal. The smooth white surface and the durability and density of the material has great appeal for him. The strong bond between the glassy body and his glazed surfaces also appeals to him. Then too, the character of the porcelain allows him to contrast sharp crisp edges with soft billowing forms. Cochrane continues to teach at Sheridan College and to create utilitarian pots. His forms and ideas are still strongly influenced by his time working in earthenware and he continues to use forms and imagery that are loose and decorative. In these pieces he combines the human touch of the low-fire ware with the elegant sobriety of wood-fired porcelain.

Bruce Cochrane. This photo was taken at a workshop and shows Cochrane demonstrating how he alters the lip of a thrown porcelain form.

Greg Pitts

Greg Pitts has been active in the field of ceramics for a number of years and has worked in a great variety of ways. Wherever his explorations have taken him, he has worked with intensity and commitment. He does not want to limit himself to any one material or work strategy. His work is about the material and he does not care to identify himself with either the sculpture or vessel format. He has carefully looked at ceramics from all over the world made in many different eras and knows that no one format or style or material or work strategy is the "best." He is distrustful of arbitrary limits. He wants the whole field of ceramics, with all of its possibilities, to be open to him. As a result, we see from him pieces with a strongly sculptural identity and others that are functional, vessel-oriented, and ornamented with painted imagery.

In the middle of the 1980s Pitts' work had to do with sculptural issues. He wanted to make sculpture without making the forms normally associated with sculpture and sculptural pieces that did not have the formality we normally associate with sculptural work. He also became very interested in trying to resolve issues of the material. His goal was to be able to treat clay like stone or

Photo credit: Greg Pitts.

Tools, 5" x 5" x 8", 1987, sculptural piece. Pitts made the white colored, rock-like form using a porcelain body and added 15% molochite and 5% silica sand to it. Pitts made these pieces from solid blocks of clay because he wanted them to be massive and dense. He made the blue colored pipe-like form using a copper bearing barium glaze. He lightly stained the unglazed clay to give the form on the left a tan color. He fired these pieces to cone 9 in a wood-fired kiln. He wanted to use these mysterious, half recognizable forms to illustrate the idea of tension between dissimilar objects.

Three Legged Stool, 9-1/2" x 14" x 14", 1986. Sculptural piece. Pitts used a dense earthenware body composed of red clays, stoneware clays, grog, and sand to make this piece. He painted a black vitreous slip on the base, then painted the orange colored area with a terra sigillata made from PBX Valentine clay. He made the white colored area with a porcelain slip. He fired the piece to cone 2.

wood. Pitts began to make tool-like sculptural forms. He formed these abstract constructions from solid lumps of clay. They speak of form and of their materials in a very direct and natural way.

In 1988 Pitts went to Korea for three months to build Western-style kilns. He took the opportunity to study Korean pottery. He responded very strongly to the pottery he saw and handled there, especially to the unpretentious pieces intended for everyday use that he saw in the villages. He was very impressed by their casual

mastery. He feels now that a dramatic change in his work came from his exposure to the Korean pottery tradition. He started moving back to a functional orientation in his work.

The result was his next body of work, a group of utilitarian vessels with painted blue and white imagery. These pieces are meant for the very specific function of holding bulbs and the plants that grow from them. In this way Pitts has combined his interest in the pottery tradition with his interest in flowers and plants. In making this work he followed an important histor-

ical model, that of the decorative Delftware utilitarian ware known for its blue and white imagery made by applying a blue slip on a white ground. This kind of work, a product of the Netherlands and England, was very popular throughout 17th century Europe. Pitts' work, however, is the product of a somewhat wary and ironic sensibility; though he hews closely to the traditional style, the piece has a very contemporary look. He wanted to "make marks on the vessel form that had purpose; to help define the form and shape the character of the piece. The problem, as he saw it, was to do this without making the form into a mere "vehicle" for carrying the ornament. He wanted the forms to be very assertive.

In this recent work Pitts uses a white stoneware clay body. The soft white color and opaque character of the body produce an elegant surface. This body is midway in workability between porcelain (very difficult to throw) and stoneware (very easy to throw). Pitts finds that it is possible to make complex forms with this body, furthermore, it is far less likely to slump in the fire than porcelain. Pitts loves throwing and has made it an integral part of his building process. He does not form his pieces solely on the wheel, however. He starts with thrown forms, then cuts these apart and rejoins the fragments to create new and complex forms. He says of this process, "Essentially I am deconstructing a thrown form, then reconstructing it to make the piece." This process of forming, deconstruction (cutting), and reconstruction (building) is time-consuming and quite complex. Though pieces like this are the result of hard work, he does not want this to be obvious. He wants his finished pieces to convey a sense of naturalness, ease, and nonchalance.

Pitts uses a blue underglaze slip under a clear glaze to decorate these pieces. He makes his own warm colored blue slip; he is searching for the rich warm colored cobalt mixtures used in Delftware from England and Holland. The warm color of

the original slips was caused by impurities in the cobalt. Pitts admired this color and set out to make a similar slip with contemporary materials. Generally, ceramists add some cobalt to a white slip and leave it at that. Pitts, however, adds a bit of manganese and iron, as well as cobalt. He mixes these materials with an equal amount of china clay and puts it in a ball mill for 24 hours. He then lets the mixture dry because he prefers to keep the slip in a dry form until use. When he is ready to use it, he takes a bit of the dried mixture, adds a bit of gum and some water, and mixes it in a mortar and pestle. He uses French watercolor quill sable brushes to apply the slip. He says these brushes are better than any other he has worked with. They load well and can hold a good deal of slip without dripping. They can be used for a wide variety of line widths from very fine to broad. After he has drawn his imagery, Pitts bisque fires the ware to cone 02. This produces a very dense bisque ware which he likes because it enables him to create thin brilliant layers of slip and glaze. He now applies a clear alkaline glaze using simple dipping methods. The application looks uniform and no dip line shows because of the smooth flow and transparency of the glaze.

Pitts fires in a fuel-burning kiln. He puts the kiln into body reduction at about cone 08 and keeps it in this state until cone 04. This turns red iron oxide into black iron oxide. The result is a white body with a bluish

undertone; this makes the body look whiter. Once the temperature goes beyond cone 04, Pitts fires to his maturation temperature, cone 9, in a strong oxidation atmosphere. He finds that it is not difficult to achieve an oxidation atmosphere and yet fire the kiln evenly. He does have to monitor the firing carefully, however, as the firing chamber becomes hotter. Interior gases are released during combustion; these expand as the firing chamber becomes hotter. This expansion can cause the kiln atmosphere to go into a reduction phase unless he opens the damper a bit. Pitts has to be careful not to have any reduction after cone 04 to avoid carbon trapping. Glazes that have a high percentage of soda, such as his clear glaze, are particularly vulnerable to carbon trapping and the result will be a muddy looking glaze.

Pitts first worked in clay in high school in 1973. He was living in a small town in Oklahoma named Ponca City. He says it was a wonderful place to grow up. People had a sense of community and were concerned for each other's welfare. It was, however, an insular and a limited world and Pitts began to feel the weight of these limitations. Though he was obviously bright and wanted to do well, he felt he needed things from high school that he was not getting. He acknowledged the importance of the courses he was required to take, but felt they were not speaking to him. He had hints of a wider world that was completely ignored in these courses, a world that

Photo credit: Greg Pitts.

Vase with Mermaid, *length 12", 1996. This piece shows how Pitts can use altered wheel shapes to create unexpected forms. In its frilly lip, thickened rounded edges, and full billowing walls it tells us that Pitts made it, at least in part, on the wheel. In its sharp edges it shows us that Pitts, in part, built it with hand-forming methods.*

Detail of **Vase with Mermaid**. *Notice the elegant watery shading of the blue underglaze slip seen very clearly in this photograph.*

Photo credit: Greg Pitts.

dealt with his need for a rich expression of self. He took an art class and saw that this was a different kind of study, one that would challenge him and one with which he could identify. A fellow student taught him the rudiments of throwing on a wheel made from a kit. He kept on taking art and making ceramics in high school. He also made ceramics in an art center where he taught himself

more about throwing. He feels now that though these pieces show little personal vision they are witnesses to his commitment at that time to make forms on the wheel. He went to college in 1975 at the University of Tulsa and here too he ran into difficulties with his classes, particularly the large introductory, liberal arts classes. He did do well in his art courses. He studied ceramics with Tom Manhart

who encouraged discipline in all areas of ceramics, especially in wheel-thrown utilitarian ware. During this period he also worked on drawing and developed very good drawing skills. Again, however, he began to feel restless and decided he needed to study with Robert Turner. He had seen Turner's work and had read about him. He was attracted to Turner's spiritual approach to ceramics

Left: Double Walled Vase with Perforated Dome, height 11", 1996. While at first glance this piece looks nonutilitarian it is meant for the very specific function of holding bulbs and the plants that grow from them. Pitts has designed this piece to hold tulips.

(Turner is very active in the Society of Friends, the Quakers, and his work reflects his firmly held beliefs). In summer of 1978, in his junior year, Pitts left Tulsa for the Penland School of Crafts to study with Turner. When the course was over, he returned to Oklahoma to earn money so he could take more courses of this sort. He went to work in the oil fields for six months. He describes this experience as brutal but he was able to earn a good deal of money very quickly. He then went back to Penland and spent a year there (1978/79) as a concentration student. He worked at Penland as a weekend cook to earn his board and keep. At the end of 1979 he left Penland and went back to Tulsa and worked at the Philbrook Museum on the grounds crew. He found the work very satisfying; he learned to love the refinement of formal gardens. He remains interested in growing things; he designs his pieces to contain plants and uses images of plants as his primary subject matter.

In 1980 he transferred to the Cleveland Institute of Art where he studied for three years (Cleveland's B.F.A. is a five-year program). He worked with Bill Broulliard, Judith Salomon, Kirk Mangus, and Eva Kwong. He liked the Institute of Art and began to do really well in school. This was a period of breakthroughs. He made art ware - vessel-like forms of no utility. They were low fired with brilliant color and lots of visual texture. Pitts took his degree in 1983 and was accepted in the M.F.A. Program of the New York State College of Ceramics at Alfred. He was determined to make as much of the experience at Alfred as possible and dealt with as many faculty as he could. He studied with Val Cushing, Tony Hepburn, Wayne Higby, Scott Chamberlin, Tom Spleth, Anne Currier, and John and Andrea Gill. All of his work there had to do with sculptural issues. He became very interested in trying to resolve issues of the material and explored ways to use clay to make sculpture that didn't have a vessel identity or a container space. He explored ways of turning everyday objects into sculptural forms by stripping them of their utility and looking at them purely as forms. He began to make tool-like, solid, sculptural constructions. Pitts graduated from Alfred in 1985.

The next few years were marked by a good deal of travel and work in many places. During the school year 1985/86 he took a job as the studio technician at the Rhode Island School of Design. There he worked with Larry Bush and Jacquelyn Rice. He continued with the sculptural work he had been doing while at Alfred. In 1986 he went to Morgantown, West Virginia, and set up a studio. Again, he took up his sculptural work. In 1988 he went to Korea for three months to build Western-style kilns. He started moving back to a functional orientation in his work. He feels now that this came in good part from his experience in Korea. From there he went to Chicago to teach in the summer program of the Art Institute of Chicago. Soon he was making wood-fired porcelain vessels. These were utilitarian pieces such as pitchers and creamers. Pitts began to draw on the surface of these pots and worked to get the forms and drawing to influence each other. He was living a very nomadic life at the time, jumping from one task to another. It was an interesting time for him but very difficult. Indiana was his base until 1992. During all of this he kept on working and took up making vases with complex shapes in white stoneware. In 1993 he went to Portugal to teach and spent three months there. Then he settled in New York City; he continues to live there. He is trying, as much as possible, to live and work in one place for a time. New York City can be difficult for a ceramist. It is an expensive and crowded city. Even with its problems he loves New York, he likes its tense and alert city life, the feeling of being in the center of things, the wonderful choice of places to eat (like many ceramists, eating is very important to Pitts), the world-class cultural life, and the rich exhibition calendar. He has traveled far from his roots in rural Oklahoma and has become a true New Yorker.

Imagery is very important to Pitts in his work. In the middle of the 1980s Pitts used an imagery based on modest everyday forms such as modest furniture and hand tools. Though based on reality these were highly abstract and stylized. In his recent work he paints expressive portrait heads and plant imagery on the sides of his pieces. Pitts has also used the image of a formal garden a great deal. These images are figural but tell no story and have no plot, myth, or allegory to communicate. They are images he likes to use and are old friends. He is thinking now of trying to use images that show more than just the head of a figure, that show the whole figure from head to toe. He would like to include at least some references to anatomy. He is also thinking about what he can learn from painted pre-Columbian pottery. In these pieces the artists altered the forms of the vessel walls by pushing in or pushing out from the inside. This made the contour of the piece more interesting and gave the drawn imagery greater realism. These manipulations suggest anatomical forms such as navels, elbows, penises, breasts, and noses. Pitts likes to learn from pottery of the past. He is drawn to certain forms and ways of working and tries to introduce them into his work, blending the imagery of the past with his own. He is fascinated with the tulip imagery he has seen in Delftware. He admires French Faience and Rococo Chinoiserie. He loves their self-consciousness, their over saturation of embellishment, and their overflowing visual invention. He says of these pieces that they are "unashamed pots."

Greg Pitts.

Wayne Higby

Wayne Higby makes his ceramic work in Alfred, New York, and teaches at the New York State College of Ceramics at Alfred University.

Photo credit: Brian Oglesbee. Collection of Barry and Irene Fisher.

Lake Powell Memory - Rain, *17-3/4" x 19-1/2" wide x 12-1/4" deep, 1996. This piece is nearly solid and its weight is approximately 50 pounds. This is an example of Higby's work in porcelain and his exploration of its reserved character and ability to accept imagery.*

Higby made a porcelain body for this piece from Grolleg clay, Kona F4 feldspar, and silica. Finally he added a small percentage (3%) of the plasticizing agent Macaloid. He had the body made for him at school and repugged it in his studio at home in a de-airing pug mill. He formed the piece using thick chunks and laminated slabs of porcelain. Though this piece is a constructed form, Higby did not join any of its elements together until after he fired it. He made the front panel and the sides separately. He drilled holes in the elements so they could accept steel pins to bind them together. These pins hold everything in place. The piece can be disassembled and reassembled at will. After the firing Higby tied this piece together by pinning the tile elements into elements he used to support the piece.

Higby made plaster slabs and carved into their surface. He used these to impress the slabs with a complex carved relief imagery. He then removed the slabs from the plaster molds and combined them with support elements to create the form. Once the piece was cheese hard, he carved into the back of the piece, cutting the surface away and developing its imagery.

He finished the piece with a simple high-temperature transparent glaze applied with a brush. The color of the piece varies depending on flashed effects in the firing. The surface of the piece is marked by cracking and crazing which he feels enhances the richness of the drawing. He fired this piece in reduction to a hot cone 10.

For many years Higby worked in the low fire and effectively exploited its possibilities for brilliant color and flamboyant forms. Very recently he has taken up work in porcelain and is exploring the cool reserve of this medium. In this work Higby uses a very simple clay body of the standard porcelain type. He had always thought that he might work in porcelain someday and was intrigued by its special status as the most aristocratic and unique clay material. Higby had seen a great deal of porcelain in China and even worked with it there for a short time. He still couldn't work in the medium, however, until he went to "Kaolin Mountain" in China. Higby knows himself and knows that his work must start from a strong personal experience. He says, "This is where art comes from." He now felt that he could work in porcelain and even that he *had* to work in it.

He had never really worked in porcelain in the past and he was fascinated with the idea of "thinking like a beginner." He wanted to explore the special character of this material and, respecting it as he did, he decided to see where it would take him rather than forcing it to act in a certain way. He set out to avoid any preconceptions and had no idea of what kinds of work he was going to make. Though he was fascinated by the mystique of porcelain, Higby felt that most ceramists, awed by the medium, tried to make things in it that conformed to a conventional picture of what was appropriate to it.

Close up detail of **Lake Powell Memory - Rain**. Here we see how Higby has exploited porcelain's fine grain surface. He carved imagery onto a plaster bat, then transferred these clear precise marks to the surface of his porcelain slabs.

Higby sees himself as gaining power when he acts as an iconoclast and ignores conventional expectations. He began to work with the clay body in very direct and simple ways. He worked out a way of using thick chunks and slabs of porcelain and laminating them to create thick blocks of clay. He developed this method of working while manipulating the porcelain in a playful way. In this way he was able to completely ignore the conventional limitations of the medium. Thin-walled porcelains are difficult to form. His pieces were thick-walled and easy to form. Porcelains crack and warp; he welcomed this.

He found that taking this approach, he enjoyed working with this medium and began to exploit its character. Higby first forms his porcelain pieces as separate elements. After the firing he uses steel pins to tie the elements together. He uses the pins to mate one porcelain element with another. He can assemble and disassemble these pieces at will.

Higby wanted to exploit porcelain's smooth surfaces and imagery possibilities. He began to create imagery on the porcelain slabs that made up the piece. He didn't draw on the porcelain directly because he wanted to explore what the porcelain could do rather than what he could do with it or to it. As he was wedging the porcelain, he saw that it was picking up every little mark on the wedging bat. He realized that he could draw and incise on a plaster bat and transfer this imagery to the porcelain. The imagery had come from the process itself. He made plaster slabs and carved into their surfaces. He used this strategy to impress the slabs with a complex, carved relief imagery. In this way he could explore the special character of porcelain in his imagery. He then removed the slabs from the carved plaster bats and began to combine them with other slabs to create the form. Once the piece was cheese hard, he carved into the "back" of the piece, cutting the surface away and developing its imagery. He ended up with a piece with a dense and visually weighty character. Its look is that of a heavy block-like form

composed of multiple layers with frayed edges. His aim was to tightly integrate the surface and the form of these pieces. He has always aimed for this in his work, though he has used different methods to achieve this goal. Higby finished the piece with a simple high-temperature transparent glaze applied with a brush. The color of the piece varies depending on flashed effects in the firing. The surface of the piece is

marked by crazing which he feels enhances the richness of the drawing.

He fires his porcelain pieces to a hot cone 10 in a reduction atmosphere in a gas kiln. Since he has resumed work with high-fired reduction only recently, he is still learning how to best do this. He has not fired in reduction for many years and so has had to relearn it. He wants the piece to slump to a point "just short of disaster." Because he

Photo Credit: Steve Myers.

Orange Grass Marsh - Landscape Box (an older piece), 1976. Earthenware, clay inlay, hand-formed, raku-fired. In the mid and late '70s Higby made a group of richly colored covered boxes. In these pieces he was aiming at creating containers in which he rendered his landscape imagery in a three-dimensional manner. He did not, however, lose sight of their identity as container forms.

is taking so many chances, he sometimes goes too far and has a high loss rate with these pieces. He very much enjoys this challenge.

Higby is very concerned with the physical experience of working in clay, of ceramics as a sensual, tactile activity. He loves the way the ceramist weaves back and forth between the sensual and the cerebral. He doesn't worry about the cerebral as much as he worries about control. Over the years he has come to feel that ceramists try too much to control the clay. Though this is a very natural response, he believes that ceramists must be alert to this and have the courage to let the clay do what it wants. He wants to exaggerate the physical characteristics of the body and encourage the clay to crack, open, and slump and encourage the glaze to craze and blister. He is trying to make work that is on the edge between something he has done and something that he has watched happen, between the cognitive and the spontaneous. He wants to establish a balance between these two tendencies. He says with a characteristic mixture of irony and intensity that his next step will be to mix the porcelain body, take it out of the mixer, let it dry, and fire the resulting objects.

In his youth, Higby spent a lot of time raising horses and rode alone for hours every day through the unpeopled landscapes of Colorado. He loves landscape imagery, it reminds him of the silence he experienced on these rides. He sees the landscape as a vehicle to make introspective yet sensual images. In this imagery he is especially interested in the horizon line, using it to signal that the image he has created is that of a landscape. He has a fantasy that he will travel to the horizon line and will slip through it. He will then get to a special place of complete acceptance and complete knowledge.

Higby had a little exposure to art as a youth. He regularly took art classes both in school and in various art centers. He especially remembers a visit when he was in grade school to the Van Briggle Pottery (a famous art pottery started in 1904). He remembers his fascination with the potter's wheel and the throwing process. He was never aiming for a career in art, however when he thought about any career at all, he half accepted that he would take up his father's profession of the law. At this time he probably wanted to become a horse trainer more than anything else. He was very introspective and not very verbal. School meant little to him except the opportunity to compete in sports. He says of himself that in high school he had never read a book from cover to cover. He did like acting and participated in the high school drama program. Like many introspective people, he enjoyed acting because he could immerse himself in the characters he was playing.

College for him was a duty that he undertook because he was expected to attend. He was accepted at the University of Colorado at Boulder in 1961 in the pre-law program. In the middle of his first, very frustrating, semester he visited the law building. He went in and began to look at a few of the law books. He is still, many years later, quite able to communicate his feeling of panic when he read what was in those books. The language of the law is full of arcane terms and convoluted phraseology. He says that at that moment in the law library, it dawned on him that he would *not* be a lawyer. At that moment instant terror seems to have been mingled with relief. He was released from the duty of following in his father's footsteps. He asked himself what he would do now. Persuaded of the usefulness of exploration in libraries, he explored more. He came to the art section of the main library and found art books. He saw with interest and relief that he could deal with these books and found them fascinating. He switched his major to the art program and it was immediately clear that this was something he could do. In fact he did very well and his grades went up. He began to feel empowered. Most important, he proved to himself that he could get decent grades and do well, even very well, in college.

In 1963 and 1964 Higby took a year off from college and took a six-month trip around the world, starting in Japan and ending in New York City. An experience that was to prove especially influential on this trip was a visit to the Heraklion Museum on the island of Crete.

Cloud Bank Bay, a landscape bowl, 12" x 20-1/2" x 14-1/2", raku, 1991. Higby says this piece is directly inspired by the Maine landscape and its seacoast. He likes the piece because he feels in it he was able to reinvent his approach to the bowl form and the imagery he creates for it. He likes the rumpled surface, distorted form, and the folded lip of this bowl. The imagery calls up the surging energy of the sky, wind, and water on the Maine coast. He feels a sense of tension between his form and this imagery.

There he first saw Minoan pots and they moved him very deeply. He was especially interested in their decoration. He had discovered art, now he discovered ceramics and resolved to work in this area. When he came back to Boulder, he talked with one of his teachers, the painter George Woodman. He asked Woodman if he knew anything about ceramics. Woodman had him talk with his wife, the ceramist Betty Woodman. At that time Betty Woodman was teaching at a local art center. Higby took a noncredit course from her and after a time served as her assistant. At this time Higby was taking many art education courses. Along with Betty Woodman's classes, he began to study ceramics in the education department, studying with Ann Jones. Though this class was very different from Betty Woodman's classes (and much more limited) he remembers Jones as a fine teacher. He completed his undergraduate work at Boulder in 1966, earning a B.F.A. degree. In that same year he and Donna Bennett married. He says of Bennett, a painter, that she has given him very important support in his work. She serves as a sounding board and is a totally committed believer in his work.

He now had to make a very important decision: should he go on in ceramic art or go into art education? The Woodmans advised Higby to talk with Paul Soldner who had quite a bit of experience in both areas (Soldner had worked in the field of art education with great success before becoming a ceramist). Soldner was teaching at that time at Scripps College in California. Higby talked with Soldner who encouraged him to

Left: Intangible Notch, a tile installation for Arrow International Inc. in Reading, Pennsylvania. 12' x 10' x 14" deep. An earthenware body fired in raku. Here we see how Higby was able to translate the imagery on his vessels and sculptures to this large mural.

work in ceramic art. He invited Higby to apply for the M.F.A. program at Scripps. Higby decided to throw in his lot with ceramic art. However, before he could attend Scripps, Soldner left teaching for a time. Higby now had to find another M.F.A. granting institution with a good program in ceramics. In their conversation, Soldner had spoken very highly of the ceramics program at the University of Michigan in Ann Arbor. Higby visited Michigan, applied to the program, and was accepted in 1966. There he worked with John Stephenson and Fred Bauer. He was especially close to Bauer. Studying with Bauer was very informal and mostly consisted of studio visits. Higby loved the feeling of independence. He set up his own studio away from the school and built a raku kiln. He worked in raku and spent a good deal of time developing his own raku lusters. Working outside the department, he didn't interact a lot with the other graduate students. Though he did work with John Stephenson during his second year of graduate school, he says that most of his learning from Stephenson took place in a postgraduate context. He says now, "It is difficult to say how important John Stephenson was to my work." At this time Higby was making angular, slab-formed boxes, using a press mold work strate-

gy. After a time he softened the corners of his angular forms to give the pieces a softer appearance that spoke more clearly of the character of the clay. He became very interested in concepts of decoration and embellishment. He worked with ornamental, rhythmically patterned abstract imagery. He became interested in the self-glazing clay bodies called "Egyptian faience." He asked himself, "How do you get decoration into the structure and off of the surface of the ware?" His work with Egyptian faience grew out of that question. While continuing to work mostly in raku, he made some pieces that attracted a great deal of attention using inlaid pattern imagery made with Egyptian faience. He earned his M.F.A. degree from Ann Arbor in 1968.

With the help of John Stephenson, Higby got a job at the University of Nebraska in Omaha where he taught from 1968 to 1970. It was a very good first job and he felt lucky to get it. He had his first big show at the Joslyn Art Museum in Omaha. In a few of the pieces in this show Higby began to use the landscape imagery that is now at the core of his work. Though he was living in the flat plains of Nebraska, he kept on seeing, in his imagination, the hilly landscape of his youth in Colorado. These images are still the source of much of the landscape imagery in his work.

The exhibition at the Joslyn led to other exhibitions, including "The Young Americans" exhibition at the American Craft Museum and "Objects U.S.A." at the Smithsonian Institution. Both these exhibitions opened in 1969. In 1968 he met Howard Kottler at an NCECA meeting in Kansas City, Missouri. He and Kottler became good friends. In the summer of 1969 Higby was a visiting lecturer in ceramics at the University of Washington in Seattle.

Though he liked Nebraska, Higby wanted to move on. He applied for a few jobs including one at the Rhode Island School of Design. When they offered him a position there, he was quite enthusiastic because he had never lived on the East Coast and he thought he would enjoy the opportunity. Higby liked the School of Design and thought he would stay there for the rest of his teaching career. He found it to be a dynamic and interesting school. He shared an office with Norm Schulman and Dale Chihuly. He liked working with Schulman and felt Schulman gave the best critiques he had ever heard. In 1973, however, a position opened up at the New York State College of Ceramics at Alfred. Ted Randall called and asked him to talk to them about the job. He flew there, met with the faculty, and liked what he saw. He felt that the opportunity to teach along with Bob Turner, Ted Randall, and Val Cushing was especially appealing. He decided the opportunity was too good to pass up and he has taught at Alfred ever since. It has been an exhilarating and demanding job. Alfred is an isolated and intense place. Higby gets lots of talented and interesting students.

For many years Higby continued with his brilliantly colored work in raku. This work is highly admired and he has had many opportunities to exhibit it. In the early 1970s Higby began to teach in the summer at the Haystack Mountain School of Crafts. Haystack is set on a high point of land at the edge of the Atlantic Ocean. He has returned there often and feels that the Haystack landscape has exerted a very strong influence on his work. In 1975 Higby began to work with a large bowl form. He took up work with this form because he wanted a looser form than the press-molded slab-formed boxes he had been working with until this time. Though Higby used no inlay imagery in these pieces, his control over his glazes is such that they often look as if he used an inlay work strategy. Form and glaze are strongly bonded.

Over the years Higby has traveled a good deal, first around the world, then to Europe, and most recently to China. When he first went to China in 1991, he found himself responding to a culture in a way he had not before. He thinks this response was partly to China's ceramic tradition and partly to the energy of its people. Since that time he has been closely associated with Chinese ceramists at the famed ceramic city of Jingdezhen and is an honorary professor of ceramics at the Ceramic Institute there. Higby has returned often to China and has had many good experiences there. He has had a great deal of exposure to porcelain at Jingdezhen and in 1994 he decided to take up work in the medium.

During a sabbatical that year (1993/94) he attended a family reunion on Lake Powell in southern Utah. This is a huge and hauntingly beautiful lake with a very complex coastline. The family lived on the lake on a houseboat. Later as he began to work in porcelain, he came to see that the medium would be perfect for picturing the images and feelings he remembered from this time on the lake. This is the source of the imagery we see in his new porcelain pieces.

In 1995 Higby carried out a large raku tile wall commission for Arrow International, a medical technology firm based in Reading, Pennsylvania. This commission is the largest piece he has made so far. He found it quite daunting at first but it has given him a new feeling of confidence that he can tackle difficult technical problems. He continues to work with both raku and porcelain but feels he is moving steadily toward greater involvement with porcelain and expects to spend most of his work time with that medium in the future.

Wayne Higby in his studio.

Sandi Pierantozzi

Sandi Pierantozzi makes hand-formed pots. She means them to be both decorative and utilitarian. We sometimes associate a deep concern with the utilitarian aspects of ceramic work as a leftover from attitudes common in the 1950s. This is not true of her work. Her forms and decoration have a strongly contemporary character.

Photo credit: Sandi Pierantozzi and Neil Patterson.

Covered Box *(an older piece), raku, 5" x 12" x 5", 1988. When Pierantozzi made this piece her work had very sharp, highly controlled contours and hard edges. She made the piece from leather-hard slabs. The viewer is quite conscious of its geometric form and its crisp edges. Its surfaces have a somewhat different mood, they are more atmospheric and marked by soft visual textures.*

Left: Carafe, 12" x 5" x 5", 1996. Pierantozzi began making this piece from a flat slab ornamented with relief patterns. She then took the slab and formed it into a simple straight-sided cylindrical form. She placed her hand inside the cylinder at its middle and pushed outward to stretch the walls. She then cut darts into the upper edges of the piece. These let her narrow the top and gave the form its swelling contour at its base. She gathered together parts of the base to create the three tapered feet. She formed the foot area by folding and pinching. As she folded the base of the slab, she was able to create a structure composed of three arches. She turned the base of each arch into a foot, creating the tripod form we see here. She designed the narrow textured neck so the piece could be easily grasped by the user.

Pierantozzi bisque fired the piece to cone 05/04. She then applied cone 04 glazes to finish it. She first poured a clear glaze on the inside of the piece, then applied the glazes on the outer surfaces of her work using a brush. She glaze fired to cone 06/05 in an electric kiln. The color is reminiscent of patinated metallic surfaces.

Pierantozzi makes her pieces using a red terra cotta clay body. She bisque fires her work to cone 04. It is a very smooth, tight clay body with no grog. Grog would help the body withstand stress but would cause other problems. She needs to have a smooth, finely textured clay body. Grog or another aggregate would encourage a coarse texture instead of the refined surfaces she needs. Furthermore, grog would cause tearing and cracking as she forms the piece. It would be certain to cause problems when she stretches parts of the surface to create a full form. Her grog-free clay body allows her to create the smooth buttery surfaces she needs for her pieces. Her clay body's fine grain works very well with her complex textured patterns in relief. Pierantozzi forms her pieces using a combination of slab and pinch forming. She often folds her slabs to create complex volumetric forms. This puts stress on the clay body, so she requires a strong and plastic clay body that will stand stress during the forming, drying, and firing processes.

Pierantozzi starts her pieces using flat slabs. She often starts off by creating elaborate patterns in relief on the surface of the slab. She then joins the two ends of the slab to create a simple straight-sided cylindrical form. Next she forms the foot area by cutting, folding, and pinching. She places her hand inside the cylinder at its middle and pushes outward to stretch the walls to give the form a swelling contour. To complete the form she often cuts darts into the upper edges of the piece. This gives the piece a rich full form. These darts encourage an informal and pieced together look. She creates complex forms that seem to spring naturally from her building methods. Her work strategies require a very flexible clay body because her manipulations of the clay can cause stress cracks. They put a good deal of stress on the clay body. It is along the grooves caused by the textured pattern that the clay is especially liable to crack. She must carry out her work without threatening the integrity of the piece.

Pierantozzi's forms are simple and volumetric. Her use of cuts and darts lets her create forms that have an appealing full look. With their tripod feet and exaggerated handles and spouts, they are dramatic and convey a sense of ritual. Furthermore, they give the work a pleasing informality. In her complex surface textures we see her trying for highly active patterns in relief. She creates these patterns by pressing materials into the clay surface. She loves to find objects in the street that she can use for pressing into the clay. She often creates patterns on the surface of her pieces with a piece of plastic or wire mesh. This pattern does a number of things: the resulting surfaces are very appealing and interesting, they help the viewer to read the volumetric character of the form, and they work with the glaze to encourage rich surfaces. In her use of color we see a color sense that does not strive for a natural feeling but rather one that is luxurious, harmonious, and somewhat reminiscent of patina on metal.

Pierantozzi uses cone 05/04 glazes to finish her pieces. She makes her own glazes in the studio. At one point she was working mostly with decorative

Ruffle Vase detail. In this slide we can clearly see Pierantozzi's way of placing rich patterns and colored and textured glazes next to each other.

Far Right: Ruffle Vase, 9" x 6" x 6", 1998. Pierantozzi has filled out the form in this piece to give it a swelling volume. The gathered clay feet also contribute to that feeling of volume. The dark area under the raised feet is quite dramatic and conveys a sense of ritual. To make the neck, Pierantozzi first created a series of grooves on a flat slab. She then formed the slab into a cylinder. The grooves at the neck contribute to the sense of drama. This is not the only pattern on the piece, however. Pierantozzi has decorated this piece with a variety of highly patterned surfaces.

covered boxes. She used terra sigillatas almost exclusively to finish these pieces. She loved the rich waxy surfaces of the sigillatas. The sigillatas were quite appropriate for these decorative pieces; though practical considerations were important, they were not all-important. When she began to make vases, she decided that glazes would be much more appropriate and useful for finishing her work. She needed their durability and sealing characteristics. She has learned to use glazes and achieve a look that is reminiscent of her terra sigillatas. She has made sure her glazes are lead-free and as food-safe as possible. She pours a clear glaze on the inside of her pieces, then, using a brush, applies the glazes on the outer surfaces of her work. Pierantozzi bisque fires her work to cone 04 and glaze fires to cone 05/04. She fires exclusively in an electric kiln.

As a potter making utilitarian production pieces, Pierantozzi must confront problems related to their functionality and to the way she carries out the production process. She sees these as an integral part of the overall character of her work. She tests her pieces for utility before she makes a whole group. She wants to make sure the piece is effective in terms of both the visual design and the way it works when it is used. She feels that as a production ceramist she must maintain an aspect of challenge in her work.

She knows that the process must be satisfying. Otherwise tasks that were originally daunting and interesting will become boring and repetitious. Pierantozzi makes it a point to periodically make changes in her work so she can keep up its energy level. Function has another aspect that is very important to her. This is the idea that she is in some way connected to those who use her pieces. This communality of maker and user is an important part of utilitarian ceramics. Even in an era in which ceramists often ignore utility, this idea keeps bobbing to the surface. Its irrepressibility shows us its power and relevance.

Pierantozzi has worked as an artist during all of her adult

Chimney Cap Tea Set, the teapot is 8" x 7" x 5", 1997. This is representative of Pierantozzi's way of making a tea setting. Her use of templates results in a successful grouping of shapes, sizes, and forms. The sense of playful invention is very strong in these pieces.

life but for a long time she was not a ceramist. She was a successful graphic artist who worked in the field for 20 years. For 12 of those years she owned her own graphic arts business. Pierantozzi began her work in ceramics because neighbors invited her to the Christmas sale at The Clay Studio of Philadelphia, a very successful institution where classes and workshops are offered and ceramic artists may rent studio space. She had never seen so much pottery and had never thought about it very much. She really enjoyed the Clay Studio. After another

visit in 1984 she decided to take an introductory course in ceramics. She loved to cook and wanted to make pots for the kitchen. After the introductory course she took a course in throwing on the potter's wheel. When she began working in clay, it was as a hobby, a way of relaxing from the tensions of deadlines and client demands. As she puts it, she "wanted to get away from the pencils." A year later, in 1985, she enrolled in the next level, the Clay Studio's "Associate Artist Program." This was a program for serious students who wanted 24 hour access to the facili-

ty. Her work was beginning to take on a professional character. During these years her pieces had very sharp and controlled contours. She made them from stiff leather-hard slabs. As she says of this work now, "I thought about 'shape' more than 'form.' Clay is soft, responsive, and those were the things I loved about it. Yet I was unable, at that point, to make work that reflected those qualities. I felt stuck." In 1990 she went to a one-day workshop on making cups with soft slabs. Though she found the experience disconcerting, she couldn't get it out of her mind and soon she was using soft slabs for all her work. She began stamping patterns in relief into her clay at this time as well. The work took on a new life for her. She still uses these strategies in her work.

Pierantozzi went to Anderson Ranch Art Center in Snowmass, Colorado, in the summers of 1987 and 1989 as a student. There she met the potter Neil Patterson, who had come as a workshop assistant (see page 120). During the 1990/91 school year Patterson attended the Cardiff Institute of Higher Education in Wales (England) as an exchange student. She and Patterson corresponded by letter and exchanged visits. She remained in the Associate Program of the Clay Studio until 1990 when she applied for "Resident Artist Status." This program was for those advanced ceramists who wanted to have their own work space in which they could develop their work. She worked in the ceramic studio during the evenings and on days off. From 1984 to 1992 she continued to run her graphics business. In 1992 she gave up her business and went to work for other graphic artists, dividing her time between ceramics and graphic arts. In the summer of 1992 Pierantozzi and Patterson again worked together at The Anderson Ranch Art Center. In the fall of that year Patterson moved permanently to Philadelphia.

In 1993 Pierantozzi began to use cut and dart forming methods to soften and fill out her forms. She wanted to develop other ways of forming her work as well as paddling and she liked the resulting pieced together look. This method has become an important component in her work. There is a five-year limit at The Clay Studio for those in the Resident Artists Program and in 1995 Pierantozzi rented her own studio. At this time she became a full-time studio potter making utilitarian vessels.

Pierantozzi and Patterson now share a studio in a loft in the Old City section of Philadelphia. She supports herself by selling at craft shows, galleries, and at studio sales and by teaching private classes. She and Patterson have had local publicity and their work has a following in Philadelphia.

Pierantozzi wants to create a sense of unity and harmony in her work. She works hard to create a balance between clay body, clay surface, form, and glaze surface. Her strong clay body allows her to work with complex building strategies. Her forms work well with the patterns in relief that she places on their surface. These patterns create interest and a feeling of richness. No one aspect of the process dominates - neither the forms, the patterns in relief, nor the color. The result is an example of the partnership of clay body, forming, and surface creation methods. Pierantozzi balances these aspects of her work to create a sense of unity and balance.

Photo credit: Richard Zakin.

Sandi Pierantozzi in her studio in the Old City section of Philadelphia.

Neil Patterson

Neil Patterson is a studio potter who lives and works in Philadelphia, Pennsylvania. Patterson works a great deal in thrown and then altered forms, though he has also begun to work on slab-formed containers and tiles. In the past he most often worked with vase or bottle forms but recently has begun making a group of covered boxes as well. He makes pieces that combine utility with an interest in form and surface. Patterson ornaments his surfaces with textures in high relief, which strongly influence the look of the piece. He wants to

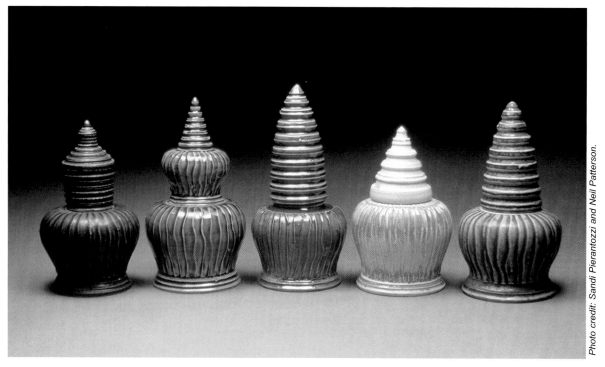

Potion Bottles, *6" x 4" x 4", stoneware clay body, 1996. Patterson has used a highly flowing, low viscosity glaze on these pieces to emphasize the relief imagery.*

make visually pleasing craft objects that work well and that he can price reasonably. He also wants his pieces to challenge the imagination and to speak of the contemporary visual culture. In a time when much of the focus in magazines and at conferences is on sculptural work, the production potter can feel neglected. Currently there is no well understood and generally agreed upon goal or direction for this sort of work. As a result, the production potter has great freedom but must develop a personal sense of direction and goals.

Patterson buys vacuum pugged clay body from a ceramic supply house. It is very consistent and highly workable. The body contains kaolin and a good deal of fire clay. It is quite plastic, which is extremely important to him because he often bends and folds the body in forming his pieces. He feels the plasticity is derived from the vacuum de-airing and a great variation in particle size due to the presence of a variety of clays in the recipe. He especially values its rich burnt orange color when he fires it in a wood kiln (he wants this color, not a chocolate brown). Patterson forms his pieces on the potter's wheel. He often cuts, alters, and assembles pieces after he has thrown a basic form. He creates his strong patterns in relief on the wheel as well. He looks for glaze recipes that enhance the relief, particularly glazes with a strong visual texture. His recipes mostly come from colleagues and from notes he made during his time at the

Penland School for the Crafts. Once he finds a useful glaze recipe, he likes to tinker with it by substituting materials or varying the amount of the materials in the recipe. He uses simple glaze recipe types such as gunmetal, slip glazes, and high clay glazes. Patterson applies his glazes by pouring or brushing. He fires his pieces to cone 11 in a cross draft wood kiln. He uses a heavy body reduction but fires in only a light reduction after that. Patterson uses the light reduction because it encourages brighter livelier glazes. Toward the end of the firing he may expose the ware to a light salting to ensure that the glaze has a smooth surface and the slips have a waxy sheen. While Patterson does not put the kiln atmosphere into reoxidation before finishing the fire, his light reduction firing does not require one. Furthermore, his use of light reduc-tion means that there is no black core in the interior of the body. A heavy black core can encourage a brittle clay body and he wants the clay body to be highly durable.

Patterson is interested in texture and what textured patterns can do to the form. He often creates grooved patterns in relief on the surface of his pieces. At times he has this lead the viewer around the form; at other times he uses the lines to run in a direction counter to what one might expect

Detail of **Assembled Bottle**, 1997, showing the combed imagery that Patterson uses in his work.

and "play against" the form to add a surprising note. Because of their strongly textured patterns, these pieces have a great affinity with Nigerian pottery. Nigerian pottery is highly utilitarian but the potters don't ignore the aesthetic aspects of their work. Patterson especially admires the potters' use of rhythmic pattern and rich texture. Patterson saw a good deal of this work while in England and feels he learned much from it.

Patterson thinks a good deal about the vessel format. He works in both utilitarian and nonutilitarian formats. He is very interested in the container idea and has used a great many types of container forms

Photo credit: Sandi Pierantozzi and Neil Patterson.

Left: Bottle, 10" x 5" x 4", 1996. *Patterson likes simple, strong forms and he is concerned with the stance or posture of his forms. Notice that this piece is tall with a good deal of weight at the top. This strong stance makes it a very dramatic form type.*

Patterson made this piece using a white stoneware body with an addition of fine grog. He assembled it from small segments created by first forming a thick-walled cylinder on the potter's wheel. During the throwing process he created a furrowed texture by pressing a toothed rib against the surface of the cylinder, then pushed the clay wall outwards from the inside to widen and enrich the clay furrows while continuing to throw and thin the clay wall. He repeated the process to make more cylinders. He used different tools to create different surface textures. After finishing the furrowed surfaces he removed the cylinders from the wheel and cut them into fragments of various shapes ranging in size from 2" to 5". As soon as he could touch the fragments without marring their textured imagery, he began to assemble the piece. He slipped and scored the edges of the segments and began to join them together. Starting with small elements, he built the pieces step by step. As he built the wall he slipped and scored the edges of the clay segments and joined them to other segments. He assembled these segments over a foam form to create larger sections of the piece. Patterson used the grooved textures on the segment surfaces to create ordered rhythmic patterns. Once the clay hardened, these sections became very strong. Finally, he assembled the sections to create the completed form. When he finished the piece, he covered it in plastic and allowed it to dry slowly.

Patterson made the bronze-like surface on this piece using the following recipe: 90 Alberta slip, 10 nepheline syenite, 5 cobalt. The metallic surface adds to the character of the work. He found this recipe among a large group of recipes at the Penland School in North Carolina. He glazed the interior with a high clay glaze. Patterson poured the glaze on the inside of the piece. On the outside he applied the slip with a brush using a lathering motion. Patterson has used a monochromatic color here. This choice makes sense given the sculptural form and complex relief surface of the piece. Lots of color variety would have obscured form and surface. He often uses a monochromatic glaze strategy because he feels a single glaze unifies what might otherwise be disparate elements. This piece has a strong affinity with Nigerian pottery, which has similarly monochromatic color and a grooved, textured surface. Patterson fired the piece to cone 11 in a cross draft wood kiln. He used a heavy body reduction but fired in only a light reduction after that. Toward the end of the firing he did a light salting of the ware.

in his work - covered jars, teapots, bowls, cups, and platters. At present he is interested in vases, bottles, and covered boxes. Function is important to him but more important is the visual character of his pieces. In part this is the influence of his work in ceramic sculpture. Recently Patterson has begun to work on a series of tiles and he believes they may eventually prove to be an important part of his work. Unlike his vessels these are not high fired, they are earthenware pieces. He makes the tiles using the press mold forming process and finishes them with terra sigillata. The surface is covered with patterns in relief similar to that of his vessels. They are highly decorative. Patterson intends them for both indoor and outdoor use in places like kitchens and patios. These tiles are fairly large (8" x 8"). He hopes they will prove a successful addition to his line of pieces.

Patterson has been serious about ceramics since he was in high school in Gates Mills, Ohio. He took a number of ceramics courses there. He became very involved with the potter's wheel and bent all his energies to mastering its challenge. As his involvement with ceramics deepened it became obvious to him that he would have to continue his work in ceramics in college. He enrolled in the ceramics program at the Cleveland Institute of Art. From 1981 to 1986 he studied with William Brouillard and Judith Salomon. Cleveland is a five-year B.F.A. program; the emphasis in the fifth year is on independent work. In his fifth year Patterson worked on pieces in which he used textured fragments assembled into vessel forms. Thus, during his time as an undergraduate student he was already working on the sort of piece he continues to make more than ten years later.

Upon graduation from the Cleveland Art Institute he went

Vase: Flower Arranger, stoneware clay body, 1996. These two photographs are of great interest because they show the impact of use on a container form. In this first photograph we see a vase especially designed to hold flowers, without the flowers.

Vase: Flower Arranger, here we see the same piece with flowers. It is useful to contrast views of this piece while empty and when holding flowers. This form is well designed for its purpose and strikes a note of great visual consistency when it holds flowers.

to the Penland School in the mountains of North Carolina as a "core student." Core students are given living and work space in return for services to Penland. They help make Penland the formidable institution it is. Patterson attended Penland from 1986 to 1988. There he did more work along the lines of the pieces he had made in Cleveland. He also made some production pieces. These were definitely influenced by the Penland scene, especially by the work of Cynthia Bringle, a professional potter who has a studio on land adjoining Penland. He enjoyed the freedom he had there and used his time to create a great deal of work.

Patterson then went on to study at Louisiana State University with Joe Bova. Bova was teaching at Penland in 1987 and Patterson met him there. He was very impressed with Bova and had met some of Bova's former students who encouraged Patterson to apply for graduate study with Bova.

He spent the years 1988/89 and 1991/92 at Louisiana. Bova was particularly interested in encouraging him to try new ideas. During his time there he began to work in sculpture. Some of the imagery he used was figurative while in other work he employed narrative imagery dealing with images of the sort that arise during dreams. During this period he tried all sorts of approaches. He took on, as his particular challenge, work on a group of large scale, low-fire sculptural pieces. Though he now feels that his core talent in ceramics lies elsewhere, he enjoyed working on these pieces and feels that some of the things he learned from his work in ceramic sculpture are very much relevant to the work he does now.

In the summer of 1989 Patterson went to Anderson Ranch Art Center, in Snowmass, Colorado, as a studio assistant. There he met Sandi Pierantozzi, at the time a graphic artist, who had come as a student to attend a workshop. After the workshop was over, they corresponded by letter and exchanged visits. Patterson interrupted his program at Louisiana during the 1990/91 school year to attend the Cardiff Institute of Higher Education in Wales as a student exchange student. There he worked with Mick Casson and Peter Starkey, both potters. At this time he was mostly making sculpture and received a great deal of support from Casson and Starkey. In the summer of 1992 Patterson again had the post of studio assistant at The Anderson Ranch Art Center. He now returned to his work in pottery. The potter Ron Myers was a big influence on his work and encouraged him in this return to pots. He began making both sculptural pottery and production work. He says, "It felt wonderful to return to what I feel is my own." He likens it to bird

behavior. The Oriole builds the nest in a certain shape; the vessel form is like Patterson's nest. He and Sandi Pierantozzi now were actively planning ways to share a studio and construct a life together.

In the fall of 1992 Patterson moved permanently to Philadelphia and set up his studio. By this time he felt he understood what kind of work he wanted to do and he has kept at it since. He supports himself by selling at craft shows, galleries, and at studio sales. His best customers are from Philadelphia. He and Pierantozzi have had local publicity and their work has a following in that city. Patterson divides his time between studio work and teaching stints. He has been an adjunct instructor at the Tyler School of Art in Philadelphia and has had a residency at The Clay Studio of Philadelphia. At present he is teaching homeless adults with mental health needs and finds this work very rewarding. He makes sure, however, to devote 20 to 40 hours a week to his studio work.

For many ceramists, ceramics becomes a way of life as much as a medium to be mastered. This is true of Patterson. His career has not taken any abrupt turns and he has had no crises of confidence or big change of plans. He has stayed with the medium since high school and has developed a way of working that suits him. The sense of steady growth, order,and harmony we see in his work, we see also in his life.

Photo credit: Richard Zakin.

Neil Patterson at work on a tile set.

Ron Roy

Ron Roy lives and works as a studio potter in Scarborough, a northern borough of Toronto, Canada. He is obsessive in his need to master the technical problems that accompany our craft. He works for a portion of each week as a technical consultant for a well known Canadian ceramic supply company. He is their "glaze doctor," a very demanding job. For all his understanding of the technical aspects of ceramics, however, he never ignores the artistic and aesthetic impact of his pieces. He attacks the technical and aesthetic problems of ceramics with equal energy and concentration. It is characteristic of his approach that many of his solutions to aesthetic problems have a technical or materials based cast.

Photo credit: Ron Roy.

Two Place Settings*, 1984. To make the form he wanted, Ron Roy threw a disk-like form with a shallow depression in the middle, then trimmed the edge of the disk to create the complex, highly designed lip. Roy wants these pieces to enhance the enjoyment of food and to encourage feelings in the user of harmony and contemplation.*

Ron Roy uses a highly durable cone 10 porcelain clay body. In the reduction fire its color is white with a slight gray cast. This color is derived from a significant ball clay content. In most ways this body conforms to the classic porcelain recipe. It has comparatively good workability and working strength (he feels he needs that for the kind of work he is doing). It also has excellent resistance to cracking.

Roy is very interested in the way his porcelain pieces dry. This is no surprise because porcelain is subject to warping and cracking during the drying period. Unlike most contemporary ceramists he doesn't wrap his pieces in plastic sheeting. Instead he uses a damp box (a cabinet or room that can be sealed off and kept quite moist). Damp boxes are more effective than plastic sheeting but much harder to maintain. If a damp box has an effective moisture seal and is kept moist, it can be a very useful tool for letting ceramic pieces dry slowly and evenly. Roy likes a five or six day drying pattern. In this way he can arrive at the perfect moisture content for trimming and even drying.

Roy keeps two different strands of work going at the same time, a highly utilitarian line of dinnerware and a line of decorative platters. Though utility and purpose are very important aspects of his dinnerware, the aesthetics come first. In these place settings he gives his pieces a unique personality by making the plate surface the simplest of shallow curves, by

Place Setting, 1994. Utility and purpose are very important aspects of Ron Roy's work. Here utility is expressed in both the aesthetic and physical character of this place setting. Roy used a highly durable cone 10 porcelain clay body. In the reduction fire its color is white with a slight gray cast. It has comparatively good workability and excellent working strength. If he dries the work properly, it has excellent resistance to cracking.

This plate has a smooth, unbroken, concave surface with no delineation between plate and rim. Roy threw the plate by throwing a 1" porcelain slab. He concentrated on creating the concave curve of the plate. He says that when he is throwing these pieces the contour of this curved shape is "the only thing I am thinking about." He took this piece off the bat as quickly as possible, then placed it in a damp cupboard on a rack until it was firm enough to turn over on its rim. He used a rib to smooth the surface of the plate, then used his palm to wipe out irregularities. Then he turned the plate over and trimmed it. He trimmed the edge of the plate to give it its special profile. Unlike most contemporary ceramists Roy doesn't wrap his pieces in plastic sheeting during the drying process. Instead he uses a damp box (a cabinet or room that can be sealed off and kept quite moist).

Roy designed for the glaze when he formed the plate. The basic color of this glaze is a rich deep black. Because this glaze has a low viscosity, it runs away from the edges of the form. Where it does this the thin layer of glaze that remains is marked by a rich rust color. This emphasizes the complex carved contour of the form. The glaze is smooth and durable, making it very suitable for a utilitarian plate. His application was simple. He immersed the plate in the glaze, pushing it into the glaze bucket with the front edge going in first. He then drew it back and pulled it out of the glaze bucket. He held the plate on two edges and filled in the spots where his fingers had rested and which were now left bare of glaze. He high fired this piece to cone 10 in a reduction atmosphere in a natural gas kiln.

Photo credit: Ron Roy.

Snow Plate, 12" diameter. Roy made this piece using a cone 10 porcelain clay body. He created the form entirely on the potter's wheel. In this piece the glaze work takes center stage. The orange red color is a material he calls a cone 10 terra sigillata (when a true sigillata is fired to cone 10 it takes on the character of the most highly refined slip glaze). He applied the terra sigillata over the entire surface of the piece, let it dry, then glazed the piece with a zircopax mat glaze in powder form. He sprinkled the powder over the plate, then shook the platter until it took on a pattern he liked. He carefully loaded the piece in the kiln and fired it to set the glaze.

giving the edges a special profile, and by using glazes that emphasize the character of the form. He works hard to create the smooth curve of the plate and the articulated edges of these forms. The smooth curve of the plate works well and holds food very efficiently. Perhaps most important, however, this curve is daring in its simplicity. The outline of his plates is also worthy of note. The character of the edges is that of a taut line that alternately accelerates at a curve and then slows and comes to a dead stop at a right angle. The line has a lot of energy. In his plates he is aiming for a feeling that every aspect of the piece works in concert with every other. He is interested in the aesthetics of utility. He joins aesthetic matters to use when he says he wants them to look complete only when they are used to hold food. Without food they appear empty; they ask to be filled. He wants his pieces to enhance the enjoyment of food and to encourage feelings in the user of harmony and contemplation. When utility and aesthetics are joined in this way, mundane matters become important. The act of eating becomes a ceremony and even the act of cleaning up afterwards becomes more pleasurable. For this reason he makes his pieces strong and durable, smooth surfaced, easily cleaned, food safe, and oven proof. He smooths and softens the edges of these pieces to reduce chipping and cracking. Glazes are highly durable and bond effectively with the body.

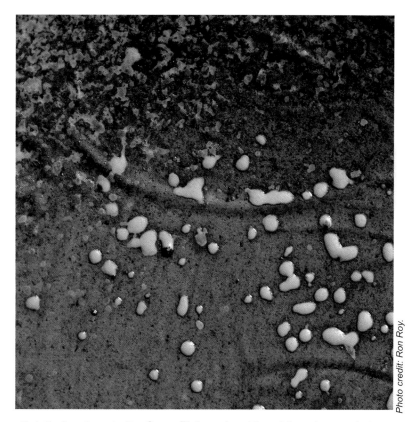

Photo credit: Ron Roy.

*Detail of a piece in the **Snow Plate** series. The white spheres of glaze result from the dry sifted application of the glaze over the terra sigillata.*

Roy makes a point of designing for the glaze when he forms the piece. A number of years ago he realized that his work would gain power if he threw, trimmed, and ornamented with the final glaze effect already in his mind. His pieces now took on a feeling of completeness that he had been looking for in his work. In the past few years he has used a Temmoku glaze to finish his dinnerware. This is a low viscosity glaze that flows away from the edges of the form and in the process goes from a black color to a burnt orange. This color change highlights and emphasizes the details of the form. Therefore, when Roy

makes one of these pieces, he forms the edges to go with the behavior of the glaze. He has designed the plate and created raised ornament on its surface that catches the glaze and exploits the imagery of the Temmoku glaze. The effect is natural to the glaze and is quite striking.

In recent years Roy has also made a group of decorative platters he calls Snow Plates. These feature a rich glaze imagery. For these pieces he uses a round platter form with a simple raised rim and a raised band a few inches in from the rim. He has designed the form to carry the surface imagery. In these decorative platters he

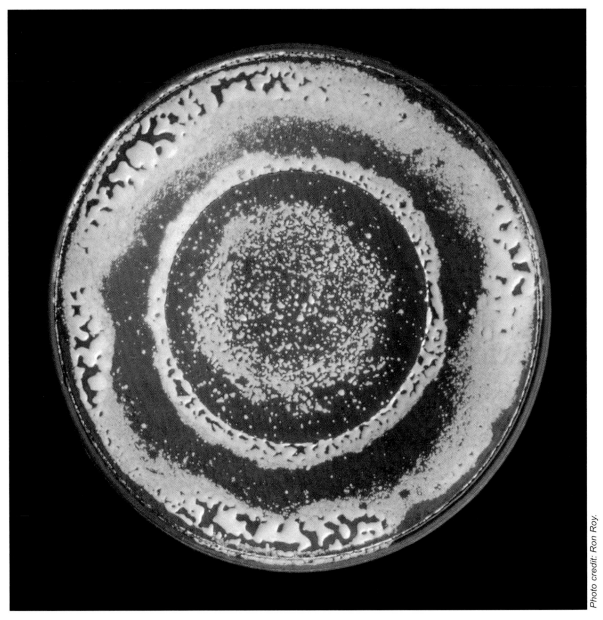

Snow Plate #12, 13" diameter. The crawling white glaze is also the result of the dry sifting application of the glaze over the terra sigillata.

creates the surface by first painting a terra sigillata over the surface. Recently a number of ceramists have taken to firing terra sigillatas to high temperatures. At these temperatures the sigillatas are thin, hard surfaced, durable, and richly col-

ored. They work well with high-fired glazes. During the firing the glazes break over the sigillata to create rich patterns and textures. Roy then sifts a dry glaze onto the surface of the piece. He shakes the plate to create a pattern of dry glaze

that pleases him. Though sifting a dry glaze over a form isn't very common in contemporary ceramics, it used to be done more frequently and is still one of the basic application strategies for the enamelist. There is no reason why we can't use it in contemporary ceramics (wearing the obligatory dust mask, of course) but not many ceramists do.

Roy arrived at these refinements after many programs of testing and experiment. Central to his work is his development of new forms and form/glaze combinations. He creates test pieces in a very instinctual way. He feels he is best when reacting to the problems he runs into when working on a real piece. When he has made an experimental piece he can react to it, analyze it, and see what needs to be improved. In this way he is able to mix the instinctual with the analytical to develop a finished idea.

Roy is a perfectionist and these form and glaze combinations are elegant and perfectly controlled. Such images are a long time in development and when they are developed, Roy stays with them for a long time. He pays for his need for perfection by accepting limitation. These days he limits his form choices quite strictly. He makes cups and bowls for his dinnerware sets but beyond that, all of his pieces are in the plate or platter format.

As important as these characteristics are, one more has equal if not greater importance - how does Roy make this work look current? Roy's approach *could* result in a body of work that wouldn't look out of place in the 1950s, yet this is not the case. His work is chance taking and has its surprises. It could only have been made at the present time. The austere

curved surfaces of his utilitarian plates serve as a good example of this. This is not how plates used to be made. His glazing too has a contemporary character. In the glazing of the *Snow Plates*, he is willing to create a complex multi-part work strategy. These strategies would never have been accepted in the '50s. They would have been rejected as unnatural.

Roy attended the Ontario College of Art in Toronto from 1959 to 1963 as a special student in their three-year program. He studied ceramics with Arthur Handy, an Alfred graduate who specialized in sculpture and wall pieces with a strong artistic content. While attending school Roy worked for the department as a helper in the ceramics laboratory. At this time he was not very interested in the technology. He learned the basics - how to make clay bodies and glazes and how to fire kilns. Upon graduation he set up his own studio in Toronto, where he did commission work and made a line of decorative vessels and planters. He also made a line of utilitarian plates and platters. He was trying to make and sell his work while carrying out a rigorous program of exploration of ceramic forms and surface textures. His careful approach and low key attitude to ceramic imagery didn't encourage popular acceptance and his work was not selling well. In fact, until recently, his work hasn't met with great public acceptance. From 1968 to 1983 he taught ceramics (mostly to adult

learners) at Centennial College in Toronto. In 1971 he founded a clay business, Rodaco Clay. He now says of this period that his teaching plus his work at Rodaco kept him (just) in the black.

In 1983 he purchased his first computer and was able to run the powerful glaze analysis program *Insight.* This encouraged him to explore the technical aspects of ceramics in a way that was very different from the piecemeal approach he had taken previously. He began an organized program of experiment and reading. At this time he was trying to attain a level of mastery that had seemed beyond him before. This included mastery of the wheel, of clay bodies, glazes, utility, and technical analysis of ceramic materials. During this period he began to feel that his supply business was taking too much time away from his work as a potter. In 1981 he sold the business and returned to full-time studio pottery. Simultaneously he made a big change in his work and switched from a stoneware body to porcelain. His glazes looked much better on porcelain and the character and seriousness of the work was intensified. Porcelain requires a very strong commitment and Roy, with his intensity and tenacity, has the perfect temperament for this medium. He felt the materials of porcelain were more refined and therefore more reliable and less variable than the materials found in stoneware bodies. These investigations slowly lent his work a new austerity and intensity. He continues to explore the possibilities of the medium with great intensity and commitment. The two poles around which this work revolves are form and utility. He considers that in the area of utilitarian pottery, he is almost entirely self-taught and is proud of his contributions to the field. He wants his forms to be beautiful, serene, pleasing, and personal. He also wants his pieces to be useful. When asked which impulse takes precedence, he replies that he wants both but says, "The aesthetics must win if there is a conflict between aesthetics and utility."

His work is better known in Canada than the U.S. but this is changing. More people know about his work and he is often asked to give workshops. His work has proved to be especially appealing to potters who understand what he is trying to do. His intensity and will to perfection has gained him an audience.

Photo credit: Ian Sinclair.

Ron Roy.

Eva Kwong

Eva Kwong uses the events of her life as a springboard for her imagery. This imagery is a kind of personal language. The imagery reflects such intangibles as the microscopic world, fertility, genetics, the growth cycle, faith in life, her children, the way we bond with others, and serious illness.

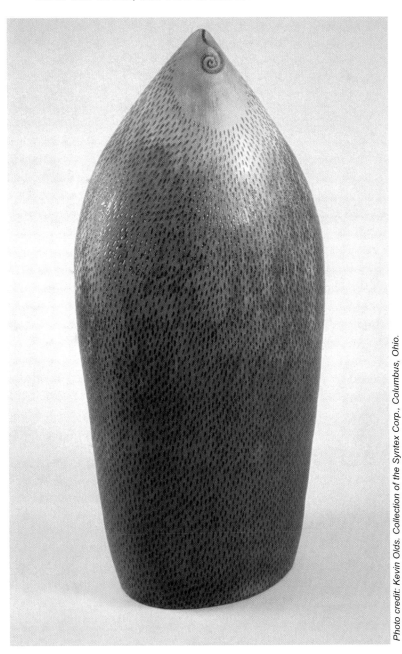

Passion Fruit, 48" x 22" x 15", salt glazed, 1990. Kwong is known for her richly colored surfaces. Here we see her using a combination of sgraffito and brushwork to create a complex fabric-like imagery. She painted five different colored pink slips and three different yellow slips on the surface to produce a rich carpet-like effect. She then created a dense pattern of scooped out marks and filled these in with a dark blue slip. Once the piece dried, she fired it in a salt kiln to give it a transparent finish.

Photo credit: Kevin Olds. Collection of the Syntex Corp., Columbus, Ohio.

Kwong uses cone 5 sculpture clay body for her work:

Fire clay	50
Redart clay	50
Silica sand	10% to 20%

Kwong makes her pieces with stoneware clay bodies. She forms her pieces using a fat coil 5" or 6" in width. She simultaneously thins the wall and shapes it. She also uses potter's ribs to thin the wall and shape the contour of the form. She then adds another coil and repeats the process. Each time she does this, the piece grows by about 10". As she gets to the end of the process, she uses thinner coils.

Kwong paints the surface with colored slips. She may paint the slips in a simple additive strategy or may paint multiple layers of a thick slip, then carve back to reveal lower slip layers. She then uses a sgraffito strategy to carve lines into the slip imagery to delineate and refine the imagery. This combination of slips and sgraffito has been used for millennia. It is particularly effective with painted slip imagery because the brush applied imagery is soft and atmospheric, while the sgraffito has a hard etched, linear imagery. The two image types complement each other very effectively. She then finishes the piece by firing it in the salt kiln or applying a clear glaze. She likes the salt surface because it has a lively and pleasing texture and its uneven surface discourages reflections. If she uses a glaze to finish the piece, it will often be a commercially manufactured

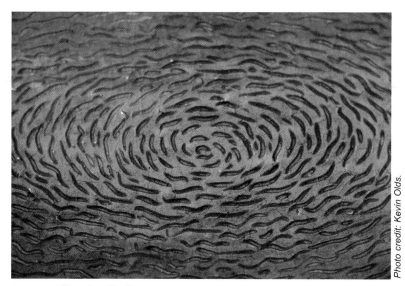

Photo credit: Kevin Olds.

Detail of **Passion Fruit**. *This photograph clearly shows the way Kwong combines slip painted and sgraffito carved imagery to create her colored surfaces. She uses the slips to create a soft color field, while the carved lines are linear and active. She combines these to make a complex multi-layered image.*

glaze, intended for cone 04 firing. This glaze is useful at a very wide range of temperatures, however, and she uses it at cone 5 with excellent results.

Kwong works very hard to create rich surfaces. She wants to create complex movement and rhythm on her glaze surfaces. She has developed an intricate imagery, painting spots on top of spots and using inlay imagery. She is very interested in rich and unusual glaze color. She likes the colors she can get from the high fire. She often uses bright colors such as pink, green, and blue. These are not the assertive colors of the low fire but rather the slightly muted colors of the high fire. She likes their harmony and sense of reserve. She once fires her pieces. Once firing has great appeal for her. It allows her to create her rich imagery. It is very difficult to carve a sgraffito

line into bisque-fired ware. She fires to cone 5, preferring this midfire temperature because it is not anchored to a particular look. She can create a high-fire or low-fire effect. She fires in either an oxidation or reduction atmosphere. She likes this choice because it gives her a much wider variety of colors than she would have if she limited herself to one or the other. She says she does a great deal of testing to come up with the kinds of surfaces she wants. She doesn't limit herself to recipe testing, she also tests work creation and image creation strategies because they all have a profound influence on the look of the work.

Kwong's work also shows the influence of her study of the scientific method. As an undergraduate student during the year 1973/74 Kwong had a work study position at the

Nature Laboratory at the Rhode Island School of Design. She has written of this, "I had the opportunity to spend hours with all the objects there. I would study the seashells one week, insects the next. This work study program turned out to provide me with many visual resources. This experience gave me a sense of the under-lying structures and principles that govern all living things."

Kwong is fascinated with the idea that complex ideas can be conveyed by visual means. When she was young she learned to write using the Chinese calligraphic system. These calligraphic characters are beautiful and powerful. Because they stand for words rather than sounds, they can stand for a word in any lan-guage. In China one set of writ-ten characters is used by peo-ple communicating in a broad variety of spoken languages. Learning about science and the

Drop of Water, 34" x 25" x 25", 1994. Kwong made this piece using a stoneware clay body. She formed it using a fat coil 4" or 5" wide. She simultaneously thinned the wall and shaped the piece, then added another coil and repeated the process. She also used potter's ribs to thin the wall and shape the contour of the form. Each time she did this, the piece grew by about 10". As she got to the end of the process, she used thinner coils. When the piece was dry, she painted its surface with colored slips. Kwong then used a sgraffito technique to refine the imagery. She covered the piece with a commercially prepared clear glaze. Though this glaze is meant primarily for work at cone 04, it has a very wide range and Kwong has found that it is useful at cone 5. Kwong fired the piece to cone 5 in a gas kiln in an oxidation atmosphere. She fired in the gas kiln because this very large piece wouldn't fit in any of the electric kilns she had access to.

The origin of the idea for this piece came to Kwong in the mid 1980s after she had recovered from a serious illness. At one point in the course of this illness, the doctors thought she might have a life-threatening cancer. It turned out that she had suddenly developed a strong allergy to pollens. Once the doctors arrived at the correct diagnosis, they were able to cure her. The experience was a very difficult one. She dealt with it by undertaking a program of research on the microscopic structures of pollen from a visual and artistic point of view. The tech-nology that allowed her to see and study these tiny structures was brand new and very exciting for Kwong as an artist. The images the technology revealed were awesome and beautiful. She talks of this now with expressions of great gratitude, "What a blessing to be alive! Life is like a gift of heaven. I wanted to make a celebratory piece, I wanted something that would reflect my faith in life. I decided to search for an image that would convey my feel-ing for life. It came to me that the form it should take would be a drop of water."

scientific method, Kwong was fascinated to learn about the way scientists illustrate their complex ideas with an extensive symbolic vocabulary. This reinforced her interest in visual symbols. In her own work she has learned to use visual symbols as the basis for her own personal imagery.

Kwong was born in Hong Kong in 1954 and moved to New York City when she was 13 years old. New York and life in the U.S. in general was a real shock for her. In the manner of many young newcomers to the U.S., she chose to assimilate its culture. She attended the High School of Music and Art and studied painting and thought she might be a painter. Kwong was awarded a scholarship to the Rhode Island School of Design in Providence. She was required to choose a major and in her freshman year she chose sculpture. At Rhode Island the sculpture major encompassed ceramics, wood, glass, metal, stone, and plaster. You could specialize but students were encouraged to try many media before settling on any one of them. The sculpture major was further divided into sculpture, glass making, and ceramics. She decided to specialize in glass making in her sophomore year. She studied with Dale Chihuly, who encouraged her to find her own individual way to create art and she liked that. In the second half of her sophomore year, she took ceramics merely because it was required of all sculpture majors (she asked for permission to waive the requirement but was told

she had to take the course). She then found that she liked ceramics a great deal. In her junior year she switched to a specialization in ceramics major (still within the sculpture major). She did most of her ceramic work with Jun Kaneko and Norm Schulman. She felt she could manipulate clay more freely than other media and she liked clay's tactile working qualities.

Kwong felt at a disadvantage in the ceramics program. She knew little about ceramics and was taking classes with fellow students who had been in the program for two years or more. Though this meant she didn't consider herself a "star," it allowed her to look at ceramic processes in a nontraditional way. She used unusual work strategies whose origins were from sculpture and painting. She was not sure of what clay could or could not do. She tried experiments that her fellow students believed would not work. For example, she made thick-walled porcelain pieces and large porcelain pieces. Those who saw this work told her that was not the way to handle porcelain. She quietly rejected these views and because of this she was able to find her own personal way to work in clay.

She feels she was very lucky in the teachers she had. They were very tolerant of her experiments. They let her be herself and pursue her own way. At this time, during the height of the popularity of low-fire glazing, she began working in the high fire using stoneware and porcelain clay bodies. She

valued the subtlety of the colors she could get from the high fire. She was strongly influenced by the Chinese, Japanese, and Korean pots she saw in her classes in Asian art history. She feels these ideas became very important to her and feels that for her, "form follows ideas." She graduated from the Rhode Island School of Design with a B.F.A. degree in 1975.

At the NCEA meeting of 1975 in Philadelphia her teacher Dale Chihuly introduced her to Rudi Staffel who taught at the Tyler School of Art in Philadelphia. Kwong and Staffel had an instant rapport. In the fall of 1975 she received a scholarship to study for her masters degree at Tyler. There she studied with Staffel and with Bob Winocur. She enjoyed her studies at Tyler, especially her work with Staffel. "I think that he really understood my work and encouraged me. Over and over again he said, 'Don't worry about what other people are doing, don't worry about fitting in.' Because of his interest in Asian art he was able to understand the background and the nonverbal qualities of my work." This was a time of introspection for her. She started on a series of tile pieces she called *Gardens of the Mind*. They were inspired by Japanese gardens and Buddhist temples and earthworks by the contemporary American sculptor Robert Smithson.

Her first pieces in this group were small white sculptures and tiles (she had a tiny studio space - she made pieces that fit well with the size of her studio). She wanted these pieces to be complete worlds in miniature. A little later she made a group of slab pieces finished with colored glazes. Many of these pieces were in the tile format. She made them using a porcelain body. She used porcelain because she liked the way the material looked. She didn't want to use a white colored low-fire body. She far preferred porcelain to white low-fire bodies because she felt these had an undistinguished character. She also liked the way the porcelain body influenced the color of her glazes and liked the high temperature colors she used with it. She painted these tiles using pictorial imagery. She wanted these pieces to seem like windows into another world and to deal with the character of light. She worked in a small space with only a small window in a basement - she thinks this may be why she was interested in light.

Unlike many of her contemporaries Kwong did not feel that the reduction fire limited color, rather she felt it allowed for a very wide range of color possibilities. Nor did she use reduction in the way it is so often used - we never see black spots on an earth colored field in her reduction work. Rich as this surface is, its proponents probably relied on these familiar effects too much. Kwong did a lot of high temperature experimentation at that time and these experiments helped her to understand much more about glazes and helped her create her own personal ver-

Photo credit: Eva Kwong.

Radiance Spiral, tile panel, 19" x 16" x 1", reduction fired to cone 10. Kwong made this piece in 1977 at an early stage in her career. Kwong reports that in this piece she was exploring the metaphysical character of light and the feelings that this evokes. Kwong used a porcelain body to make this piece. This gave her a white ground for her color. She pounded the slab to make it dense, then placed it on a sand base so it would dry evenly. She let it dry undisturbed for several days to discourage cracking. She applied her glazes with a brush and a spray gun, using stencils to encourage sharp clear edges. She used a flashing fire to encourage color variations. We see an example of this variation in the spiral form at the center of the piece. Its color changes from burgundy to green depending on the influence of the flame.

*Right: Pink Tendril. This vase is from the **Opposites Attract** series. It is 12" x 6" x 5", made from a stoneware body and salt glazed over colored slips, 1997. Kwong threw the elements for this piece on the potter's wheel. She says she threw more parts for this piece than she thought she would need. She likes to have a large selection of shapes to choose from. To prepare for assembling the piece, she kept the parts in plastic overnight. In the morning they were workable and homogenous in moisture content. The excess number of parts meant she could achieve a good match of size and shape. This allowed her to "play" with a variety of combinations so she could choose the most satisfying one. Once she settled on the form, she joined the parts and let them become very firm. At this point she painted the form with slips and then fired it to cone 5.*

sion of a reduction surface. She wanted to emphasize the atmospheric character of the reduction glazes. She experimented with high temperature color and the effects of reduction on glaze color. This was the era of greatest interest in low temperature prepared glazes. She didn't want the bright cheery colors or the flat enamel-like surfaces of these glazes. Instead she wanted the reserved character, broken color, and dappled surfaces of reduction. Furthermore, she loved the way reduction firing combined aspects of chance and skill.

She and Kirk Mangus (a fellow student at the Rhode Island School of Design) were married in 1976. In the summer of 1976 they attended a wood fire workshop run by Rimas VisGirda (see page 27) at the Earth, Air, Fire, and Water Program in Grass Valley, California. At the workshop they gained experience firing a seven chambered wood-fired kiln and a large domed roof salt kiln. This experience showed her how organic the firing process can be. She saw that the firing could shape glaze color and character and could play a very active part in the creation process. She learned to play with color using

flashing and experimenting with variations in the reduction process. She used these tools along with variations in the application process. For example, she was able to get Shaner Green to produce green, pink, yellow, and black colors. She wanted each firing to be a unique experience, a record of a unique moment and wanted her glazes to have a different look in each firing.

In 1977 her husband was accepted in the graduate program at Washington State University in Pullman. They lived in Pullman until 1980. After graduate school they went to the Archie Bray Foundation for three months where they shared a studio and worked on blue and white porcelain.

In the fall of 1980 she and Mangus moved to his hometown of Mercer in western Pennsylvania and set up a studio there. They had a salt kiln and she did a lot of work in porcelain fired in salt. Kwong was fascinated with odd materials and the way they behaved. She experimented with slips on porcelain, salt resist strategies, the use of locally available clays (they are a source of a great variety of colors), and the use of unusual melting materials such as vanadium sulfates and

chlorides. She remembers with great fondness being given pink colored silicon carbide chunks. They stayed pink in both oxidation and reduction. Their look was very unusual, most closely resembling small chunks of pink colored grog. She built a wood-fire kiln with Mangus and made a group of sculptures with local clays that she fired in this kiln. She created an installation of these sculptures that she called *Fertile Garden*. Much of the work of this period is figural and is about fertility and growth. These things were very much on her mind because she and Mangus were thinking of having a child. In 1982 she and Mangus taught with Bill Brouillard at the Cleveland Institute of Art. She made plates, slab tiles, and coil built sculptures there and remembers it as a very exciting time. She continued to work in porcelain, fired to cone 9.

In 1985 she switched to colored slips and firing in the midfire temperature of cone 6. It gave her the same range of image possibilities she had when firing in the high fire but allowed her to use all sorts of kilns including electric kilns. She likes the midfire because it has a lot of possibilities - she can fire in oxidation and reduc-

tion and in either case work with a great variety of colors. She still has access to the dappled effects and the subtle color that she previously associated with the high fire.

During this period Kwong started on a series she calls *Opposites Attract*. This was the period when she had her children and this experience had a profound influence on her work. She continued to explore imagery that referred to the cycle of birth, maturity, and death. During this time she made a piece she called *Double Balls*; it is about the process of cell division and the process of conception. In these more sculptural pieces she no longer used the pictorial imagery she had used on the tiles. The new imagery was more abstract and fabric-like.

She continues working on large pieces using simple shapes and complex dappled glaze imagery. Recently she has been making prints and installation pieces as well as clay work in order to broaden her range. She continues to center her work, however, around clay, creating pieces with simple forms (often quite large) with richly colored imagery.

Kwong has made her work her own in two ways: in the character of her surfaces, and in the way she has created a personal imagery. She is known for unusual ceramic surfaces. When she creates these surfaces she pays special attention to the application. She uses a combination of sgraffito and brushwork to create a highly personal fabric-like surface. She has made her imagery very personal by using the events of her life as a springboard for a kind of personal language symbolizing these events. She likes to use images from the world of science as a basis for this symbolism. It is interesting as well that she does not need to refer in her work only to the good things in her life. She is able to use many different events as the inspiration for her work. She used her extended bout with illness as a source of some of her most evocative images.

Photo credit: Richard Zakin.

Eva Kwong working on the surface of a large piece.

Chapter 3: Idea and Object

When we look at a ceramic piece, we are dealing at once with a *material substance* and a *matter of thought*. We are seeing a blend of the material and the intangible, of idea and object. I see the artists in this section as having been strongly affected by the impact of an idea or principle. Some of these artists work in a purely sculptural idiom and are driven by such ideas as the structure of natural or manmade forms. For example, I think that Virginia Scotchie, Joanne Hayakawa, and Jamie Walker take this approach. Some of these artists deal with the idea of sculpture and vessel form, Kirk Mangus and Mary Barringer are examples of artists who take this approach. Other artists in this section are concerned with an exploration of the idea of use. Both Jim Lawton and Neal Forrest have wrestled with these issues. I see these ceramists as having developed an idea as the central axis of the work. For these artists the idea is the seed; once the seed is planted, then the artist creates the piece. This gives the work a sense of focus and intellectual toughness that is very persuasive.

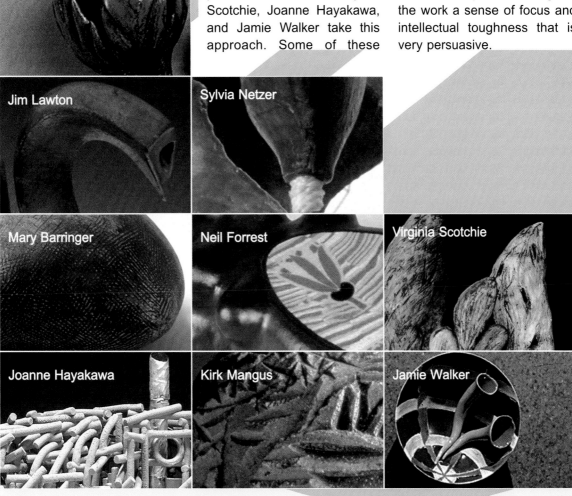

Linda Huey

Jim Lawton

Sylvia Netzer

Mary Barringer

Neil Forrest

Virginia Scotchie

Joanne Hayakawa

Kirk Mangus

Jamie Walker

Linda Huey

Linda Huey is a sculptor whose medium is clay and whose subject is the natural world. She is tied very strongly to both the clay medium and to her subject matter, the world around her. In recent years this has changed from a city environment to the world of nature. She loves the clay medium for its challenging character and great flexibility. She sees in her subject matter beauty, contradictions, and the energy of the life force.

Cruddy Versus Beautiful*, leaf bowl, 10" x 26" x 23", 1995. The title comes from the contrast Huey felt between the smooth inviting terra sigillata surfaces and a rough highly textured clay body she calls "hay clay". This is a combination of hay and clay. Huey calls this piece a leaf bowl and sees the imagery as suggesting leaves randomly falling into a pile that takes on the shape of a shallow bowl. She made this piece in a bisque-fired bowl to support the piece until it became firm and self-supporting. She relates, "In the firing some of the pieces pulled widely apart from each other. This opened up the form in an unexpected way, making the leaves appear as if they were in the act of moving through space even more than I had intended."*

Huey uses a low-fire terra cotta clay body to make her pieces. She uses slab-forming work methods and adds the relief imagery while the clay is still quite wet and easily worked. She doesn't work from her imagination, instead she works directly from nature. She says, "I like to do a lot of studies because I have a huge collection of little buds, dead flowers, seed pods, sticks, and leaves. I go through my boxes before I start working. I pick out a few and put them on my worktable and use them as reference." When she was working on the leaf bowl, she placed a whole group of leaves on the table and used them as models. She likes the way these forms help her see nature more closely and help her make her pieces while studying objects that have the liveliness and variation we see in nature. She uses a broad group of strategies to create the imagery, including adding pinched or coiled clay elements and impressing patterns in the clay.

In the last few years she has made many of her pieces in the form of wall hanging groups of small elements that gain power by association with other pieces in the group. When she works this way she makes a great many of the small elements, then chooses those that she will place together. She is very particular about the way she arranges these pieces together, for the whole gains much from the sum of its parts.

In some of her most interesting pieces Huey works the clay sheets around wire, embedding the wire into the fabric of the piece. She wants the clay body to crack. It is a very important and visually exciting part of her imagery. In the fire there is tension between the wire (which does not shrink) and the clay (which does). This causes cracking. To most ceramists, cracking would not seem like an advantage. Huey is distinctly in the minority in her preference for cracks in her work.

Huey first fires her work to bisque, then applies glazes and/or terra sigillatas. She uses both glazes she has made in her studio and commercially prepared glazes. She applies her surfaces with a brush. She sometimes uses a slip she calls hay clay made by adding hay to normal clay slip. She adds glaze to this mixture for durability. The contrast of the tangled hay clay and her smooth low-fire clay body mirrors forms in nature. She makes this slip in an impromptu fashion and must test it before using it. She says she is constantly firing test tiles. She loves the way they allow her to combine all sorts of materials, many of which are as difficult to predict as this one.

Huey bisque fires to cone 08 to prepare the piece for the application of the glazes and terra sigillatas. For the final firing she fires to cone 06 in an electric kiln. During the firing the clay may slump and Huey feels this falls into the category of the happy accident. She says, "If I could get more accidents of this sort, my work would be much better. I get a lot of my ideas from accidents." She feels part of the ceramist's job is to accept the nature of the clay in the firing. She has learned to accept the idea that the clay may slump and crack, to allow this to happen, and even to welcome it.

In recent years the jumping off point for Huey's imagery has been the world of natural forms. Huey has always liked to walk, study nature, and collect objects if they interest her. She has enjoyed collecting these objects and curiosities.

Huey's pieces can be understood as accurate representations of natural objects. Not representations of the skin of her models, but representations of the natural forces that make these objects function. Huey's pieces also have a significant metaphorical content. For her, clay is the perfect medium to express ideas. She uses her imagery to deal with issues of control, birth, death, and decay. In the work she made when she lived in Boston she used images of the growth and decay of the city. Since moving to Alfred, New York, a rural setting, she uses images of the natural world. To Huey this imagery tells us a great deal because it so clearly embodies juxtapositions of decay and life. "Real seed pods crack so that the seeds can be released for new life. Thus the emotions of fear (death) and desire (life) are combined in one piece. It is important to get over the fear that the clay might crack, or the fear of nature, because we cannot fully control it." Huey has come to realize that the central theme in her work is the relationship of growth to decay.

Collapsed Pod, *clay, glaze, wire, and hay clay, 22-1/2" x 30" x 28", 1993. In this piece Huey explores the associations with birth and death that pods have for us. Huey has combined the sinewy, tensile, linear support system of wire with the sheet-like, turning, and curving surfaces of clay to make her version of a seed pod. Huey is tied very strongly to both the clay medium and to ideas that we associate with her imagery. In this piece we see how Huey deals with this familiar but powerful natural object. The resulting image is an exploration of the clay and at the same time an exploration of a familiar and powerful form. This piece has been exhibited outdoors in the midst of a wooded grove among weeds, trees, and scrub. The piece blended very well into its environment and at the same time retained its power and identity.*

Huey used a low-fire terra cotta clay body and added grog to the body (approximately 10%). She used slab-forming work methods, working the slabs around the wire, embedding the wire into the fabric of the piece as she carried out the construction process. She used the grog to control the amount of cracking she got in the fire as the clay shrank over the wire. In the fire there was tension between the wire (which did not shrink) and the clay (which did). Huey wanted the body to crack. She likes the way the cracks help to delineate the form. They open it up and make it very dramatic. Of course, if the piece cracks too much it will not survive the fire and she will have to discard it. Huey must walk a fine line to create work that is strong enough to survive but not so strong as to resist the cracking she needs. She says, "I have to be careful not to use too much grog because then the clay won't crack at all during the firing, or too little grog, making the clay not crack enough." To most ceramists, cracking would not seem like an advantage. She is distinctly in the minority in her preference for cracks in her work.

Huey first fired the piece to cone 08 for the bisque fire. She then brushed on an ocher colored vitreous slip; over this she brushed on terra sigillata. She made the tangled forms at the top of the piece with a material she calls hay clay. To make this, she first made a slip from her clay body, then added hay to the slip. She added a glaze (by eye) to the mixture to enhance durability. She tested the slip to make sure it was fairly durable and would stick to the other elements of the piece.

For the final firing she fired to cone 06 in an electric kiln. The body contains frit and manganese and is fairly dense when it comes from the final firing. During the firing the part of the piece that was resting on the kiln shelf slumped, taking on an interesting shape.

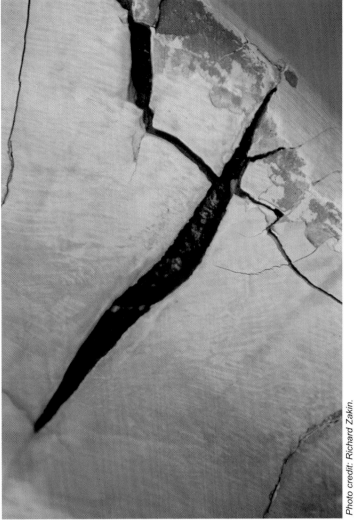

*A detail of one of the cracks in **Collapsed Pod**, revealing the texture of hay clay on the inside of the piece.*

She feels by understanding nature she can begin to understand death and accept it as a natural part of the cycle of life. She thought of this when she had to deal with her father's death. Huey sees such natural forms as trees, bushes, flowers, and seed pods as speaking of such things as "transience, fragility, and struggle." She has a strong urge to explore the bonds and conflicts of the forces of vigor and decay symbolized in her seed pods and branches. Huey wants to make very sure her work ends up with a symbolic rather than an illustrative character. As she works she becomes "lost in the mysteries and goes beyond the merely descriptive." Though she starts with reality, she wants to move toward poetry so that what can be seen will suggest the intangibles of the natural world.

Huey went to Upsala College in New Jersey, a liberal arts college with a small art department and no ceramics program. This disappointed her because she responded to ceramic objects she had seen and used. She wanted to try to make her own dinnerware. After graduation she settled in Boston and got a graphics job. She was able to take night classes in ceramics at the Massachusetts College of Art and the Boston Museum School. She enjoyed clay a great deal and "fell in love" with the medium. She began to

Industrial Landscape (an older piece), 1990, 31-1/2" x 16" x 16". Huey made this piece using a terra cotta clay body. She painted the imagery with commercially prepared underglazes and covered this with a clear glaze. This piece is an example of the work Huey made while she lived in Boston. As is the case at present, she deals with images of growth and decay in her immediate environment. In this piece it is the growth and decay of the city. She pictures old industrial buildings, smokestacks, chain link fences, power lines, and the distant skyline of down-town Boston.

spend as much free time as possible working with it and made great progress. After a year or so of working in clay, she decided to quit her graphics job. Though it offered economic security, she wanted to work solely in ceramics. She went to work as an apprentice to William Wyman, a well-known ceramist who worked in Boston at that time. She is still grateful for his mentoring and support.

When she finished working for Wyman, she wasn't sure what she should do next. Finally, a friend suggested she try to make her living from pottery. Wyman encouraged her in this as well. In many ways she was well prepared for the life of a production potter. Her skills were improving dramatically and she was dedicated to ceramics. She had good work habits and had a good sense of organization.

She could live on very little money. She had a very inexpensive apartment and was paying a very small fee for her share of a cooperative studio space. She ate inexpensively and until she was 30 didn't own a car, traveling exclusively by bicycle. During the next years she worked in a succession of co-op studios, making pots for a living and honing her skills. She sold her work out of these studios and began to make a living from clay. Now she felt ready to set up her own studio. She enjoyed this challenge a great deal. She found she had the organizational skills and "business sense" necessary to make a living in ceramics. Furthermore, she is very personable and knows how to make connections to people. She developed a mailing list of her customers and they came back to buy more work. She did

feel, however, that sometimes the demands of the business got in the way of creativity. She found she was under pressure to work too hard and to repeat herself too often. She could make a living with $18 mugs but understood the dangers of this kind of repetitive pottery production. She realized that for her this route would lead to burnout, so she began to slow the pace of her production and to develop custom items and individual pieces. She began to use very complex imagery made from underglaze slips covered by a clear glaze. The forms were the ones she had been working on for quite awhile but the complexity of the imagery was new. She used a great deal of city imagery. This was the imagery she dealt with every day in her real life.

She began to attend a wide variety of workshops and

continued this practice over a period of many years. She found the workshops challenged her and encouraged her to grow. These workshops were held at such places as the Penland School of Crafts, Haystack Mountain School of Crafts, and the Rhode Island School of Design. She also took many night classes and workshops in the Boston area.

In the 1980s she was working in an artist's area in Boston called Fort Point. It was full of old warehouses and commercial buildings made from brick. It was a neighborhood that for a long time had been ignored and it was perfect for artists. The communal aspects of this life were very nurturing; Huey loved working there and interacting with the community. However, Boston was booming and development was coming to the area. Great office towers were going up in nearby districts and the developers were eyeing the Fort Point area. The artists saw that they would lose their area to the developers unless they fought to regulate development. They founded an organization called the Fort Point Art Community and Huey played a significant role in it. She began to believe that the presence of artists conferred benefits on the whole community and played a significant role in making their city a special place. She became deeply involved in this art community and the conversations and intellectual challenge of this time still seems valuable to her. She was making a living and beginning to feel successful. She was

happy with her work and was able to use it to comment on life in the city. She was painting imagery on her pieces and she loved this work. The city was her subject - she painted every aspect of it. Even the ugly aspects of the city interested her.

At this point her feelings started to change. She had everything she wanted from the city and it didn't seem to be enough; she started to think of the city as a place in opposition to nature, threatening to crush it. She began to think of living in a more natural setting. She had always had a yearning for nature and now she strongly desired a release from the pollution, chain link fences, and trashed environment of the city. At the same time she started feeling uneasy about the pot forms she was using. She began to suspect that her forms did not relate to her painted imagery. If not, what forms should she use? What is an appropriate ceramic form for painted imagery? She needed a new challenge. The idea of going to the New York State College of Ceramics at Alfred struck her as the answer. It was in a rural location, far from any city. She wanted to study clay full time, she wanted to go to art school, the time was right, and she felt she needed that challenge.

She applied to Alfred and was accepted. Now she had to deal with the challenge of an entirely different environment, a very rural environment. Looking back on it now she says, "It was quite a courageous thing to

come to Alfred." It shook her world as she knew it would and it changed her work. Alfred is situated in a beautiful and relatively unpopulated part of New York State. As she grew used to the Alfred landscape, she began to use this landscape in her imagery. Her imagery was now of leaves, branches, and seed pods. Her work changed in other crucial ways as well. She moved from a painterly approach to a more sculptural approach. In this work she used the same imagery she had used in her painterly pieces, but now created them in sculptural form. She was no longer painting illustrations on the form, but rather creating imagery from form. "The imagery became the form." She remembers how this began - rather than making the pot and painting leaves on it, she made a pot out of "leaves." People responded strongly to the piece and she developed it into the core of her work. In clay, this form oriented approach has many advantages because clay is a medium with form and space as centrally important attributes. She sees it as ironic that she went to Alfred to learn about making forms to paint on and she never did do that. Instead she learned how to make form the center of her work. When she broke away from painted imagery, she also began to break away from the vessel format. She moved toward the creation of sculptural pieces and now most of her work is in the sculptural format. Since graduation she has stayed in Alfred and has made her life

Photo credit: Linda Huey.

Six Specimens, *wall piece made with metal additions, 19" x 21" x 2-3/4", 1995. In this wall piece Huey has used more compact imagery than she uses in her sculptures. She added pinched or coiled clay elements to create the imagery in these pieces. She added metal parts to two of the pieces, the brown grid-like object in the piece at the top left is a piece of scrap metal and the spiral wire O-shaped form on the piece on the bottom left is a metal plate handle from an old wood stove. The models for her imagery come from nature. She has a large collection of natural objects that she uses as models for form, color, and texture. She goes through this collection before she starts working on one of these pieces. She combined these nature-based forms to make a piece with some of the character of an exhibition of specimens in a museum of natural science.*

there. She makes sculptural pieces which she sells at galleries around the country.

Huey has come to want to mirror the clash of energies and the fragmented forms she sees in nature in her work. She says, "I have stopped worrying about 'finished product' and feel satisfied making unfinished bits and pieces. For example, I have played with spare parts of branches and pods made of clay, not knowing how they will work together as a wall piece later. This open approach has helped me to explore more freely. I like to surprise myself by glazing in ways that seem illogical, since nature can seem that way also." Recently she has been trying to use "unlikely" colors, contrasting her natural forms with geometric shapes and accenting areas in the glaze that don't correspond to centers of interest in the form. For her, a feeling of surprise and wonderment is the issue and a sense of wholeness must include the things that don't fit easily, must allow for images that seem to clash. She sees these kinds of difficult harmonies in nature and their energy seems to her to be the stuff of life.

Linda Huey.

Jim Lawton

For many years *Jim Lawton* played a game of "tug of war" with surface and form, playing two-dimensional against three-dimensional space. Most recently he has placed most of the emphasis on three-dimensional form. He has been exploring the idea of three-dimensional space by creating complex combinations of solid and pierced forms. These complex volumes take some time to understand. Lawton wrestles with them and these pieces convey a sense of tension and vitality.

Left: Suspended "A" Funnel, 11" x 10" x 9", 1998. Fired to cone 06 in an oxidation atmosphere. This piece is part of a group called **Suspension Series.** It is composed of a funnel in the form of an upside-down "A." Lawton surrounded the funnel with a pierced form he calls a cage. The cage supports the funnel and simultaneously reveals it and makes the space in this piece more complex. Capping the piece is a thick flat top that can be lifted off, allowing access to the funnel. This top is solid and weighty, making a strong contrast to the open form of the pierced cage and the inverted A-shaped funnel.

Lawton began this piece with wheel-thrown forms that he used as a point of departure. From this point on, he used hand-formed strategies. He assembled groups of thrown forms and cut parts away from some of them to create complex structures. He threw a cylinder and by making darts at the top, created the tapering funnel form that is partially obscured by the cage. It is a very full and volumetric form. It is irregular in outline; the imagery changes as the observer moves around the piece. This is a crucial aspect of the piece that a still photograph cannot reveal. Lawton threw a cylinder for the cage, then drew and carved the many openings with a sharp blade. He threw and trimmed the lid, then carved the two holes in the top piece. These can be used to grasp the top for removal from the form and are very much like the grasp holes in a bowling ball. He then fired the piece to bisque.

Lawton was now ready to glaze. In this piece he used a good deal of a glaze fluxed with a lead frit and lithium carbonate.

Villendorf Glaze Base, cone 010 to 06

Lead frit 3304	51.7
EPK kaolin	26.1
Lithium carbonate	22.2
Magnesium carbonate	+10.0

Lawton added the magnesium carbonate in this recipe to encourage cracked and cratered surfaces. He did not sieve this glaze, he wanted the varied textures and bursts of color he got from the unmixed chunks of glaze and colorant in the unsieved mixture. The glaze has a pleasing mat surface. Lawton created the orange rim at the bottom of the lid using a terra sigillata made of 65 Lawton Redware body (without the grog and kyanite) and 35 Newman clay (orange red clay from California).

Lawton glazed the lid with the Villendorf glaze base colored with 3% cobalt carbonate, 1% copper carbonate, and 1/2% iron chromate. He glazed the cage with the same glaze base with 2% copper carbonate and 1% chrome oxide. Lawton glazed the hanging A-shaped form inside the cage with the Villendorf base as well. Its yellow color comes from the addition of 15% tin oxide and .15% chrome.

Lawton used a brush to apply the Villendorf glazes. He purposely used a very uneven application, varying its thickness from thick to thin in an abrupt manner. We can see the results of this on the surface of the cage. Where the glaze is thin it is green, and where it is thick its color is orange. Lawton brushed a thin layer of terra sigillata on the thin orange band at the base of the lid. Even thin sigillata applications are quite opaque, so a thick application was not necessary.

Lawton fired to cone 06 for both the bisque and glaze firings of this piece. He fired in an oxidation atmosphere in a standard top-loading electric kiln. He fired quickly and didn't soak at the end of the firing. Chrome orange and chrome yellow are enhanced in the quick firing. The out-gassing of the lead glazes fumed the sigillatas during the firing. These lead fumes deepened the color of the sigillata and gave its surface a rich patina.

Though the ideas and intangible aspects of the work are important to Lawton, he is very aware of the tangible and material aspects of the work as well. A look at his clay body recipe, for example, shows that he is very careful when choosing materials for the recipe and that he has a clear idea of what constitutes a good clay body.

Clay body:
Lawton Redware, cone 04

Fire clay	20
Red clay	35
Goldart	12
Ball clay	14
Kyanite	4
Talc	10
Grog	4
Bentonite	.5
Barium carbonate	.5
Red iron oxide	2

This is a dark colored body with good plasticity and working characteristics.

Lawton begins his pieces with wheel-thrown forms that he considers as a point of departure. His manipulations of the forms from this point on fall into the category of hand-forming strategies. He assembles groups of thrown forms and

Teapot with Trousers, *10" x 11" x 4-1/2", 1985. This teapot is very shallow - barely 2" deep at the base. Lawton flattened its dimensional volume and exaggerated the resulting squashed imagery. Though this piece is almost slab-like in its lack of volume, it is still a very strong and emphatic form, not one that is impoverished. It might be suggested that in this piece Lawton was very interested in the form and its lack of volume. He was not ignoring form so much as pushing it as far as it would go and then just a bit further. He says of its thin base, "This piece is about not being balanced."*

cuts parts away from some of them to create complex structures (he sees a similarity to the way a tailor cuts a garment). Many of these pieces are constructed with movable parts

in a manner reminiscent of lids on utilitarian pots. His pieces have a strongly assembled feel and are fit together in a careful manner. Lawton makes his pieces in groups. By doing this

he has a chance to try many versions of an idea.

Lawton fires to bisque to prepare the work for glazing. He begins the glazing process by painting a white terra sigil-

Teapot with Script, *8" x 13" x 4", 1989, saggar fired to cone 06 in an oxidation atmosphere. This is a highly personal version of a teapot. The volumetric character of this form is very important to Lawton. Three years before, he had taken his forms to an almost slab-like point. His piece **Teapot with Trousers** is an important representation of that approach to volume. Lawton feels this piece marks the recovery of the sense of volume in his work.*

Lawton threw and altered the piece to give it its sinuous irregular shape. He made the spout on a tapered stick (pulling the clay against the stick to create the form), then curved the spout and let it become firm. He pulled the handle, then attached these elements to the body of the piece. Lawton fired the piece to bisque and painted its surface with a terra sigillata colored with 10% crocus martis (a water-soluble form of iron oxide that gave him the warm ocher color). He then fired the terra sigillata in a saggar fire to cone 04. He painted the script-like imagery using a very thick cone 06 foaming glaze containing a black stain. Because this script is thick and raised above the surface of the piece, he says it is "Braille-like." The imagery takes on both the character of an abstraction that articulates the surface of the piece and the meaning laden character of script.

lata over the surface of his piece. This serves as a base coating and ensures brilliant color. Many of his glaze recipes contain lead frits. Lawton applies these glazes on the outside of his pieces. Lead containing chrome orange and chrome yellow colors are particular favorites. He also uses high percentages of materials such as magnesium carbonate that encourage cracked and cratered surfaces. He doesn't sieve glazes of this sort. He wants the varied textures and bursts of color he gets from the unmixed chunks of glaze and colorant in the unsieved mixture. Lawton uses a brush to apply his surfaces. He uses a very loose and irregular application, varying the thickness from thick to thin abruptly to create strong and active textures.

Lawton uses cone 06 for both the bisque and glaze firings. He fires in an oxidation atmosphere in a standard top-loading electric kiln. He fires quickly and doesn't soak at the end of the firing. Chrome orange and chrome yellow colors are enhanced by the quick firing. The out-gassing of the lead glazes fume the sigillatas during the firing. These lead fumes deepen the color of the sigillata and give its surface a rich patina.

At one point Lawton used

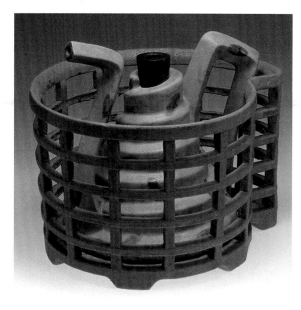

Ziggurat Teapot and Cage, 10" x 11" x 10", fired to cone 06 in an oxidation atmosphere, 1996. To make the pot form in the center of the piece, Lawton threw a solid conical form on the potter's wheel. He then applied a trimming tool at the top of the form and brought it down to the bottom to make the spiral imagery. He then made a cast of this form and used it as a slipcast mold to make the stepped form inside the cage. He made the handle spout and the stopper for the stepped form, then threw a cylinder for the cage and drew and cut the many openings with a sharp blade.

flattened forms painted with complex imagery. For a time Lawton fell under the influence of the great painted Oribe pots from 18th century Japan. These richly painted pieces influenced him strongly. He came to feel that what he called "re-contouring" forms with painted imagery was at the heart of Oribe work. It was his belief that Oribe potters used painted imagery as a tool to modify the way the viewer saw the forms. He began to "dissolve" and "flatten" his own forms by literally squeezing the volume out of them and by painting them with repetitive linear designs to further manipulate their space.

He says, "The 27th Ceramic National in Syracuse provided an opportunity for me to reflect on where my work was going. The teapot I entered was shallow - barely 2" deep; it had to be waxed down to the high narrow ledge provided for it." He describes this teapot (made in 1986) as so shallow that it might as well have been a hanging wall piece. The question that came to mind was, "Why bother with the shelf?" He had flattened the dimensional volume and concentrated on the pictorial image. He was especially interested in the way form and surface could influence each other. He saw the interplay between the two as creating a dynamic equilibrium. In this work the vessel form should have been volumetric but instead was flattened and the image that should have been flat was given the illusion of volume. Lawton was now faced with a clear choice - hang the piece on the wall or make the interior important again. Choosing the latter course he said, "This particular American experiment with the nonutilitarian pot had, for me, come to a close; pottery's sole virtue was no longer as a prop for pictures." He decided to return to the vessel form. He wanted to lessen the importance of the skin of his pieces and expand the inner space, the volumetric aspects of his pots. He has done this and feels he has taken his work back to a point where form and interior space matter again. He has been using forms that are more full and volume oriented. "My efforts since have involved a type of CPR, expanding the inner space and therefore the tangible life of the pots."

In his latest work, the *Suspended* series, volume and dimension take center stage. He is trying to translate the two-dimensional imagery he formerly painted on the surface of his forms into three-dimensional forms that he forms from clay. In this recent work he has created a group of pieces with complex three-dimensional images in which he explores space and volume. He uses his volumetric forms to create objects that float in the revealed space of pierced "cages." Dramatizing these pieces still more, their volumetric elements are not symmetrical and their imagery changes from every angle.

Another important aspect of this work is its references to utility. He refers to the funnel as a "funnel form," implying that it cannot be used. In fact, though Lawton knows that this will rarely happen, his funnels can be used as functional funnels. Lawton trained as a functional potter and he still has affection for this kind of ceramic work. On the other hand, he is also very taken with the theoretical foundations of ceramics. He is very interested in the idea of

Twisted Bottle with Waist *(an older piece), 17" x 6" x 3", 1987. Lawton threw this piece on the potter's wheel, then altered it to give it its twisted shape. He made the imagery using airbrushed colored engobes. He covered it with a clear glaze, then painted the background with a lepidolite copper glaze and fired it in a raku firing.*

Lawton wanted the irregular walls of this piece to remind the viewer of the human figure. He liked the way this garment image worked on the pot form. It reminded him of fabrics billowing in the wind. Lawton feels he began to use garment imagery as a reflection of the irregular forms of his pots. In this fabric imagery Lawton echoed the emptiness of the disem-bodied garment in his use of a pot form that could not be used. He also echoed the billowing form of the fabric garment in the irregular flapping form we see in this thrown and then highly altered pot form.

the funnel as a kind of archetypal form. He is so fond of the form that he has collected a number of utilitarian funnels. Lawton likes to use forms that resonate visually. He is very fond of fonts and letter forms (the letter A is one of his favorite forms). He also likes sieves, cages, and lids. He likes the cage form because it partially shields and partially reveals what is inside. Its space is very complex. He is interested in the way people handle his pieces and designs them for easy handling. He likes to develop new ways to make it pleasant to hold his pieces. For example, his handles come in all sorts of unusual and outlandish shapes but all leave plenty of room for the hand and encourage comfortable holding. In other pieces we see him placing grasp holes on his lids instead of handles. They too work both visually and functionally.

In high school Lawton was interested in the fine arts and in graphic design. He was also interested in areas allied to art, such as font design, mechanical drawing, and architectural drawing. It was at this time as well, that a love of nature and water, boats, and boat design became important to him. In 1972 Lawton entered the art program at Florida State University in Tallahassee. Until he took his first pottery course, he thought he would major in painting. He became obsessed with ceramics and moved away from canvas painting altogether. Though the ceramics lab was across campus and the atmosphere in the education

department was very different from that of the art department, he went there willingly and learned the basic skills of the craft. He also remembers an art history class in which he saw a slide of a painted Greek vase, "The Berlin Painter Kylix" (6th c. B.C.). He says, "The irony of Dionysus lounging in his boat adrift in the interior sigillata 'sea' of a wine cup was not missed, even by that quite unripened 18 year old. The pot, therefore, was where I began to find a place and purpose to my urge to paint on clay surfaces."

The well-known enamelist William Harper taught at Tallahassee and became Lawton's mentor. Harper, who had taught at Penland School of the Crafts, encouraged Lawton to take a course there. He first went to Penland in 1975 (in the summer before his senior year in college) to study with Michael and Sandy Simon and was very impressed by this experience. Lawton graduated from Florida State in the spring of 1976. For the next few years he moved a good deal and amassed a group of experiences that were to prove extremely important in shaping his career as a professional ceramist. In the spring of 1977 he attended an eight-week concentration session at the Penland School with Byron Temple. He says of this experience, "We fought vigorously but I learned more from Byron than anybody." Lawton then entered the Core Scholarship Program at Penland. In return for assisting the Penland program he was given tuition, room and

board, and a place to work. He especially remembers the opportunity to meet and work with such faculty as Robert Turner, Cynthia Bringle, and Angela Fina. In the fall and winter of 1977/78, while things were quiet in Penland, he "holed up in the glaze room of the ceramics studio." He sees this time as one in which he was highly focused on ceramic work. He worked in raku, in part so he could see the results of his experiments most quickly. He says that wintertime at Penland is very spiritual; there is snow on the ground and the school seems to be hibernating and is a quite special place.

While a Core Student at Penland, Lawton met Joe Bova who was head of the ceramics program at Louisiana State University in Baton Rouge. Bova persuaded Lawton to come to Louisiana's graduate program. Lawton arrived in the fall of 1978 and found a rare group of people who got along with one another and who were immersed in their work. He says they were tough on each other but supportive as well. He talks of Bova's incredible ability to arrive in his studio with a comment at just the right time. He characterizes Bova's teaching style as astute, magnetic, and assertive but adds that Bova had the ability to listen well and understand a student's needs. Lawton got his M.F.A. from Louisiana in the spring of 1980.

During this period he made lots of work in the studio, exhibited at such galleries as the Garth Clark Gallery and the

American Hand, gave workshop presentations, and took on a series of half-year stints as assistant to the director at Haystack Mountain School of Crafts.

Because he had taken on so many projects, he found it hard to keep up with his ceramic work. Therefore, in 1983 he joined the resident program at Penland. At Penland he was able to make as much ceramic work as he wanted. He stayed in the program for almost two years. In 1984 he was awarded a National Endowment for the Arts Visual Arts Fellowship grant; he used the money to buy ceramic equipment. In the next few years he was a visiting artist or sabbatical replacement at Louisiana State University, The New York State College of Ceramics at Alfred, the School of the Art Institute of Chicago, and the University of Michigan at Ann Arbor. He says of these teaching experiences that he learned a great deal about the life of a teacher including some of its rough and tumble aspects.

In the summer of 1986 Lawton went to England and Europe on a three month bicycling tour. In 1987 he took over a house in South Carolina that had been in his family for many years. It is on a salt marsh estuary in the lower part of South Carolina. It is a very beautiful place and he spends as much time there as he can. In 1987 Lawton got another N.E.A. grant and used the money to build a studio on this land.

Lawton then declared a moratorium on teaching and decided he would take no more teaching jobs for two years. In the fall of 1991, however, the part-time job at the Art Institute of Chicago was converted to a full-time tenure track position; Lawton applied and was hired for it. During the next few years he clarified his thinking about the role of an educator in ceramics and decided he really did have an aptitude for teaching. He spent six years in Chicago and enjoyed teaching there a great deal. He talks of arguments with other faculty at the school about the relevance of ceramics to contemporary art. Though they reflected a dismissive attitude toward object making on the part of many of the faculty, these were challenging and exciting conversations. He spends winter breaks and summers in his house and studio in South Carolina with his wife, the printmaker Yvonne Leonard. In the spring of 1998 he was asked to become part of the ceramics program at the University of Massachusetts Dartmouth. He looks forward to more teaching and more work on his own pieces.

Jim Lawton altering the thrown form.

Photo credit: Yvonne Leonard.

to combine clay and nonclay materials, a move her teachers did approve. She says she faced a constant challenge: "Why do you use clay?" She feels that though this constant questioning made her uncomfortable, it forced her to think about her work and to express her thoughts in a clear and intelligent manner. She finished her work for a Master of Fine Arts degree from Columbia in 1976.

During the summer of 1976 she studied at the New York State College of Ceramics at Alfred with instructors Jeff Staller and Val Cushing. At Alfred she continued the sort of work she had been doing in graduate school, especially in mixed media sculpture. She also was interested in the technical aspects of ceramics. She found Alfred a storehouse of information on such topics as sculpture bodies and saggar firing. Some ceramic sculptors ignore the technical aspects of ceramics. They feel that technical matters should be de-emphasized and the aesthetic aspects of the work emphasized. A surprisingly large group of ceramic sculptors, however, pay great attention to technical matters and feel this knowledge will help them in their work. Netzer is in this latter group and feels that she is very much part of the ceramic community.

After graduation from Columbia University, Netzer set up her own studio in the Chelsea section of New York. She began to teach in adjunct positions at such schools as the

For Jenny, installation piece, Low Library Rotunda, Columbia University (an older piece), 10' x 8', 1976. Netzer made this piece in porcelain and fired it to cone 10. She suspended the structure from the ceiling using narrow steel cables. This piece is important because it was Netzer's first work with suspended forms. Since that time this has become one of her favorite formats. Netzer points out that the undulations in this form came about as a solution to a number of problems she was dealing with at that time. The undulations strengthened the piece, allowed her to work with lighter forms, and also allowed the piece to stand in the kiln with no supports. Netzer made the parts of this piece using a press mold made from plaster bandages. She developed this strategy because the molds made with plaster bandages had a limited flexibility. After she draped her clay forms in the mold, Netzer was able to give them a small shift or bend. This allowed her to free the clay forms from the mold without cracking them. She used this strategy to help her make shapes that otherwise would not have made it through the mold-forming process.

Pratt Institute, Jersey City State College, the Parsons School of Design, the City College of New York, and Greenwich House. She has particularly good memories of her teaching at Greenwich House (1971-90). This was a difficult time for her because all her jobs were part-time, none of them paid well, and travel from one job to another often involved a long subway ride. Aside from these teaching stints she had supplemental jobs at this time to keep her studio going. She might have found better paying work outside of New York but she declined to leave her city. In 1990 she was appointed to the faculty of the City College of New York on a full-time tenure track basis. She now has tenure there and since 1996 has served as chair of the art department.

Netzer has been working with multiple modular units or elements since the mid-1970s. She uses both geometric and organic forms in her work and likes to combine these two form types. Netzer usually works in a series. She learns from each previous piece in the series so that by the end of the series, she can do things that were not possible at the start of the work. She says of her approach, "I feel that I can make anything that I can imagine or draw. Even though I am often frightened that the work will collapse or split or crack, I try. I figure the worst that can happen is that it may fail - and if it fails I will have learned something anyway!"

Sylvia Netzer.

Mary Barringer

Mary Barringer's work shows her concern for establishing a sense of unity. She has devised her work processes so she can slowly and carefully build form and surface at the same time and in this way unite them. Her emphasis on unity gives her work a sense of control and inevitability and a very personal and introspective cast.

Photo credit: Wayne Fleming.

Toi Tende, *18-1/2" x 8-1/2" x 8", 1996. Commercially prepared light colored clay body fired to cone 6 in an electric kiln. Barringer used a combination of coiled and pinch-building strategies to build this piece. She began by pinch forming a rough shape. She added coils or pieces wherever the mood struck her without establishing a base for this piece. Here we see how Barringer's novel coiling method enabled her to create a very unusual form.*

Some of the textures here are artifacts of the way Barringer paddled the coils together as she was forming the piece. She created other textures by scraping, drawing, scoring, and smoothing its surface. While it was still unfired, she applied slips, stains, vitreous engobes, and glazes. She used these as lightly applied washes over the surface of the clay. Barringer used a brush to apply the slips in multiple layers. At the leather-hard stage, when the piece was barely out of the building process, she drew through the slip. She applied layers of slip after the bisque firing as well. She then sanded and scraped the slip layers.

She then fired the piece. Once the kiln reached temperature she allowed the temperature to drop a bit and held it at that point for a time to keep her surfaces in a semi-molten state. She did this to further encourage rich slip and glaze surfaces. For the same reason she also "fired down" for a time before fully finishing the firing.

Untitled Sculpture, 4" x 18-1/2" x 7-1/2", 1997. Commercially prepared light colored clay body, fired to cone 6 in an electric kiln. This piece is not a vessel form but rather an open, ring-shaped form (Barringer compares it to an inner tube). To make this form, Barringer started with a very thick solid coil of clay. She then pinch formed it into a U-shaped form. As she progressed, she thinned the walls of the form, shaped it, then closed the top. Where she ran out of clay, she added coils. Where she needed to pull the surface in, she cut spaces or darts into the form. This is a very compact shape, one that lends itself to the ceramic medium.

Barringer uses a commercially prepared light colored cone 8 to 10 sculpture body to create her pieces. She likes this body because it has good working properties. The clay body is strong, resists cracking (even when she varies the wall thickness), and allows her to attach parts as she wishes. Since she fires this very high-fire body to cone 6, it resists settling and warping. Furthermore, it is not particularly grainy and lends itself to the creation of defined edges and Barringer likes to contrast her full forms with highly defined edges.

Barringer's forms are compact and strongly volumetric. She uses a combination of coil and pinch-forming strategies. For many years she began her pieces at the base and built from the bottom up. When she got to the top, she finished the piece. This is the normal manner for coil work. In recent years, however, she has wanted to build in a different, much more "all over" way that allows her to develop the form at many points simultaneously. She now begins many of her pieces by pinch forming a rough shape and adds coils or pieced

forms wherever the mood strikes her. She no longer feels she has to begin the piece at the base. She has developed this strategy because she wants to be able to work with a wide range of forms. This freer approach allows her to concentrate on the relationship of all the parts to each other as she works. Even more important, it frees her from the insistence on growth only in a vertical direction - growth can take place in any direction she wishes.

Rich surface textures have become a signature of Barringer's clay work. Some of

*Detail of **Untitled Sculpture**. Barringer has spent a lot of time and thought on the bone-like surface of this piece. It doesn't look applied but simply seems to be the surface expression of the form.*

these textures are artifacts of the way she paddles the coils together as she forms the piece. Among the surfaces she creates in this way are overlapping seams, subtle dips, and raised areas running along the surface in a rhythmically repeated pattern. She creates other textures by scraping, drawing, scoring, and smoothing the surface of the piece. Barringer finishes her work with slips, stains, vitreous engobes, and glazes. She uses these as lightly applied washes over the surface of the clay. These washes modify the light color of the clay body and the result is a highly muted color and a slight sheen. Glaze and stain colors are caught in the textures engraved on the surface of the piece. She doesn't want thick glaze surfaces or strong color to obscure her textured clay surfaces. Instead she wants to use a thin surface that helps her emphasize this imagery.

She has said of slips, "For me, slips are both the material and conceptual 'missing link' between clay and glaze, between the process of building and finishing. Their physical compatibility with the body, and the accretive process of building up the layers, allows me to feel that I now keep on working on the piece, experimenting with it and simultaneously changing form and surface."

Barringer uses a brush to apply her slips and thin glaze washes in multiple layers. She applies these both before and after the bisque fire. At the leather-hard stage, when the piece is barely out of the building process, she draws through the slip and glaze layers. She

Photo credit: Mary Barringer.

Baby Jars *(an older piece), height 5", 1987. Barringer made the forms from a commercially prepared clay body fired to cone 9 in a fuel burning reduction kiln. She made each piece by resting a slab base on a pillow. She built on this base using coiling methods. Barringer says of these pieces that they are "playful" but also that they "are examples of the persistent influence of the figure" in her work. She feels they also recall pre-Columbian figural sculptures, especially from western Mexico.*

also sands and scrapes them. Some of the slips and glazes are highly reactive and contain lithium, ash, and magnesite (the mineral source of magnesium carbonate). These reactive, highly melting slips can cause anything applied over them to melt and to create strong visual textures. Barringer feels that she is bridging the gap between form and surface with her slip and glazes and that they have the physical character of clay but the texture and fluid character of glaze.

All these layers of slip and glaze react with each other in the kiln and thus create complex interactions and transformations. Barringer notes that in a fuel-burning kiln this can happen as a result of the reduction atmosphere. In the neutral atmosphere of the electric kiln she makes this happen by using these multiple layers of slip and glaze and by using highly reactive recipes. Though slips change less than glazes during the firing, layered slips and active slips have the potential to surprise. She can build color, depth, and sheen with slips of varying degrees of activity, vitreousness, and color saturation. The thickness, number, and sequence of the layers also affects the character of the melt and encourages rich broken textures.

Barringer fires to cone 6 in an electric kiln. She is very interested in the effects of her actions on the course of the firing. She is experimenting with various firing schedules. Once the kiln reaches temperature she allows the temperature to drop a bit and holds it at that point to keep her surfaces in a semi-molten state. She does this to encourage her slip and glaze layers to create a rich

Two Creamers, stoneware with slips and glaze, height 5", 1997. Barringer made these forms from a commercially prepared light colored clay body fired to cone 6 in an electric kiln. She used a slab-forming strategy to build the basic forms. After creating the forms she modified the shapes by paddling and scraping the surfaces.

surface. For the same reason she also "fires down" for a time before fully finishing the firing.

Barringer's image creation methods have much in common with the natural growth processes of forms in nature. They too are incremental. As a result, these pieces seem to be the product of a natural growth process. They bring to mind such things as mineral outcroppings, animal forms, shells, and coral. Rather than imitating nature she uses process to create work that mirrors natural processes and shows us the inner workings of the natural process. She is also interested in the human form, not so much as a beautiful form, but as a container of energy and as the embodiment of movement and rhythm.

Barringer has a love of making and a great belief in its inherent value. She knows her material and takes joy in her understanding of its ways. She sees this understanding as in some part intellectual but in good part coming from a deeper, more intuitive level. She has said of her work, "Craft or technique functions for me as a groove along which my ideas flow. A certain mastery is important so I don't get bogged down in problem solving. It sometimes seems that 'creativity' doesn't begin to operate until I have figured out how to work."

Barringer attended Pratt Institute in New York City in 1968 and 1969. She then transferred to Bennington College in Vermont where she took ceramics from Stanley Rosen. Rosen, a brilliant man, was famous for finding his own way both in his personal style and his ceramic work. He was a very special teacher and Barringer learned a great deal from him. She received a B.A. degree in art from Bennington in 1972. She started her schooling with the intent of being a sculptor; her imagery was centered on the human figure. She worked with many media and created her imagery with both carving (a technique she does not use often in her ceramics) and modeling. As she began to work intensively with clay she was seduced by the tactile character of the material. At this time she also saw that she could make a living as a potter and this too strongly attracted her to clay.

As she became convinced that she wanted to be a potter she discovered the attractions of the vessel form. Both its repertory of forms that work so well in clay and its references to utility appealed to her. She also discovered that pottery had a marginal place in the art world. Many ceramists dislike the dismissive or patronizing view of ceramics held by many in the world of the "fine arts." Others, however, enjoy this outsider status. These ceramists believe

this lack of status encourages freedom, independence, and a spirit of cooperation. Barringer is in this group. Finally, she came to enjoy the challenge of having to deal with the market and the taste of its audience and she felt it made her stay open to aspects of art she might otherwise have ignored.

Barringer apprenticed to the ceramic artist Michael Frimkess in 1971. In 1973 she established the Park Street Studio, a community studio in Hartford, Connecticut. She managed the studio, taught in it, and produced functional pottery there. In 1976 she moved on to become resident potter at the Farmington Valley Art Center in Avon, Connecticut (1976 to 1982). She now maintains a private studio in Shelburne Falls, Massachusetts.

For many years, after deciding to make her living in ceramics, Barringer worked solely in the vessel form. She still makes some pieces that are functional or reminiscent of functionality. In recent years, however, she has turned to sculptural forms. Though these pieces are strongly sculptural, they are rooted in the ceramic medium. In this new work she makes forms that look like they have a particular use and identity. This use and identity, however, is never revealed.

Barringer is unusually intent on creating a sense of unity in her pieces. She has developed a group of work strategies calculated to encourage a smoothly uninterrupted flow of work from start to finish. She has modified her finishing

process so it is very similar in the character of its action to her forming process. She slowly constructs her pieces, coil by coil, then slowly and carefully constructs her surfaces, layer by layer. In this way she works to erase the barrier between the way she creates form and the way she creates surface. Barringer notes that in the normal way of making our work, we think about making and glazing as separate activities. She acknowledges that there are practical reasons for this, but feels many ceramists experience a feeling of bafflement about how to create the surfaces of their ceramic work. "We loved making pots, but we dreaded glazing them." She feels these sentiments are very common and that her move from gas to electric firing made her confront this problem. She could no longer rely on the richness of the reduction atmosphere; the burden was now on her to create rich surface finishes. She says of this challenge, "I needed not just new techniques, but a new attitude." It is this that led her to adopt the use of slips and to use them both during the final part of the building process as well as after the piece was dry or fired to bisque. Her present way of working "suits both what I want to make and the way my ideas take shape: incrementally and by the way of addition, subtraction, and the accidental." She relies on the process to act as a kind of "feedback loop" that will allow the piece to talk back to her as the work proceeds.

At the core of her work as a

ceramist is Barringer's wish to break down the walls between creating the form and creating the surface. She has developed strategies that allow her to continue working with the form as she creates the surface. This has restored a sense of discovery and creativity to what used to be merely the "tidying up" part of the creation process. While she cannot substantially alter the form at this point, she can shift the visual weight and rethink the relationship of one part of the piece to another. As she brushes on her layers of slip and works the surface of the piece, she can see and feel the piece in new ways, and renew her sense of what she was after in the first place. This allows her to shape the character of her work right up to the moment when it goes into the kiln and "the kiln gods (yes, even in an electric kiln) take over."

Mary Barringer.

Neil Forrest

Neil Forrest lives and teaches in Nova Scotia, Canada. He uses a modernized version of an Egyptian faience clay body (also known as Egyptian paste) and has done a great deal to revive interest in it. This is an ancient and very striking clay body type. Egyptian faience appeared in Egypt as early as the late pre-dynastic period (approximately 3300

Photo credit: Steve Farmer.

***Trivet: Shadows and Pockets**, earthenware and an Egyptian faience element set in grout, 26" x 24" x 2-1/2". Neil Forrest made the decorative element in the center of this trivet form with an Egyptian faience clay body (also known as Egyptian paste). He made the supporting structure from an earthenware body. In this piece we see the way Forrest's earthenware supporting structure works with the faience element in the inset section of the structure.*

Forrest started out by making a rectangular tile which he shaped after firing into a tile element. He also made a hollow, volumetric form which serves as a supporting structure for the tile element. He made the supporting structure with an inset section designed to receive the tile element. He dried, glazed, and fired the supporting structure and set it aside. He made a rectangular tile (21" x 11") from various colors of Egyptian faience. Forrest made the Egyptian faience element using various colored clay strategies including inlaying and marbling. He created the faience imagery and let the tile dry. He fired the tile, then cut it into the shape he needed using a tungsten tipped tile cutter. It would obviously be easier to cut the tile before the firing but Forrest waited until after firing. At this point it had shrunk as much as it was going to and the imagery detail (including its color) was now defined. After he cut out the tile element, Forrest placed it in an inset section of the terra cotta supporting structure. He used grout to integrate the tile element into the structure. He used the Egyptian faience tile element to create rich imagery that he couldn't get with normal terra cotta clay and he used the structure to create a volumetric character that he couldn't create with the Egyptian faience clay body. Forrest fired the structural part of the piece to cone 04 and fired the tile to cone 010 in an electric kiln. In this tile element we see decorative imagery of beetles placed on a marbled, colored clay ground. To create this marbling he mixed clays of various colors, then cut against the grain of the mix. Forrest says he is playing with the decorative imagery suggested by the kind of spatial treatment he has seen in Roman mosaics. He cites the way the Romans used shadows in mosaics to create their illusionistic imagery.

B.C.). It was used for jewelry, amulets, small sculptures, and vessels. Through his use of Egyptian faience, Forrest creates work in which the color and glaze are completely integrated with the form. This clay body shapes the personality of his work and informs it with its unusual character. This is a very difficult medium; Forrest has learned to deal with the difficulties.

Egyptian faience bodies contain significant percentages of high alkaline, water-soluble fluxes. These fluxes encourage the waxy surfaces and rich colors integrated with the clay body. Unfortunately, the soluble materials that give these bodies their special character also give them the rubbery boneless feel that makes them difficult to work with. Some form types and forming methods lend themselves to work in Egyptian faience more readily than others. The ceramist can use hand-forming and press-mold methods with these bodies but they don't encourage throwing on the potter's wheel. Because these bodies have a limited workability they don't lend themselves to the creation of complex forms. We frequently see small solid formed pieces such as jewelry and scarabs and tile pieces made from Egyptian faience; we see far fewer vessels and sculptural pieces. Egyptian faience bodies have lots of limitations but a few ceramists such as Forrest have been willing to take up their challenge.

This clay body contains ingredients that encourage the

Photo credit: Steve Farmer.

Trivet: Ombra, *earthenware and an Egyptian faience element set in grout, 13" x 13" x 3-1/2", 1998. There is no meaning, no story to be understood in Forrest's tile compositions. These images are about color and the idea of the decorative. He plays with the space of these pieces using the insects and the complex backgrounds they hover above or crawl upon. In this piece Forrest pictures gray colored moths on a geometric, marbled, colored clay space. He is very interested in insects and the way we see them as simultaneously beautiful and dangerous.*

formation of a glaze on the surface of the piece. Such clay bodies are known as "self glazing bodies." To make a self glazing clay body the ceramist adds water-soluble melters and colorants to the clay body. As the piece dries, water migrates to its surface. The water-soluble melters migrate along with the moisture and form a film of soluble salts that covers the surface of the clay body. Upon firing, this filmy layer of melting materials unites with the clay to form a thin glaze-like layer over the surface of the piece. Egyptian faience encourages satin surfaces and strong saturated colors. Color and gloss don't look like an applied overlay but seem to come from within the

piece. Body color is often very subtle and enables the ceramist to create tonalities that are not often found in ceramic work. These bodies, with their unusual surface character and color response, look as much like glass as they do clay.

Ceramists have access to a number of useful recipes for contemporary versions of Egyptian faience. They have a number of characteristics in common: they are high in silica, low in clay, and contain water-soluble melters. The following recipe is originally from Richard Behrens. It is a contemporary version of a self-glazing Egyptian faience and is made from materials easily available to contemporary ceramists. The suggested firing temperature is cone 08 to 06.

Feldspar	35
Flint	35
China clay	12
Bentonite	2
Sodium bicarbonate (or borax)	6
Sodium carbonate	6
Copper carbonate	2 to 3

The color of Egyptian faience bodies is distributed evenly throughout the fabric of the clay. Because these bodies are vitreous, they are similar to glazes. Like all glassy clay bodies they require very little colorant. Forrest adds 3% of most stains and 5% of the new zirconium encapsulated stains to get the saturated colors he needs. He has encountered an interesting phenomenon with the stains. They encourage slightly different shrinkage rates. He has noticed that if you run your hand over the tile you feel very subtle height differences from one stained clay to another. This phenomenon is extremely difficult to see. Forrest noticed it when he ran his hand over the surface of the pieces.

While most of the soluble melters are deposited on the top of the tile during evaporation, it is still a good idea to fire pieces made from Egyptian faience on a material that will protect the kiln shelf. Forrest uses a piece of glossy (kaolin enriched) paper for this purpose. Though this is not protection against extreme melting, it works very well for Forrest's Egyptian faience.

Forrest has created work that is highly ornamental but at the same time rooted in use. He is fascinated by the faience objects the Egyptians made for everyday use. He is particularly interested in the carefully designed objects that functioned as containers for cosmetics. We look upon them now as arresting objects; we are not conscious of their utility.

Forrest likes to use Egyptian faience for tile work; though it would be possible to use it for vessel or sculptural pieces, its limited workability discourages this kind of use. Forrest wants to "let it do what it likes to do best." The body must be used with great attentiveness and care; it can be the source of real problems and he must pay special attention to his materials and the way he handles them. He must sieve his soluble fluxes because overly coarse soluble fluxes may cause blisters and pock marks in the fired body. He must make sure the piece dries at a steady rate because if it dries too slowly, the solubles remain buried in the interior of the body and don't come to the surface. This is a real problem in the winter when Forrest's studio stays quite damp. He also must control his firing temperature very carefully. If he fires at a

*Detail of **Ombra**.*

Photo credit: Steve Farmer.

Forrest uses his Egyptian faience clays to create a highly stylized imagery based on forms found in nature. A few years ago he was using floral imagery; he now works with images of insects. His favorite subjects are dragonflies, houseflies, and beetles. He doesn't picture these creatures with realistic accuracy, instead he wants to create a rich surface pattern based on the insect's silhouetted form. He notes that our reactions to insects are mixed. We are at once squeamish and fascinated. It is no wonder that we find insects frightening, disgusting and fascinating; they may bite, sting and transmit disease. However, their forms and colors are truly intricate and beautiful. They lend themselves to use in ornament.

Forrest sees the language of the crafts as allied, but in some crucial ways very different from the language of painting and sculpture. He believes the crafts have decoration at their core. He works with a decorative shallow space - he uses textile-like patterns that would never work in painting but work well in the crafts. He feels that figure and ground relationships that work well in painting are inappropriate for his work. Forrest is wary of using the imagery of true three-dimensional space in his work. This kind of space will punch holes in the walls of the forms used by artists working in the crafts. Forrest says, "I am a frankly decorative artist - it's so out, it's in!"

Forrest is also intensely interested in the service role often played by ceramic ware. This is another aspect of the work that is limited to the crafts. This utilitarian aspect of the crafts has been in good part neglected in recent years. Forrest, taking a contrary stance, has moved away from wall ornaments to work that is meant for table use. To Forrest, the utilitarian role of these pieces is very important; they protect the table and serve as a stand for a serving piece. It is important to him that the piece has a function and has a place in the ritual of the festive meal. The trivet holds the hot or cold serving piece and when the serving piece is removed, the trivet becomes the centerpiece of the table setting. Forrest takes an unusual route to utility and encourages us to think again about utility and how best to make contemporary utilitarian work.

Neil Forrest was born in Toronto in 1952. He attended Sheridan College outside of Toronto, studying with Angela Fina and Bruce Cochrane. He took part in its three-year program and received a diploma in 1970. He worked with earthenware sculpture and sculptural vessels. He had as role models the ceramists Robert Turner who taught at Alfred in the U.S. and Gordon Baldwin who taught at Eton College in England.

From 1979 to 1981 he studied with the sculptor Jun Kaneko at Cranbrook and received a B.F.A. degree. During this time he made figurative sculpture pieces in red earthenware. From 1981 to 1983 he worked in his home city of Toronto. He received a Canada Council Grant which allowed him to work on his own for an extended period of time. He worked on a series of large vessels with forms that suggested architecture. He was very concerned with ornamental shapes and studied ornament from a great many sources including furniture and other areas of the decorative arts. He created his pieces using an earthenware clay body painted with terra sigillatas. He once fired these pieces to cone 04. From 1983 to 1985 Forrest attended the New York State College of Ceramics at Alfred. He worked with Tony Hepburn, Wayne Higby, Tom Spleth, John and Andrea Gill, and Ann Currier. His explorations of ornamental form continued. In the work he did at this time he created ornament by taking decorative fragments from architecture and enlarging them many times their original size. He made these pieces using earthenware clay bodies fired to 018 with low-fire enamels painted on bisque.

From 1985 to 1987 Forrest lived in New York City. He says of this that he and his wife "wanted to live, for a time, in what we saw as the center of art world." It was here that he started to use Egyptian faience. He made this decision because he needed a way to work in a very small test kiln. This was all he had room for in his New York apartment. Furthermore, the kiln required only the normal house current that he found in

Scotchie builds her pieces with a clay body that is off-white in color. She adds kyanite and grog to help the body resist heat shock and cracking and to enhance building strength. Kyanite is similar to grog but is more pure and free of color and melting impurities. It is made from small granules of aluminum silicate. Scotchie builds her pieces using strip coils. She uses a wooden paddle (one she made in graduate school) to move the clay and shape the form. She makes her pieces in sections. She scores these sections, then joins them with slip. Between work sessions she keeps the pieces covered with plastic sheeting. When Scotchie finishes a piece, she removes the plastic sheeting and lets it dry. Her clay body doesn't seem to require special care during the drying process. Once dry, she sands it with a woven plastic scrub pad to refine the surface, fires it to bisque, and applies her surface coatings. Scotchie uses many different surfaces to create her pieces, including metallic surfaces and dry crawling surfaces. She brushes multiple layers on the surfaces, applying some when they are in a paste-like consistency thus creating a thick coating. Scotchie's final firing is at cone 6. She fires in a highly insulated top-loading electric kiln that holds heat very effectively, so she doesn't need to control heat loss by soaking.

For many years Scotchie worked in the low fire. Since spending the summer of 1995 at the European Ceramic Work Center in the Netherlands she

*Detail of the glaze surfaces of **Andriana's Crawl**. In this detail we see a crawling glaze set next to the bronze colored luster.*

has been working in cone 6 oxidation. She likes clay bodies fired at this temperature for their workability and durability and values the durability and color range of glazes fired to this temperature. She also likes change and finds it a good engine to move her work ahead.

A lot of the impact of Scotchie's pieces lies in her fascination with forms and forming. She has thought a good deal about the act of joining forms together. She has studied the way objects in nature are joined and finds the junctions between one form or part of a form and another very exciting. In nature they often occur as a way to allow for a change of direction, a mechanism to aid the form in the way it can twist and bend. Scotchie has tried to put the same kind of structural logic in her pieces. She works to make her forms powerful and gestural. She

likes to juxtapose contrasting forms, colors, and textures. She places shiny metallic surfaces alongside crusty, organic, highly textured surfaces. She also contrasts static elements with highly active elements.

Although pure form is very important to Scotchie, she also refers in these pieces to imagery from the real world; her visual resources are strongly connected to her life. Scotchie has a great curiosity about the world and its objects. She has a fondness for forms that surprise the viewer and convey a sense of the unusual, quirky, and ironic. She also uses forms that have very personal sources. Her work is strongly informed by her connections to family, children, and culture. The genesis of much of her recent work is in such objects as watering cans and other tools. Her grandfather was an avid gardener and she has some of his tools. This tie to her grand-

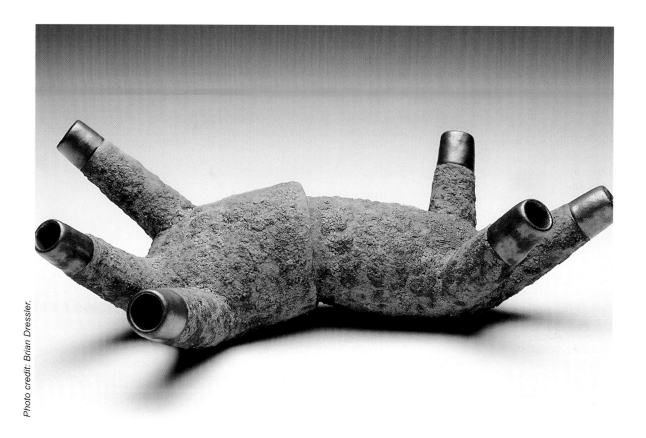

Photo credit: Brian Dressler.

father makes tool-like forms special to her. She also likes these forms because she sees them as a tie to her original work with functional pottery. Scotchie's forms also bring figural images to mind. She sees this figural character as having its roots in children's toys, especially dolls. She believes a lot of her visual resources are connected to her life and that her children's sense of curiosity and wonder has strongly influenced her work. She would like to mirror the directness of a child's vision in her work. She evokes the child's vision by using surprising forms and images in her pieces.

Scotchie did not intend to become an artist, she thought she would end up in one of the helping professions. She always loved art but never thought about making art as a career. She entered college at the University of North Carolina in her hometown of Asheville in 1973. She attended school there until 1975, majoring in sociology and religion. She took her first ceramics course at Asheville during her sophomore year as an elective outside her major. She studied with Elma Johnson, a graduate of Southern Illinois University. She really liked the course and subsequently took a variety of art courses including more courses in ceramics. In the fall of 1975 she transferred to the

much larger University of North Carolina at Chapel Hill. She took a few courses in art but majored in sociology and religion. She graduated from Chapel Hill with a B.A. degree in sociology and religion in 1977. In the summer of 1977 she went on an archeological dig in Israel organized by two of her professors at Chapel Hill. This turned out to be a very important event in her life because much of the material she and her fellow students were unearthing was made from clay. This renewed her interest in clay.

After graduation, Scotchie returned to Asheville. She went to work for a UNICEF program for latchkey children in

Left: Turquoise Funnels, 7" x 21" x 10", 1998. This complex piece is composed of a large central form with six tubular forms attached to it at various angles. Scotchie contrasted the cracked and caked textures of the green glaze with the metallic smoothness of the luster surface. She used a mid-fire off-white clay body to make this piece. Scotchie values this body for its great workability. She added grog and kyanite (a white grog-like material) to help the body resist heat shock and cracking and to enhance building strength.

Scotchie sculpture body, cone 5 to 10

Fire clay	40
Ball clay	20
Red clay	15
Kyanite	15
Fine grog	5
Medium grog	5

Scotchie built the central form of this piece using strip coils made from thick strips of clay placed one next to the other to create the form. She added four or five of these clay strips at a time, thereby adding from 4" to 6" to the length. The walls are about 1/2" thick. She used a wooden paddle to move the clay and shape the form. She made the central section in two halves, then joined them together. She made the funnel forms by wrapping a slab around a dowel covered with newspaper. She slipped and scored the parts before joining them together. Between work sessions she kept the piece covered with plastic sheeting. Scotchie says her clay body doesn't require special care during the drying process. When she finished the piece she removed the plastic sheeting and let it dry. Once it was dry she donned a dust mask and sanded the piece with a woven plastic scrub pad.

Scotchie used two different surface finishes to create this piece, a bronze colored material that derives its color from its high percentage of manganese and a dry crawling glaze.

Scotchie's bronze luster glaze, cone 2 to 6

Red clay	44
Ball clay	4
Silica	4
Manganese dioxide	33
Gerstley borate	7
Copper carbonate	4
Cobalt carbonate	4

Metallic bronze surfaces of this sort are identified with the material manganese dioxide. It is the crucial ingredient required to create this color effect. Its dust is toxic and ceramists must wear a mask and gloves and apply it carefully with a brush. Manganese gives off toxic fumes in the fire, so the kiln room must be vented.

Bone ash crawling glaze, cone 6 oxidation

Bone ash	75
Cryolite	13
Barium	4
Soda feldspar	8
Copper carbonate	4

This recipe is extremely low in silica and alumina, which accounts for its very dry surface. Scotchie added the copper carbonate to create the turquoise green color. The alkaline nature of the recipe accentuates the green color. She used the unstable materials - bone ash (calcium phosphate) and cryolite (sodium aluminum fluoride) - to create this highly textured surface. Cryolite gives off toxic fumes in the fire, so the kiln room must be vented.

After the bisque firing Scotchie applied multiple layers of the bronze recipe with a brush. She first mixed the green recipe to a paste-like consistency, then applied it in a thick coating using a sponge. After this firing she reapplied it to create a thicker, richer coating and fired it again to cone 6. Scotchie likes clay bodies and glazes fired at cone 6 for their workability, durability, and wide color range.

Vera's Garden *(an older piece), 5' 6" x 5' 6" x 4' (including base), 1984. Scotchie single fired this piece to cone 04. The body is a low-fire red terra cotta. She painted the imagery with colored terra sigillatas. Scotchie made this piece in segments, then assembled it after firing. All the vertical forms fit in the horizontal base. She built each vertical piece with a clay post that fits into an appropriately shaped opening in the base. She made this piece in memory of her late grandmother. Her grandparents were farmers - earthy, direct people whose ties to the land and to clearly understood values made a big impression on Scotchie.*

Asheville. Later she taught art at an experimental high school in Asheville. Her interest in clay had been revived by the archeological dig and she wanted to take more classes in ceramics. When she mentioned this to a good friend, he told her she had to go to Penland. He said that ceramics was something she was good at and should explore in depth. Penland is only an hour and a half from Asheville, so the idea seemed quite reasonable. In the fall of 1979 she went to Penland for the first time and studied ceramics with Angela Fina. Scotchie was strongly moved by the class and began to see ceramics as a possible career. In the fall of that year she attended her first ceramic conference, the combined meeting of Supermud and NCECA. At this time Scotchie was making porcelain production pottery. From 1979 to 1981 she apprenticed to a production potter, Don Davis. For the next few years she kept moving and learning. She served as a studio assistant at Penland. She moved to

Baton Rouge, Louisiana, for a time and worked in a studio there. During this time she was making progress and was getting positive responses to her work. When she talks about it, it sounds very natural and uncomplicated but she needed to work very hard, and not just at ceramics. Though she lived very frugally, she had to supplement her income to pay for rent and food. She worked at all sorts of jobs, as a waitress, tutor, and part-time teacher.

During this period she worked with slab forms and nonfunctional vessels and experimented with color and the manipulation of her surfaces. She spent an increasing amount of time on nonfunctional and sculptural forms and began moving in the direction of sculpture. At Baton Rouge she met Wayne Higby, who liked her work and encouraged her to apply to Alfred. In the fall of 1983 she entered Alfred as a graduate student. She worked with Andrea Gill. She assisted Tony Hepburn, working closely with him and learning a lot. He worked very hard for his students. At Alfred, Scotchie's work changed dramatically. She stopped making vessels and took up sculptural work.

She stopped working with porcelain and began using low-fire glazes and terra sigillatas. She worked with brilliant primary colors. Her forms became more organic. She started working with fat coils, making very large, heavy pieces. She began to work with repeated organic forms, piling them up to make large mounds. She remembers her time as a graduate student with great fondness. She graduated from Alfred in 1985 with an M.F.A. degree.

From 1985 to 1988 she held her first teaching position at West Virginia University. She

Photo credit: Brian Dressler.

***Odd Balls**, 12" x 6' x 6', 1992. Scotchie is very interested in texture. Here she created it by applying the glaze using loose sketchy motions. She used commercially prepared cone 04 ceramic enamels for some of the surfaces here. She painted others using a studio made, satin mat glaze base. She colored this base with commercially prepared stains.*

taught three-dimensional design and hand-formed ceramics. She enjoyed the work and learned a lot. She spent a good deal of time and effort on her own work which was by now entirely sculptural. She had been making repeated small forms which she piled into large mounds. Now she decided to take some of these small forms and make them in a much larger scale. During these years she began to work with large geometric forms, influenced by minimal sculpture. In these pieces Scotchie combined the loose textures so natural to clay with the geometric forms and imagery used by many of the minimalist artists. As she made her individual pieces larger, she no longer placed one on another. In her shows she clustered a small grouping of these pieces together. She also explored ways of arranging her forms for exhibition and worked hard to make these arrangements convey a sense of harmony and organization. She placed some of her pieces on the floor and others on pedestals. She started designing geometric and sharp-edged pedestals to go with her pieces because she wanted them to contrast with her softer, organic clay forms. During the 1930s the Romanian sculptor Constantine Brancusi had explored these problems in some depth in his work and these explorations became very important to Scotchie.

In 1988 Scotchie left West Virginia to take a teaching position at Indiana University in Bloomington. She feels that her already minimalist orientation was reinforced by the flat landscapes of western Indiana. For Scotchie, who had grown up in the mountainous landscape of the Southern Highlands, this was a very different environment. She saw lots of limestone set in a very austere landscape. At this time there was a great deal of newly awakened interest in the use of clay as a fine arts medium and she began to show her work at a wide variety of galleries.

Scotchie was later invited to teach at the University of South Carolina. She talks of the climate and the small town life of the south, with its pervasive friendliness. Her work was changing and she began to use complex multi-part forms in her work. In the summer of 1995 she worked at the European Ceramic Work Center in the Netherlands. This competitive program is highly selective and has highly sophisticated laboratory facilities. She enjoyed using the facilities at the center and enjoyed working with the other participants; participants came and went but there were always ten or 12 artists in attendance. They were from many parts of the world and held a wide range of ideas and attitudes. During her stay at the Center she met artists who worked in other media and who had very little experience in working with clay. These artists went to the Center to learn about clay and how to use it in their work. She now began working in the cone 6 firing temperature. Her experience at the Center encouraged her to develop her work in both its technical and aesthetic aspects. In her most recent pieces she uses cone 6 bodies, highly textured glazes, and figural and tool-like imagery. This work is complex and has many sources. Scotchie has a sensibility marked by a restless curiosity. Some of her sources are from her life, from children's toys, and old, well-used tools. Others come from the work itself, from the forms and colors that are the basis of this work. Still others come from the world of art. Scotchie's art is often about art but it is also about clay and she never strays far from her identification with clay.

Virginia Scotchie.

Photo credit: Jason Wallace.

Joanne Hayakawa

Joanne Hayakawa is a ceramic sculptor. Her work is complex and has a strong architectural feel. Because of their size and complexity and Hayakawa's interest in visual symbolism, these pieces have the character of ritualistic objects.

Aqueduct (an older piece), 22" x 16" x 31", 1990. Hayakawa used a terra cotta clay body and slab-forming methods to make this piece. She finished the piece with stains and glazes and with unfired materials. Note an imagery that resembles flowing water on the front of this piece. She made this using underglaze stains. She fired the piece to cone 04, then mixed water and salt and dripped this down the front to give it texture. She did not fire this mixture. She finished the piece by adding rods made from copper and by sifting rock salt dust on the top of the piece and on the stairs. Hayakawa says, "This torso-like structure depicts a passage for water in a desert environment."

Photo credit: Joanne Hayakawa.

Hayakawa makes her work using stoneware and porcelain clay bodies. She uses hand-forming methods. These include slab, coil, extrusion and pinch methods. Her work is fairly large and she usually works in sections for ease of handling, firing, and exhibition. Hayakawa likes to work in a steady manner, setting up a rhythm of work. She builds and then allows the piece to become firm, then repeats the cycle until the piece is finished. She says when she is constructing a piece she doesn't let a day go by without working on it. In this way, she feels, the piece will have a uniform moisture content and she will be able to create a strong structure. During the building process she works each day for five hours or so. It takes about ten days for her to build the piece from start to finish and two days to complete the cleaning process. She then dries the piece under plastic, which takes about two weeks.

Though her work usually centers around forms made in clay, she enjoys combining clay with other materials. Sometimes the nonclay materials end up constituting an important part of the visual character of the piece. At other times they are important for structural support but are not visible in the finished object. For example, some of her pieces are supported by a metal rod that fits inside the form.

Hayakawa doesn't like to shroud her forms and clay surfaces with thick surface

Photo credit: Joanne Hayakawa.

Primal Courage*, 10" x 42" x 10", 1994/95. In this piece the imagery depicts a human spine. For Hayakawa the human form symbolizes the human spirit.*

188

Blade, 28" x 12" x 28", 1994, stoneware core with a steel screen. Hayakawa says this piece is about "maintaining oneself in the midst of turbulence or chaos."

coatings. Therefore, she avoids thick glaze surfaces. She may sift a layer of dry glaze on the top part of a piece or may color the clay with a stain. An exception to this is her use of a gold luster in some of her pieces. Hayakawa fires her work at various temperatures and in various types of kilns. These include temperatures ranging from cone 018 to cone 10 and a wide variety of kiln types.

Hayakawa is very conscious of dualities. She likes to contrast the private character of the interior and the accessible character of the exterior of her pieces. She deals with the contrast between strength and vulnerability in her work and between the plastic and flowing character of the medium when it is wet and its rigid character when it is fired. She has as her goal the creation of a harmony between these dualities. She says a primary source of her imagery is a need for structure. She struggles to balance her need for structure and surety with a wish to take chances and explore the unknown.

Hayakawa says another important source for her imagery is the human body. She uses the human form as a metaphor for the "insistent effort humans make to establish and maintain the uniqueness of the individual spirit." She feels that her figural structures speak of primal instinct and our struggle to enable this core aspect of our nature to survive in an industrial and highly socialized environment. To make this happen she starts off with an architectural format and tries to infuse that structure with imagery that has human connotations. To symbolize the human she uses elements of the human form such as heart, brain, and spine. Hayakawa feels it is important to use these images of body parts - it helps her find a balance between feeling and the intellect. Since this imagery is symbolic in character she feels it is appropriate to simplify and stylize it. She wants to pare this human imagery down to its most elemental forms. It is Hayakawa's experience that viewers may not initially perceive these pieces as images of human forms. When the viewer sees several pieces together, however, it becomes very apparent that the images are human. She uses size and position to indicate that these are to be perceived as human parts. She feels her pieces must be life-size or a little larger to encourage this understanding. Many of her pieces are meant for floor placement. When placed in this way they look like they are emerging from a structure built in the earth.

Hayakawa wants her work to have a symbolic meaning and a spiritual character, but doesn't ignore the very physical character of her work. Hayakawa says she takes great joy in sports. It is from this joy in the physical that she gets her feeling for balance and strength. For her, some of the best moments in life involve the sense of timing, momentum, and energy associated with physical activity. In these peak moments we experience ourselves in a timeless, perfect moment. Hayakawa has experienced these moments while swimming and surfing. She tries to put the energy of these moments into every piece she makes.

Hayakawa entered the University of California at Santa Barbara in 1967. She started as a painting major; her B.A. degree required that she take a good many courses in the humanities as well. At Santa Barbara she studied ceramics with Michael Arntz and Sheldon Kaganoff. She enjoyed her undergraduate years, many visiting artists came through and contributed to the feeling that ceramics was an exciting field. The atmosphere of innovation and experimentation that prevailed during that era greatly appealed to her. In her work she experimented with Funk imagery; she used punning imagery and tried to make people laugh. She made a series of "Woman Kits" in which she dealt with issues of contemporary women. Her senior project was a performance called "The Wedgettes." In this dance performance piece she persuaded some of her fellow students to use the movements and gestures of ceramic artists. She received her B.A. degree in art from Santa Barbara in 1972. In the fall of 1972 she went on to the University of Washington in Seattle to pursue an M.F.A. degree. She studied with Howard Kottler, Patty Warashina, and Bob Sperry. She studied alongside a very

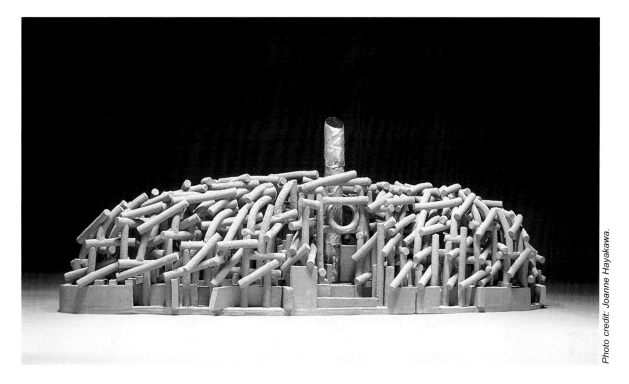

Photo credit: Joanne Hayakawa.

Cage, *ceramic sculpture, 26" x 53" x 16", 1995. Hayakawa made the main part of the form using a gritty, red colored, mid-fire body. She used this body because it is strong and has a low shrinkage. She made the tube in the center of the piece using a porcelain clay body.*

Hayakawa conceived of the piece as a large shoulder-like form with a spine-like tube running up a channel in the middle of the structure. She started building the torso-like form by making a large thick slab (5/8" thick) for the base. She let the slab become cheese hard, then began to place the small rectangular slabs at the base of the piece to wall off the base and give it structure and support. It was on this foundation that she built the piece. She let the piece become firm and she cut it into three separate parts. She did this to allow for easier loading and firing and to make the piece easier to move. She made these cuts as unobtrusive as possible. She now began building on top of the foundation and created an elaborate labyrinth out of extruded dowel-like clay pieces. She scored and slipped these forms and joined them together. She built this structure in such a way as to create a web work that became stronger as she kept adding parts. She left a channel open in the middle for the later placement of the tubular form.

The tubular form in the middle of the piece is about 16" long and 3" in diameter. Hayakawa made this form from an extruded porcelain tube. She covered the tube with whipped porcelain (she added vinegar and whipped the porcelain into an air filled mixture). She slathered it over the surface of the tube. When she finished, she cut the tube into two parts so she could fire it without warping. During the building process she worked each day for five hours or so. When the piece was nearly complete, she cleaned and finished it. Hayakawa wanted the viewer to see the contrast between the tense, linear, spine-like tube and the labyrinthine torso form. It took approximately ten days to build the piece from start to finish and two days to complete the cleaning process.

Hayakawa glazed the torso by sifting a dry powdery glaze on the surface of the wet clay. This glaze has a strong crawling texture and a dry surface. She applied the dry glaze with a kitchen sieve of standard design (eight or ten mesh). She applied the glaze until it was quite thick and appeared to have completely covered the clay. She always wears a mask when she uses this application strategy. When she had finished forming and glazing the piece, Hayakawa covered it in an airtight bag for 24 hours. She then began to expose it to air. At first she only allowed this exposure for a few minutes but each day increased the drying time. The drying process took two weeks.

Until firing, she had to be careful when touching the surface, as it was easily disturbed. She placed the piece in the kiln as soon as possible, carrying it carefully so as not to disturb the dry powder. Hayakawa single fired the large form to cone 2 in an oxidation atmosphere in an updraft kiln fueled with natural gas. Once fired, the glaze was quite strong and durable.

Hayakawa now began to glaze the porcelain tube. She sprayed a clear glaze on the surface of the porcelain tube and fired it to cone 10 in a globar kiln in oxidation. She then sandblasted the tube in an uneven pattern, creating a partly shiny, partly mat surface. After this firing she painted a gold luster on the porcelain surface and fired that to 018. In the photograph you can see the luster painted tube inside the complex structure of the torso.

strong group of students including Mark Burns, Bob Milnes, and Ann Currier. She worked on a series of small bird cage environments, another of fish, and another of shirts (made from clay). She used her environment as a source for her subject matter. She made fish pieces because she was in Seattle on Puget Sound. In her work at this time she was swept away by the energy and persuasiveness of the Funk movement. Her work differed from much of Funk only in its insistence on a very elegant design sense and a strong tendency to deal with visual/verbal puns and rebus images. She earned an M.F.A. degree in ceramics in 1974. Hayakawa took her first teaching job in 1974 as an instructor at California State University in Los Angeles. She was finishing up her work for the M.F.A. degree at the same time. While this was difficult, she enjoyed teaching and felt she learned from it.

In the fall of 1974 Hayakawa went to teach at the University of South Florida in Tampa. Again using her environment as a source of subject matter, she made work using images of birds. The region around Tampa is known for its bird life. At this time, however, she began to change the character of her work. She began to feel that she wanted her work to be truly her own and less influenced by any movement, including the Funk movement. She no longer wanted to make work marked by irony and punning, instead she wanted

Detail of **Cage**. Here we can clearly see Hayakawa's strategy of building with densely packed groupings of peg-like forms.

her work to be calm and serious in character and convey a sense of dignity. She looks back on this time as one in which she made some difficult decisions. She felt she was at the end of the line and needed another place to go. She had to trust that her audience would respond to this more serious mood, would not dismiss it, but instead be moved by it. Though the process of change took a number of years she began making these changes in her work while she was still in Florida. The manifestation of this new mood took the form of a series of pieces with an auto-biographical theme. In these

pieces she used the image of the fan and folded paper. It has been pointed out that the fan is a strongly Japanese image. Though Hayakawa is very much an American, born and brought up in California, she is also very much aware of her Japanese heritage.

Hayakawa taught in Tampa for three years, then decided to return to southern California. Her family and her roots were there and she liked its cultural atmosphere influenced by a large Asian population. She moved back to California in 1977. The move was not without its difficult consequences. She could only find part-time teaching jobs and from 1980 to 1982 had to work as a legal secretary to supplement her meager earnings as an adjunct instructor in various ceramic programs. Her work suffered as a result. In 1982, however, she obtained a full-time teaching position at San Diego State University. She was now able to return to intensive creative work in clay. The process of taking up the work again was difficult. It taught her a great deal, however, for she now saw that her identity was as an artist and that she had little choice in the matter. She began new pieces - first a group of shelf-like structures and later, architectural structures. She became interested in making pieces that establish a relationship with the viewer because of their human scale and their figural position and attitude.

In 1989 she became very interested in architectural tile work. She traveled to Italy, to the ancient but still very vital ceramic center of Faenza. She went on to Sèvres outside of Paris. Sèvres also is an impor-

tant ceramic center with a long tradition. In the U.S. she traveled to Doylestown, Pennsylvania, to the home of the Moravian Pottery, famous for its tile work. She feels that this study is now coming to fruition; she is doing a commission for the city of San Diego and is using her imagery in the tile format. She continues to teach at San Diego State University.

Hayakawa has centered her work around its imagery from the very beginning. She has struggled in recent years to deepen her imagery and make it more personal. When she began her work in ceramics, she conveyed her imagery primarily through the medium of the painted ceramic surface. Now she uses ceramic form as her medium of expression. It is fascinating to see the way Hayakawa has transformed her work from two-dimensional imagery to three-dimensional, and from its ironic Funk-derived imagery to an imagery that has a strong emotional and symbolic content.

Photo credit: Joanne Hayakawa

Joanne Hayakawa.

Kirk Mangus

Kirk Mangus is a ceramist with a strong experimental bent. Mangus has always wanted to master as many materials and work strategies as possible. He uses a variety of forming, glazing, and firing methods. While his materials and techniques can vary a great deal, his work is unified by his imagery, which is direct and expressive.

Luster Amphora, 12" x 5" x 5", 1991. This piece has a strong resemblance to many of George Ohr's pieces. The florid ornamentation and extended handles are especially reminiscent of Ohr's work. Ohr is a potter whom Mangus particularly reveres.

Skull Vase, 5" x 8" x 4-1/2", oxidation atmosphere, glaze and overglaze enamels, 1991. Mangus used a pinch-forming strategy to create this piece. He enjoys pinch forming because it is such a direct way to make pieces. He also enjoys demonstrating that this low prestige method can be used to create strong pieces. Mangus first fired this piece to cone 1, then applied the overglaze enamel colors and fired to cone 017. Mangus developed a glaze full of small bubbles that he applied to this piece to create its foamy surface.

Mangus works with many clays and clay bodies. He likes to use the clays that are locally available near his home in Kent, Ohio. Ohio is famous for its clays, some of which are very widely used. A local clay that Mangus likes very much is the Fredricksburg fire clay from Berlin, Ohio. It has good green strength and is a very strong clay when fired. Mangus mixes it with stoneware clay and kaolin or red clay and sand. He has also found a local source for a beautiful orange clay that by itself matures in the mid-fire. Mangus feels it is especially rich when used in wood-fired bodies.

He bought 90 tons of it and had it dumped on his property. He mixes it with XX Saggar for cone 9 work.

Mangus uses a great many forming methods. He loves to throw and forms many of his pieces on the wheel. He often uses a standup treadle wheel because he finds it easy to control the speed. It is especially useful when he wants to throw very slowly. He also uses pinch and coil forming methods. He often combines throwing and coiling. The "coil and throw" method is useful because it combines the virtues of hand and wheel forming. He first

throws a base form, then joins a fat coil (about 3" thick) to the lip of the form. He then throws the coil and gains about 4" or 5" of height. He lets this section become firm, then repeats the process a number of times to attain the height he wants. He then finishes the piece.

Mangus also likes to use press mold methods. In this technique he presses clay into absorbent bisque-fired press molds. If there is imagery in the mold wall he can simultaneously create the form and reproduce the mold's embedded imagery. Mangus uses a great deal of relief imagery in his work. He

Luster Bowl, *5" x 12" x 3", 1989. To create this piece, Mangus used a very simple clay body made from 50% red clay and 50% fire clay. Its high percentage of fire clay insured that the body wouldn't stick to the press mold. Mangus formed the base structure of this piece using a pinch-form strategy. He then pressed clay into bisque ware press molds to create the sides of the piece and to reproduce the mold's embedded imagery. This piece is closely related to Arretine ware made by the Roman potters of Arretium (modern day Arezzo) in northern Italy. They used bisque ware molds to create their ware. Mangus studied this ware at Arezzo. In his version of this work Mangus uses the same sort of press mold; Mangus used imagery similar to that used by the Roman potters when he made this piece. He then glazed the piece with the following recipe:*

Luster glaze, cone 01

Gerstley borate	*60*
Nephaline syenite	*40*
Copper carbonate	*3*

This simple recipe is very high in flux and very low in silica. Because it contains no clay, it settled fairly easily and Mangus had to stir it often during the glaze application. This glaze covers the piece with a thick, rich, highly dappled surface. The luster film itself is quite thin but it must rest on a thick shiny glaze foundation. Therefore, luster surfaces are typically fairly thick. While the thick glaze layer could have obscured the clay imagery, Mangus used its highly varied surface to highlight it. Mangus used a low-fire reduction cooling method called "striking" to create this fired surface. It is this that enabled him to create the bright purple pink color and the lustrous surface. Both the color and the luster come from the reduction of copper. This type of lustering process requires a heavy reduction at a low temperature. He carried it out during the cooling cycle. The heavy reduction encouraged the copper atoms to migrate to the surface of the piece and to change from a carbonate or oxide to a pure metal. This created a reflective metallic film on the surface of the glaze. To use this method Mangus fired the kiln to cone 01 in a normal firing. He then let the temperature fall to a dull red heat 1200° F, closed the damper, sealed the firing chamber, and turned on the burners. To ensure that the temperature would not rise, he sealed the area around the burners to stop air from entering the firing chamber. He kept the burners on for five to ten minutes. Using a flashlight, he looked inside the firing chamber. When he pointed the flashlight at the ware, he saw reflections of the light bouncing off the surface of his pieces. This told Mangus his pieces were taking on a metallic sheen where the copper was turning to metal. Once Mangus was satisfied that he had good luster surfaces he turned off the kiln and let it cool slowly.

does this by carving, impressing, and incising his clay -a method he feels emphasizes the clay body while giving the piece personality and energy.

Sometimes Mangus finishes his pieces using a very thinly applied glaze. In this way he can add a light sheen to the surface of the piece without hiding the clay with a thick covering of glaze. Mangus feels that this sort of finish retains the freshness he sees in the piece while it is still moist. Contrasting with these thin clay-oriented surfaces, he also works with thick, rich, luster surfaces. To do this he works with a low-fire reduction cooling method called "striking." This enables him to create bright color and lustrous reflections on the surface of his pieces. Both the color and luster come from the reduction of copper. He reduces during the cooling cycle - a classic method first applied by ceramists in the Middle East in the 9th century and later in Spain and Italy. A heavy reduction encourages the copper atoms to migrate to the surface and change from a carbonate or oxide to a pure metal. This creates a reflective metallic film on the surface of a ceramic glaze. The subject of kiln firing in all its variety is fascinating to Mangus. He has made it a point to learn how to best use a wide variety of kilns and firing types. He fires in wood, salt, gas, and electric kilns.

Mangus foamy glaze

Kaolin	25
Gerstley borate	25
Whiting	25
Bone ash	25

Imagery is very important to Mangus. The imagery often has autobiographical overtones, illustrating events and people in his life. At the beginning of his career he felt he didn't draw well enough to use human imagery, so his first imagery was of insects, but he conceived of these insects as anthropomorphic and as stand-ins for humans. In 1977 Mangus began to use figurative imagery. It was expressive and almost childlike in character. It was easy for him to draw the figure on his pieces and he saw that these images were working well. In fact these highly stylized images went well with his forms, far better than anatomically correct imagery would have. He now uses figural imagery on many of his pieces and it has become an important feature in his work. Many see

Photo credit: Kevin Olds.

*Close-up detail - **Man with Glasses**, 1992. A carved red clay body with colored slips, salt fired to cone 2. This is a good example of Mangus' simplified and expressive drawing style.*

197

Photo credit: Kevin Olds.

Left: Big Carrot Jar, 34" x 18" x 18", reduction atmosphere, 1995. Mangus used a light colored cone 10 body to create this piece.

Mangus cone 10 clay body

Fire clay	*50*
Kaolin	*50*
Potash feldspar	*20*
Flint	*10*
Silica sand	*10*

Coil and throw methods are very effective for creating large pieces and that is the method used by Mangus for this piece. He first threw a bowl shape, then firmly joined a fat coil (about 3" thick) to the lip of the bowl. He then threw the coil and gained about 4" to 5" of height. He let this section become firm, then repeated the process a number of times to attain the height he wanted.

Mangus created the imagery on the surface by carving into the clay with a large knife. The walls of the piece are 1/2" thick so he had to be careful not to cut all the way through the clay wall.

Mangus used a very thinly applied glaze surface on this piece. He wanted to keep the freshness that he saw in the wet clay. In this way he was able to add a light shine to the surface without covering the clay with a thick and impenetrable layer of glaze. He fired to cone 10 in a reduction atmosphere in a wood-fired kiln. Notice the soft blue color at the base - this is a product of reduction cooling. Mangus built the kiln without a grate. During the three-day firing, charcoal built up in the firebox. Then at the end of the firing, he pushed the charcoal up against the piece, partially burying it. The charcoal encouraged continued reduction as the piece cooled and produced the soft blue color.

humor in this imagery; humor is very important to Mangus. He says he takes it very seriously and never wants it to slip into parody, but he values the energy and life force of humor.

Mangus consciously tries to learn as much as he can about the way pieces were made by ceramists in the past. When he finds a type of work from the past that he thinks he can learn from, he tries to replicate it in his own way, with his own materials. Therefore his "copies" become brand new objects, with a life of their own and with a unique character.

Mangus has thought a great deal about the concepts of beauty and ugliness. He feels people acquire their ideas of what beauty and ugliness are very early in their lives. He seeks to explore the frontiers of our ideas of beauty and ugliness, to make people reexamine their ideas about these attributes and to make them see the richness and energy in what they may not be willing to look at. Mangus is willing to use imagery that is raw and "unfinished." He believes it has its own kind of beauty and vitality. He notes that some of those who welcome vital and challenging sculpture are put off by pottery with the same characteristics. It is a matter of expectations. Mangus wants to be able to make pottery that, in the sculptor Jean Dubbufet's memorable phrase, can "be seen naked with all the creases of its belly."

Mangus' father was an art teacher in a high school in the western Pennsylvania town of Mercer. His father became interested in clay in the 1960s. A few nights a week he commuted to the Cleveland Institute of Art to study with Toshiko Takeazu who taught there at that time. Mangus would often accompany his father on these trips. He grew up around clay and became quite used to it and was encouraged to work in it.

In 1971 Mangus went to college at the Rhode Island School of Design. He says of this now that it was "the greatest experience of my life." He had decided to major in sculpture or painting rather than ceramics. He saw ceramics as part of his father's world. In the summer of 1972, after his freshman year, he went to Penland on a scholarship. He was a driver and a janitor and his pay was room, board, and studio classes. He wanted to take sculpture classes but none were offered at Penland at the time, so he signed up for ceramic classes. A number of ceramists taught at Penland that summer including Don Reitz, Byron Temple, Mary Law, and Warren Mackenzie. He spent the summer making ceramic pieces and immersing himself in the world of ceramics. He remembers especially, long and heated conversations about throwing, glazes, firing methods, and all sorts of ceramic work, both ancient and contemporary. When he went back to Rhode Island that fall he signed up for ceramics and never looked back. He studied with a large and very strong group of teachers: Norm Schulman, Wayne Higby, Biz Littell, Chuck Hindes, and Jun Kaneko. He started out making pots. His favorite form was a kind of abstract mug. Many ceramists were experimenting with the mug form at the time; it was a wonderful form for experimentation. Students and faculty all over the country were making great numbers of bold and experimental pieces. Mugs are small and can be made and fired quickly. The mug is an excellent teaching vehicle, it is easy to learn from them. The faculty at Rhode Island encouraged Mangus to combine his techniques to create pieces with a unique character. He loved to draw and began to draw on pots. He began to develop the work strategies and the imagery he uses today. He continued to work in other media, mainly painting on paper and wood sculpture. Mangus graduated from Rhode Island in 1975.

After graduate school he went to Philadelphia. In good part this was because Eva Kwong (who had been a fellow student at Rhode Island) was studying there (see page 133).

They were married in 1976. For the next two years he worked at the Clay Studio in Philadelphia making utilitarian pots. While he needed the income from the sale of this work, he also enjoyed making a line of pottery. "It's one of the favorite things I do," he says. He likes making the pieces and loves the intimate relationship his customers have with his pots.

In 1977 his wife convinced Mangus to apply to graduate school and he was accepted at Washington State University in Pullman, Washington. There he studied with the potter Pat Filer who also liked to draw on his pots. Mangus greatly enjoyed his two years in graduate school at Washington. He remembers it as a time of very hard and engrossing work. He made pottery, sculpture, drawings, and installations. He carried out a good deal of research in ceramic form and in the history of ceramics. He graduated from the University of Washington in 1979.

In 1980, after finishing graduate school, he spent a number of years in a succession of positions. He spent a half year as a teacher at Spokane Falls Community College in Washington, then went to Archie Bray for three months. There he worked with a local porcelain clay called Helmar. He fired it to cone 11 in a wood kiln. He and his wife Eva worked with porcelain and shared a studio. He spent a summer rebuilding a kiln for salt firing at his parents' home in Mercer, Pennsylvania. In 1981 he received a grant to go to

Kirk Mangus placing a handle.

Photo credit: Eva Kwong.

Peters Valley to intern with Katseyuki Sakezumi and learned a great deal about wood kilns there. During the following years he used Mercer as his home base and taught in various guest artist positions. The high point was a stint at the Cleveland Institute of Art during the academic year 1982/83. During this time he worked on both sculpture and utilitarian pottery. He had for a long time made utilitarian pieces to make a living from sales of this work and he liked making these objects. He says, "I make large pots and sculptural pieces because I need to and smaller pots because I like to." In the fall of 1985 he began to teach at Kent State University in Kent, Ohio, and has taught there since.

Mangus' brain is very active, he has a lot of very varied ideas about his work. He mixes and matches these to create pieces that he feels are alive and exciting. The challenge for him is to take these disparate ideas and make them all work together to make pieces with coherent and convincing character.

Jamie Walker

Jamie Walker is a ceramic sculptor who works and teaches in Seattle, Washington. His work is serious and intense but at the same time it conveys a strong sense of humor and irony. Though his imagery is purely sculptural, his medium is predominantly clay and his visual language speaks very strongly of the ceramic medium.

Photo credit: Eduardo Calderon.

Ol' Yeller, 21" x 30" x 23", 1997. Porcelain with colored glazes, fired to 2250° F. Walker used a highly workable clay body that was mixed in a de-airing pug mill to make this piece. Walker threw the forms on a potter's wheel, then assembled the various parts. All told, he threw 24 separate spherical forms. He smoothed these forms with a rib after he threw them so they were nearly finished as he removed them from the wheel. When he used these parts to assemble the piece he merely needed to smooth the forms with a rib and clean them with a sponge. Walker dried the piece by completely encasing it in plastic sheeting and then during the next few days adjusted the plastic to allow more air to enter. Finally, he slowly drew the plastic sheeting away and allowed it to fully dry.

Walker finished the piece by applying a single glaze. His glaze recipe is simple and designed to create a smooth, enamel-like surface and encourage brilliant color. He applied the glaze using a spray gun to create the smooth surface. He bisque fired the piece in a top-loading kiln and glaze fired to cone 6 in a 50-cubic-foot, front-loading kiln.

Walker has chosen to fire his sculptural pieces to maturity at cone 6. This choice is somewhat unusual for contemporary sculptural work. Most ceramic sculptors choose to work with an immature clay body, firing it to a low-fire temperature. It is generally believed that a high-fire body will deform and crack in the fire and that such bodies are not as suitable for large sculptural pieces as low-fire bodies. Furthermore, Walker uses a porcelain clay body. While it is unusual to make large sculpture using a mature cone 6 porcelain body, Walker feels there are advantages to using a body with the lower clay content of a porcelain body, which shrinks less than high clay content bodies. Most important, however, he values the dense, highly finished surfaces of porcelain. Moreover, many ceramists work at cone 6 so there is large pool of information available to the ceramist working at this firing temperature. Walker has little trouble with cracking or deformation in his pieces. Once he knows where a form is likely to crack, settle, or deform, he strengthens that area.

Walker purchases his clay body from a commercial supplier already mixed in a de-airing pug mill. As a result, the body is very well mixed and highly workable. Its recipe differs from a high-fire porcelain in two ways, it contains fluxes strong enough to cause the body to mature at cone 6 rather than cone 9 and it has a high grog content. The grog strengthens the body and

further reduces shrinkage, thus further helping to ward off warping and cracking. Most of the time Walker wants a very smooth clay surface and grog can interfere with this. To smooth these surfaces Walker holds the rib at an oblique angle and slides it along the clay. This suppresses the grog. Occasionally he wants to keep a section of the rough, pebbly, grogged surface and does not smooth this area.

Walker likes working at cone 6. He feels it offers the durability of cone 9 bodies. Cone 6 bodies resist warping and cracking and are very strong. The bond between glaze and body is stronger than it can be at low-fire temperatures. Color has always been very important to Walker and cone 6 allows the use of a broad color range. He likes the porcelain body type because it makes such a good ground for brilliant color. He likens the brilliant white surface of his clay body to the gesso ground used by painters. Light hits his translucent glazes, penetrates this color layer, reflects off the white body and back through the glaze. This "bounce effect" creates a very strong and brilliant color effect.

Walker throws many of his forms on a potter's wheel, then assembles the various parts. He likes using the wheel to make his forms because thrown forms are one piece with few seams. He can finish the forms while they are still on the wheel. After he throws them, he smooths them with a rib so they are nearly finished as he removes them from the wheel.

When he uses these parts to assemble the piece he merely needs to clean the forms with a sponge. He then assembles the piece. The wheel allows flexibility in the sizes and shapes he can make and doesn't require the creation of the many molds he would need if he used mold-forming methods.

Walker hand forms much of his work. He feels he spends about 50% of his work time at hand-forming tasks. This may mean making a totally hand-formed piece or a piece that he first throws then radically alters using hand-forming methods. Walker uses such hand-forming methods as pinching, coiling, and solid forming. He has made a number of pieces featuring tendril-like forms. He pulls the clay as one pulls a handle, then assembles the tendrils. He may use 50 or 60 of these tendrils on a single piece.

Walker must deal with the problems associated with drying complex sculptural forms. He does this in a number of ways. First of all, as has been noted, shrinkage, warping, and cracking are all caused by clay. The low clay content of his bodies assures a small amount of shrinkage, warping, and cracking. Secondly, he uses a deliberate and well thought out drying process. Walker dries his pieces by completely encasing them in plastic sheeting. He leaves them completely covered for a few days to ensure that all parts of the piece have a similar moisture content. He then adjusts the plastic sheeting so a bit of air can enter. As the days pass he continues his adjustments to allow more air to enter. Finally, he slowly draws the plastic sheeting away from the piece and allows it to fully dry. The whole process takes a week and a half, a short drying time for a large complex sculptural form, but it works for Walker.

For the first time in years Walker is using a simple application of a colored glaze to finish his pieces. For many years he created complex surfaces using colored slips, textured glazes, and colored washes made from commercial stains. He sometimes used as many as nine layers before applying the final clear glaze. He began to feel he was getting carried away with surface and decided to move toward very simple glaze surfaces and colors. He now uses this strategy to finish all his pieces. His glaze recipe is simple and designed to create a smooth enamel-like surface and to encourage brilliant color. Walker applies the glaze using a spray gun. This glaze application is smooth and devoid of texture and gives the surface an industrial character. His glaze color is clear, strong, and often quite brilliant. He likes its striking appearance. Walker fires his work to cone 6 in an electric kiln.

Walker's imagery has its roots in real objects, everyday forms that rarely claim our attention. He simplifies these images until they appear to be totally abstract. Thus he takes a real object and renders it as the most abstract of forms.

Close-up of **Ol' Yeller.** Notice the smooth, clean joins. They are important to the character of this piece and give it its "industrial finish."

Walker's form imagination is that of a potter's. His form grammar consists in good part of the classic forms of the potter - bowl, sphere, and dome. We associate these forms with clay and this helps give his work a clay identity. His choice of form imagery is in part decided by what he knows about his material and the methods he favors to form it. These pottery derived forms are at the core of his work and he is as tied to them as any potter. The difference is in the intent. He doesn't want us to see them as vessel forms but rather as sculptural forms. It is his challenge to use these familiar forms in such a way that they look not like a group of stacked pots, but rather as

components of completely sculptural pieces.

Walker had an unusual introduction to clay. When he started his senior year in high school, he was a bit aimless and unmotivated. His older brother, Steve, who was working in sculpture, was worried about this and decided ceramics might appeal to Walker. He thought it might get him involved in a positive activity and might help his general view of the world. He let Walker use his hand-built kick wheel and his electric kiln. With this encouragement Walker did indeed become very interested in ceramics and began to work on it intensively. His brother also introduced him to an

Photo credit: Eduardo Calderon.

Passages, *installation at the William Traver Gallery, Seattle, Washington, 1997. Glazed porcelain, fired to 2250° F. Walker threw most of these pieces and used hand-forming methods to alter and assemble them. He made the form with tendrils at the top of the piece by pulling the clay as one would pull a handle. He made about 20 of these forms, then assembled them to create the piece. This photograph is of a section of an installation. Walker likes the installation format because he can show us what happens when he places a group of closely related objects together. Furthermore, installations encourage a viewer to walk around them to view them from different angles.* **Passages** *was intended to completely envelop the viewer, with the individual pieces seeming to float in a dream-like state. Walker says of the pieces that make up this installation, "The pieces are autobiographical in the sense that they represent symbols and objects from my past and present memory. Toys, plants, and animals all serve as potential starting points for these forms." He wants the pieces to work on the level of physical sensation and not just on a purely intellectual level.*

accomplished local potter, Ruth Newman, and she became his first mentor. He attended college at the University of Washington from 1976 to 1981. When he went to college, he thought he would prepare for a "normal" professional life and aimed for a degree in the liberal arts program. Ceramics, he thought, would be an excellent second major. However, as time went on, he got very involved in ceramics and it began to play the primary role in his life. As a student of the University of Washington he had access to one of the finest ceramic programs in the country. He had the opportunity to work with Robert Sperry, Patty Warashina, and Howard Kottler. He worked especially closely with Sperry and considers him to be the strongest influence on his work. At this time Walker was mainly making simple, saleable, functional forms thrown on the potter's wheel. He made items such as small covered jars and sushi plates. He didn't use the abstract, materials-oriented imagery such as the patterns of poured and dipped glaze found on most utilitarian pieces. He was

Traver Installation (an older piece), 1989. In this photograph Walker is standing among his pieces in the installation. He built these forms using a combination of throwing and hand-forming methods. Walker built these pieces in segments and used metal rods to join the forms. At this time he was using surfaces that had strong visual textures. The five sculptures (Neptune, Uranus, Mercury, Venus, Earth) included in this installation were part of a body of work he concentrated on from 1988 to '90 which reflected his interest in astronomy and its history. These particular pieces began to take form based on the Latin symbol for each planet. Walker also read material on Greek, Roman, and Chinese planetary myths and modern astronomical research. He used these researches as sources for his choices of image, form, and color.

interested in highly painted, multi-layer glaze surfaces. He now characterizes this work as a marriage of abstract expressionism and Funk imagery. This was (and is) an unusual combination and it had the advantage of being highly personal. Walker had a good start in ceramics and soon, even as an undergraduate, was showing and selling his work at shops and galleries around the country. He was making a living from his pots and was quite proud of this and still is. He graduated

with two degrees and two majors; he received a B.A. degree in East Asian history and a B.F.A. degree in art with an emphasis on ceramics.

In 1981 Walker applied for entrance to the master's program of the Rhode Island School of Design in ceramics and was accepted. There he worked with Jacquelyn Rice, Jan Holcomb, and Chris Staley. His graduate thesis consisted entirely of utilitarian vessel work with a strong design aesthetic. Walker graduated with a M.F.A.

degree in ceramics from the Rhode Island School of Design in 1983. Later that year he left for Berkeley, California, to set up a studio. He thought the Berkeley area would be an interesting place where he could make a good living making utilitarian pots. However, many others had the same idea. There were many ceramists in the area around Berkeley, making utilitarian ware and the market was saturated. Furthermore, the demands of production work

Macro, 1997, 50" x 72" x 10". *Porcelain with colored slips and glazes, fired to cone 6. Lobby mural for the Metropolitan Park Tower Office Building, Seattle, Washington. This is a wall mural set in a recessed alcove. The architect designed this 5' x 6' space for an art work and Walker was asked to carry out the commission. The setting is in a high traffic area near a bank of elevators.*

Walker says, "The installation at Metropolitan Park Tower was an interesting challenge, mostly due to the particulars of the site. I remember my first visit and the solemn quality of the lobby and elevator areas surrounded by beautiful, but monolithic red granite walls. One of my primary interests was to try and enliven the lobby and give it a unique and interesting personality. I wanted the pieces to have an immediate visual impact when entering the building or exiting from an elevator and to also attract a viewer to examine the pieces closely. Close inspection will be rewarded by discovering an endless number of subtleties and relationships between the pieces and the materials used to make them."

began to make Walker restless. The life of a production potter no longer seemed as exciting as it once had. Some of the potters in the area had taken up slipcast production and were using the method to make very highly finished pieces in large numbers. While these potters were very successful, Walker saw them as more concerned with the practicalities of the field, such as studio management, sales, and shipping, than with its creative core. Walker began to take another look at teaching. He was able to find part-time teaching jobs at a number of community centers. These didn't pay well but he enjoyed teaching and found it encouraged lots of ideas.

In 1984, as his interest in utilitarian production was waning, he began to shift to sculptural work. He was showing his work a good deal by this time. At this period he mixed utilitarian and sculptural forms in his exhibitions. In the spring of 1985 he taught at Ohio State as a visiting artist. From March to July of 1986 Walker was invited to work at the Kohler Company's Arts/Industry Program. There he created some very large forms, including a group of sculptures 12' to 14' tall. During this period he labored to develop his work. He had been interested in the work of sculptors, especially contemporary sculptors for some time, now his studies in this area deepened. Sculpture became a source for his work. He combined his interest in sculpture with the forms, the work strategies, and the spatial sense of a potter. During this period, as he began to really commit to sculpture, he came to look at teaching in a positive light. In the school year 1988/89 he took his first full-time teaching position at San Diego State University. At the end of 1989 he left California for a position at the University of Washington. He feels that the program in Washington is very strong and he enjoys working alongside Patti Warashina.

He feels that in recent years he has been getting much more of his imagery from his own personal sources. He has stopped working with complex multi-layer slip and glazed surfaces and begun to use highly saturated, single color surfaces with an industrial character. He creates much of his work as groupings of mid-sized multi-part forms. He is also interested in large work. In recent years he has been experimenting with a group of large pieces meant for outdoor placement. He likes outdoor work because it is a wonderful visual environment for sculpture and allows him to work in the large scale without worrying about space limitations.

Walker loves the ceramic medium, it is in this medium that he has chosen to make his sculptures. He feels very strongly, however, that he does not want to make work in which there is a distinction between what is going on in ceramics and what is going on in the general art world. He sees the ceramic medium not as a limiting factor, but rather one that is liberating and powerful. He honors the traditions of our medium and wants to learn from them though he does not want to be limited by them.

Jamie Walker in his studio working on two hand-formed porcelain pieces with floral imagery.

develop his work in reduction cooling. In this work Neely blended European and Asian firing technologies.

As his stint in Kyoto was ending, Zeller encouraged Neely to apply for a teaching position at Utah State University. He was asked to join their program. He taught ceramics alongside the sculptor/ceramist Larry Elsner. Elsner, trained as a sculptor, invented his own way of creating surface imagery in ceramics and produced an elegant group of ceramic pieces. Unfortunately, he died at a comparatively young age; Neely remembers him with great fondness. At this point Neely knew what kind of approach to ceramic work he wanted to take. His work was then a blend of the functional and the experimental and it remains so now. He continues to experiment with clay bodies and interesting ways of firing them. For him, invention is very important and when it blends well with the demands of utility, he feels he is doing what he should be doing.

Neely's work is strongly influenced by his knowledge of clay bodies and the way they act in the fire. He first began to understand the importance of this when working in Japan. At that point he was working with blue and white painted porcelain and was very involved with drawing on the surface of his pots. When he began to fire in a wood kiln, in his own studio, he saw that the action of the wood ash obliterated his complex drawn imagery. He would have to give up either his complex

imagery or his wood kiln. He changed the focus of his work from the brush to the fire and fire has been his focus ever since. He loves the interaction of the fire and the clay.

While some contemporary ceramists have a poor opinion of experiments that have a technological basis, Neely enjoys these experiments and uses the technology as a way to encourage the creation of very special pieces. Furthermore, Neely's experiments have a special flavor because he aims for results that are not dry and pedantic but that speak of the life of the clay and the fire. At first glance the work looks very traditional and in some ways it is. Neely is

working off of such fire centered traditions as Bizen and Shigaraki from Japan and the Silla Ware of Korea. On the other hand Neely uses methods that he has invented and continues to invent to make work that cannot have been made in the past. His experiments with additions to his clay bodies or experiments with kiln atmosphere and firing require an understanding of the input of ceramic science that would not have been possible in the past. Ceramics, like any other art, requires constant renewal. Neely has chosen an interesting way to attain this goal.

Neely's imagery is marked by his long stay in Japan and his unusually rich understand-

Blue and White Bowl *(an older piece), reduction fired porcelain, diameter 4", 1975. Neely formed this piece on the wheel and fired it to cone 10. He made this in Alfred upon his return from Japan. The painted imagery shows a careful study of classic Japanese blue and white ware.*

Photo credit: John Neely.

Bowl, light stoneware clay covered with an iron bearing slip, fired to cone 9. The fuel was cottonwood. After the cone went down, Neely cooled the kiln in a reducing atmosphere to about 1450° F; then put the kiln into a light reoxidation atmosphere. This accounts for the red color. Neely says, "The yellow rivulets are the result of ash falling on the pot and the crystal growth was a fortuitous accident."

ing of Japanese culture. Many of the utilitarian Japanese stoneware pots are known for their rich surfaces. Building on this tradition, Neely creates very active surfaces marked by strong patterns. He is also a great admirer of Panari ware from Okinawa. This ware was fired to a high earthenware temperature without any glaze. This work is marked by bands of color and reminds Neely of some of his own experiments. His pieces also speak of an intimate understanding of the ceramic ware of Shino and Bizen. In Neely's pieces we see the strong influence of these traditions.

Neely's imagery is also influenced by his explorations of ceramic technology, especially of clay body and firing technology. Neely combines various technologies, centering around clay body experiments, to create rich and innovative surfaces. These pieces are virtuoso explorations of the technology but always at the service of aesthetics. In a very revealing statement (one that is often quoted) in which he deals with the mixture of technology, tradition, and aesthetics he says, "All the technology available, however, doesn't seem to make it easier to produce really good pots. Throughout history it seems that good potters have managed to make good pots regardless of the level of available technology. It does seem significant, though, that they kept pushing the limits of the technology, striving to understand the mechanism of their craft. I see many of today's potters, myself included, engaged in a similar struggle. As I open the kiln I find myself wishing that, were Kazuo Yagi or other greats of the past peering over my shoulder as I inspect the ware, one might someday let slip "Nice cooling . . . "

Photo credit: Walter Wu.

John Neely demonstrating at a symposium in the pottery town of Shui-li in central Taiwan.

Aurore Chabot

Aurore Chabot makes sculptural pieces distinguished by the crowded inlay surfaces she integrates into large, angular sculptural forms. Chabot first experimented with inlay in the late 1970s.

Chabot uses a highly plastic, white colored low-fire earthenware clay body to make her sculptural forms. She adds grog to this base clay for strength and adds sawdust to the clay to retain moisture and discourage cracking. Chabot makes some of the elements of the sculptural forms using hand-forming methods and some using press-forming methods in molds. She uses a combination of pinch and coil construction strategies for the hand-formed work. She builds the walls of her pieces a few inches at a time, letting the top part of the form stiffen to ensure that the piece doesn't slump or fall during the building process. She continues the building process, establishing a rhythm of building and stiffening until she has finished the piece.

Photo credit: Balfour Walker.

If You Cracked Open a Football While Sleeping, *6" x 10-1/2" x 17-1/2", earthenware, 1995. This is not so much a vessel form as an exploration of the interior of a form that is normally closed and hidden from view. Chabot would not want the piece to be used as a vessel since any use would hide the imagery in the interior and this is the main focus of the piece.*

Right: Changeling, 12" x 11" x 8", earthenware, 1996. This piece is an example of Chabot's inlay imagery. Chabot contrasted the brilliantly colored, sharp cornered, geometric shards with a surrounding matrix of soft looking, earth colored clay.

Chabot uses a highly plastic, white colored, low-fire earthenware clay body to make her pieces. It is composed of ball clay, a plastic fire clay, saggar clay, and talc. She adds grog and sawdust to this base clay. The grog and sawdust encourage good workability while the clay body is in its wet state, making the construction of complex structural forms much more feasible. These additions seem to let the clay stay wet but at the same time stiffen so she can add to the piece without risking sagging or cracking. She ages the clay and this enhances its workability a great deal. She will, in fact, store clay for as long as four years. This highly aged clay is exceptionally workable. Over this extended period the sawdust begins to break down and becomes very sticky. This allows her great freedom in constructing the piece. She doesn't add any specific amount of sawdust; she knows how the clay feels when it is optimum. The clay is slightly sticky but has a lot of body. Chabot used a denser version of the same low-fire clay body (without the addition of sawdust or grog) for the inlay sections.

Chabot made some of the elements of this piece using hand-forming methods and some using press molds. She used a combination of pinch and coil construction strategies for the hand-formed work. In this piece she made her forms as large three-sided constructions. They remind the onlooker of partially enclosed boxes. As a result, from some angles this piece has a strongly three-dimensional presence while from other angles it has the character of a maze-like semi-enclosed form. She constructs her pieces using a pinch-forming building strategy in which she uses short coil segments to form the walls. Like slabs, these walls are flat sided but unlike slab work, they have the busy textured surfaces we associate with coil and pinch forming. As the piece grew in height Chabot defined its edges with her fingers and with such tools as wooden, metal, and rubber ribs. She built up the walls a few inches at a time. She let the top part of the form stiffen to ensure that the piece did not slump or fall during the building process. She then continued the building process, establishing a rhythm of building and stiffening until she finished the piece.

To make her inlay imagery Chabot started with unfired but leather-hard clay elements made in press molds or from slabs (which she broke apart after she painted them). She then painted these with commercial underglaze colors. She rested these leather-hard elements face down on a fabric-covered board and forced the soft clay onto the backs of and into the spaces between the shards. The soft clay "glued" the fragments together and acted as a foil for the sharp imagery of the fragments.

The resulting panel is a flat-surfaced sheet of clay with embedded clay fragments. When these inlay panels stiffened, she joined them to outer slabs to create the piece. She used these image laden panels as a foil and a contrast for those parts of the piece that have no imagery. In other parts of the piece she introduced texture by carving into the leather-hard clay wall. In yet other areas she smoothed and cleaned the surface of the clay using ribs, scrapers, and dental tools. She then fired the piece to bisque.

Next she applied slips, engobes, and terra sigillatas to selected areas of the clay surfaces that had no inlay imagery. She applied a terra sigillata saturated with copper and black stains to produce chocolate or black surfaces. She painted various colored underglazes on the inside and outside walls of the piece. She used brushes to apply her slips and terra sigillatas. She applied and then sponged off a black copper oxide stain to add depth to the surface and fired the piece a second time. She contrasted the dark color of the stain with brilliant colors (such as soft earth pink and strong turquoise blue) to produce an imagery of strong contrasts. She used sponges to apply and wipe away the stains. Chabot fired this piece to cone 04 in an electric kiln for the bisque firing and to cone 04/06 in an electric kiln for the final firing.

Chabot makes her inlaid imagery by embedding fired clay elements in an unfired clay matrix, then firing the whole composite. With this work strategy she creates panels whose character is a mosaic of fragmented elements unified by their flat surface and soft clay surround. The inlay surfaces bring to mind the imagery we see in rocks with embedded fossils covered for a long time by the earth and freshly revealed.

To make her brightly painted inlay imagery Chabot starts with unfired but leather-hard clay elements. She makes these elements from slabs (which she breaks apart after she paints them) or in small press molds. She then paints these with commercial underglaze stains. She rests these leather-hard elements face down on a press mold or a fabric-covered board. She forces soft clay onto the backs of and into the spaces between the

Photo credit: Aurore Chabot.

shards. The soft clay "glues" the fragments together and acts as a foil for the angular fragments. She places the soft clay around and over the leather-hard clay elements. The fragments have already shrunk and the soft clay will shrink around them and hold them in place so they won't fall out. Chabot has dubbed her inlay process "reverse inlay." She uses this term because she turns the shards upside down and forces the clay around the back of the shards. The resulting panel is a clay surface with embedded clay fragments. She leaves the inlay form lying face down and builds the rest of the form on top of this surface. She needs to begin the building process immediately while the inlay panel is still moist. In this way she can safely join the rest of the form to the inlay panel. When not working on the piece, Chabot keeps it carefully wrapped. She also sprays the piece with water to ensure that it stays moist.

Chabot never knows what her imagery will look like until she has fired it. She doesn't want her process to be too predictable and she enjoys the surprising aspect of the process. Chabot realized from the start that her inlay imagery was a good idea but it must be shaped, developed and given an appropriate environment. She has created a strategy in which she uses her inlay surfaces as the focal point of large sculptural forms.

She fires her pieces to cone 04 in an electric kiln for the bisque firing and to cone 04/ 06

in an oxidation atmosphere in an electric kiln for the final firing.

There was not a lot of money in Chabot's family when she was young. Yet she and her brothers and sisters were encouraged to think that they could, if they worked hard, carve out intellectually stimulating careers. Chabot was intent on earning a college education. She was strongly encouraged in this by her parents and an older sister who was already in college. Also encouraging her was a teacher at an after-school art program at the Currier Gallery in Manchester, New Hampshire. She was accepted by the art department of Pratt Institute in 1967 and studied there from 1967 to 1971. She started in art education but quickly switched to fine arts - she was much more interested in preparing for a career in the fine arts than one in teaching and she wanted to take as many art courses as possible. She began by taking painting and photography, then took her first courses in ceramics. Though she liked clay a great deal, she was still not sure what medium she would specialize in. The period 1967 to 1971 was very exciting and marked by great turmoil. These years were marked by U.S. involvement in both Vietnam and Cambodia. It was a time when Chabot felt her beliefs and ideas tested in every way. It was a time, however, that was not always conducive to a careful and scholarly accumulation of knowledge. Her interest in political and social issues took

up a good deal of Chabot's time and some of her teachers began to doubt her commitment to art. Particularly in her junior year she was very serious about politics. In her senior year, however, she returned to her studies with renewed energy. She tried her hand at all sorts of art work and at one point thought she might concentrate on photography. She was especially fascinated by the way the images would appear, as if by magic, in the darkroom. She feels now that ceramics and photography have much in common in the importance of process to the creation of the work. Though tempted by photography, she never stopped making ceramics and always found ways to work in clay. She was not always encouraged in this, some of her teachers at Pratt had a very limited view of what you could do with ceramics but she stayed with it. Chabot received a B.F.A. degree from Pratt in 1971.

After college, Chabot gravitated toward clay as her life work. During the years 1972 to 1974 she elected to stay in New York City and took a few ceramic courses at the Brooklyn Museum Art School. She rented space in a cooperative studio and pursued her studies on her own. She took a great many "day jobs," working in a succession of office jobs. This was a time of recession but she found steady employment and fairly good salaries as well. Some of her jobs were in art related businesses and that was a further benefit.

Photo credit: Aurore Chabot.

*The reverse side of **Changeling**. The two sides have a very different character. This side has a maze-like character. From this angle we see quite clearly how the piece was put together.*

Detail of **Hip Hop Matilda - Chair Pairs From Down Under***, earthenware clay body, low fire. Chabot made this piece while on a visit to Australia. The photograph shows two elements of a large wall piece made of smaller fragments. These are representative of Chabot's most recent work in the multi-part wall piece format.*

Then in 1974 she moved to the mountainous, eastern Adirondack area of New York State. While living there (1974 to 1976) she worked for an extended period with Regis Brodie at Skidmore College. She attended Haystack Mountain School of Crafts where she studied with Joan Tweedy and Donna Nicholas who encouraged her to go to graduate school. Tweedy introduced her to terra sigillatas. Chabot was to concentrate on them a few years later. She taught ceramics at a local art center in Saratoga Springs, New York. She feels in hind-sight that as time went on she was gaining important experience in clay. Her pieces were still quite crude and unfinished but they were improving. Wanting to discover a sense of personal creative identity, she tried a great many strategies for creating imagery. These included patterned and sprigged imagery and inlay (the beginning of her work in this area). From 1976 to 1977 she lived in Garrison, New York, a small city on the east bank of the Hudson River about two hours north of New York City. While living there she worked at the Garrison Art and Craft Center and enjoyed its very active program. During this time she attended workshops given by artists such as Karen Karnes, Paul Soldner, and Graham Marks.

In 1977 she returned to New York City and again took up office jobs to support herself. She remembers with special fondness three stints at the Museum of Natural History where she spent time researching aspects of archaeology, paleontology, and natural history. At this time most of her forms were still thrown on the wheel. She applied to graduate programs in ceramics and in

1979 was accepted in the graduate ceramics program at the University of Colorado at Boulder. At Boulder she worked with Betty Woodman, Ann Currier, and Tom Potter. Though Chabot still used the wheel, she now cut up wheel-thrown forms and put them back together in new ways. Chabot says Woodman gave her a whole new way of thinking about the creation of ceramic forms.

As her work became more sculptural, terra sigillata surfaces became much more important to her. She very much wanted to bring the various strands of her work together to create an imagery that was her own. She continued her experiments with embedded shards and inlay imagery. A number of ceramists were experimenting with embedded shards at that time and she liked the resulting surfaces. Most of this work, however, was done by partially embedding a shard into a clay wall. Because Chabot forced soft clay between the shards, hers was an inlay technique and her pieces had a very different character. She found these experiments very exciting. Now her imagery was becoming her own. At this time she found that her wheel-thrown forms, even her cut and reassembled wheel-thrown forms, were no longer appropriate for her work. The thrown surfaces did not mesh well with the inlaid imagery. She started to develop the angular slab-built forms she uses now. She designed these sculptural

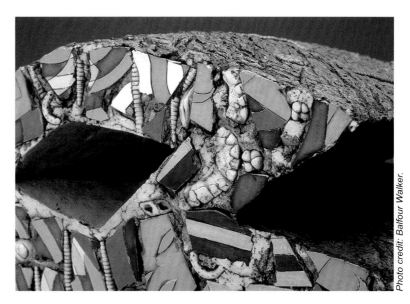

Photo credit: Balfour Walker.

Detail of **Eyecatcher**. This detail of Chabot's shard imagery gives a good idea of the complexity of her inlay surfaces. Note the earthy looking areas where Chabot pressed soft clay around the shard inlay elements.

forms to act as the armature for the angular, inlaid shard imagery.

In recent years Chabot has kept up with her explorations of her sculptural work. She has also widened her scope to include work in related formats. Aside from her large scale sculpture Chabot has become very interested in groups of small scale interrelated pieces that she hangs on the wall. Rather than trying to create a harmonious group of forms she is looking for surprising arrangements of varied forms. She is interested in the small size of the individual elements. Working with these small elements has a number of advantages: she has great freedom in the choice of forms and forming methods. Working with large forms in clay creates its own set of restraints; every time the ceramist enlarges the scale,

fewer form choices are available. On the other hand, Chabot doesn't want to be limited to small scale work. When she puts these small forms together to create a large and expansive piece, she is able to create imagery of breadth and power. Thus, she is able to have the control afforded by small scale work and the power of the large format.

Recently she has been working on the wall in a series of architectural tile installations. These have a very different character than either her sculptures or her sculptural wall pieces. This work is made for installation in a specific place and is designed to fill a specific need. Though she uses a patterned imagery that has much in common with her sculptural work, these wall pieces have a very different mood than the sculptures - they are at ease with their environment and are less private and introspective than her sculptures. It is interesting to see her characteristic imagery used in a way that is similar to her sculptural work but has been made with a very different intent.

Her forms are massive and angular. Their edges are broken and sharp, they suggest decay and aggression. She has softened these jagged forms by juxtaposing partially collapsed, softly curved forms. She uses repeated forms to create a strong rhythm. The sculptural forms work well with her clay inlay, for it too has an angular character. She combines inlaid geometric patterns, fragmented images inlaid into soft clay, and sculptural forms that carry and dramatize the inlaid imagery. The result is a body of work marked by a varied imagery that she combines to create a unified whole.

Aurore Chabot.

Jeff Oestreich

Jeff Oestreich is a thoughtful potter who concentrates on making utilitarian vessels. His pieces come from the tradition of Bernard Leach and Michael Cardew. He has been especially adept at interpreting this tradition for a contemporary audience, creating a balance between tradition and the present.

***Ewers**, soda glazed, 4" x 4" x 2", 1997. This is a scaled down version of the larger beaked pitchers Oestreich has been making for many years. He threw these forms, cut them in half, and rejoined them to make an elliptical form. He feels he can concentrate on a striking, rhythmic contour when he works with the elliptical form. The two painted pieces serve as examples of Oestreich's use of slip painted surfaces.*

Oestreich uses a light firing stoneware clay body and fires it to cone 10. Where the glaze thins out at the edges of the form, the white body encourages dramatic, light colored highlights in the glaze color that help define the form and enhance the surface imagery. He creates his pieces on the potter's wheel and often modifies the forms after taking them off the wheel. He likes leaving some throwing lines on the surface of the piece. For him, they serve as "memories" of the throwing process and he enjoys the subtle rhythms of the throwing lines.

Oestreich wants his pieces to work well when held. Sculptural ceramists rarely expect their pieces to be held, but potters who work on functional pieces are very conscious of the "holdability" of their work because functional pots are often held in the hands during use. This is very important to Oestreich and he designs his pieces so they can be held and used in a natural manner. He is very fond of the tea bowl shape because it's cradled in both hands when used.

Oestreich is fond of using relief imagery in his work. Very often this imagery takes the form of a repeated motif such as a ribbed wall. He likes to create these images and patterns right after the forming process while the clay is still fresh and easily altered. In this way, form creation leads directly to surface creation. He often uses shaping tools such as ribs, knives, or loop tools to modify the surface

Photo credit: Jeff Oestreich.

One Person Teapot, soda glazed, 6" x 7" x 6", 1997. This piece evolved from an idea Oestreich had for a different, more emphatic spout. He wanted to make a teapot that was at once sculptural and highly utilitarian. He used the striking spout form as his starting point.

of the form. He also stamps patterns into the surface of the clay. He sees stamping as a way to open up his work and introduce an imagery compatible with his more traditional surface creation methods but not associated with the work of traditional Japanese pottery. Oestreich's manipulations of the surface serve a number of purposes: they can be carried out swiftly and naturally, they allow for rich patterning, and they work well with the glazes. Furthermore, they give the inherently softly thrown forms a sense of structure - of spine. Then too, he can repeat these motifs to create a fabric-like imagery and he enjoys this a great deal. He is especially interested in African fabrics and this blend of African and Far Eastern influences may account for some of the contemporary feeling in his imagery.

It is, however, the drama of

the action of slips and glazes in the fire that is the special subject of Oestreich's imagery. Oestreich often uses slips to begin the process of creating his surface imagery. He then applies a clear surface finish. In recent years this clear surface finish has come from soda glaze firing. This surface is thin, nicely textured, durable, clear, and tightly bonded to the clays and slips it rests on. In the soda firing process Oestreich sprays soda (sodium carbonate) into the kiln at the height of the firing. The soda unites with the alumina and silica in the clay to form the clear surface finish. He has developed a group of glazes that react especially well to the soda. The application of soda encourages these otherwise stable surfaces to become active and highly flowing and the colors to brighten. In some sections of the piece, the glaz-

Beaked Pitcher, *soda glazed, 10" x 9" x 3", 1997. Oestreich threw this form, then cut and reassembled it to create the elliptical form with its sharp contour. He says of pieces of this type, "The trick is to get them to pour. The first ones didn't pour well. Then I added a slab at the top and now they do pour well." This slab not only improves the usability of the piece, it serves also to give it a visually exciting form. The checkerboard imagery is a good example of Oestreich's work with wax resist imagery.*

es pool and run off the edges of the form. The edges are light in color and highlight those areas where the form changes direction. The glazes respond strongly to his manipulation of the form. Thus they add another kind of energy to the imagery on the surface of the ware, making it richer and more complex. Oestreich chooses slips and glazes that have a mat surface. Where the soda affects them, they turn shiny while elsewhere their surface stays dry or mat. Oestreich applies his slips by painting and by dipping. He applies his glazes by dipping and splashing. He does not glaze every part of a piece. He loves to contrast the raw clay with the glazed areas. His unglazed areas are especially appealing because they have a slight sheen derived from the soda glazing. He frequently uses wax resist to create a strongly patterned imagery. He also places glaze in the cracks and crevices of the surface, applying it and rubbing the excess away to create a rich texture.

Oestreich fires to cone 9/10. He uses only a very mild reduction atmosphere because he wishes to ensure brilliant color. Toward the end of the firing he sprays soda into the kiln through an opening in the kiln wall. Soda firing (sodium carbonate) is similar to salt firing (sodium chloride). It differs in that it is nontoxic (the chloride in sodium chloride becomes a

Cornwall. MacKenzie, who had been Leach's assistant, gave Oestreich a letter of introduction and recommendation. Oestreich met the staff at the pottery including Leach and they invited him to come back in a year to work at the pottery. In his senior year Oestreich returned to Bemidji but MacKenzie continued to visit his studio and work with him. Oestreich graduated from the Bemidji State University in 1969. He was now ready to go back to England and begin his apprenticeship at the Leach Pottery. It was a very intense and rewarding experience. Leach was in his early eighties and worked in the pottery about five hours a day, five days a week. With the help of Bill Marshall, his personal assistant, Leach produced his own pots in sizable numbers. Apprentices (there were eight of them including Oestreich) learned by producing a Standardware line overseen by Marshall. After hours and on weekends, the assistants also produced their own pieces which Leach critiqued. Oestreich says the assistants largely learned by osmosis, by conversations, by the general activity in the busy studio, and from the visits of many potters. He particularly remembers the visits of Michael Cardew, Lucie Rie, and Shoji Hamada. When Oestreich returned to Minnesota he was intent on making a living from the sale of his work. Though he made very little money during the first few years, he has been able to make a fine living since then.

Photo credit: Jeff Oestreich.

*Detail of **Beaked Pitcher**. Here is a detail view of Oestreich's soda glazes. They are responsible for the soft color transition from sand to burnt orange and the texture change from a smooth surface to a highly broken texture.*

Early on, from MacKenzie and then Leach, Oestreich developed an appreciation for the quiet, understated glazes of the Far East. He was particularly interested in ash, celadon, and temmoku glazes. He used these glazes for 15 years, firing them in a gas-fired kiln. These glazes did not overpower a form or the food displayed or served on them; he valued this very highly. In 1980, however, Oestreich abandoned gas firings to investigate wood firing. He did not do this to create replicas of ancient Japanese wood-fired pots. He asked himself, "How could work using this ancient method look current?" He developed a group of glazes that would respond to the ash created by the burning of wood (fly ash). One was a yellow glaze he made quite by accident. When he applied it over a cracked slip, it looked very rich and unlike the traditional surfaces he had used previously.

In his wood-fired work, Oestreich only glazed the interiors of his pots and left the exteriors unglazed. He liked to see the flashing and fluxing of the wood ash on the unglazed clay. As time went on, he discovered that he couldn't give up glazed surfaces completely. He began to glaze the outer surfaces of his pieces again. Soon he found himself moving back to pieces that were entirely (or almost entirely) glazed. He then began to ask himself, "Why do I use wood fire when the surfaces are all glazed?" Furthermore, his wood kiln was in poor condition - if he stayed with wood he would have to rebuild it. He needed to decide whether to do this or to make a new kiln - perhaps even one suited to another mode of firing. Finally, a teaching stint at Alfred University in 1991 exposed him to oxidized soda firing. What caught his attention wasn't the overall texture of the soda surface, but the way in which glazed surfaces reacted to soda. He liked the bright colors and highly flowing and pooling glazes he got from soda. Though this was a 17th century technique, many contemporary ceramists wanted to revive it. They liked the idea of a look similar to salt fire. The gases produced in the soda glaze kiln, however, seemed to be somewhat less dangerous than the chloride gases which are a byproduct of salt firings. When Oestreich tried soda firing with his own forms and glazes, he found it very compatible with his work and he liked its unique character. After a dozen years of wood firing, he transferred his allegiance to soda firing and he continues to work in this manner. He says, however, that he is keeping an eye on possibilities for further interesting and enlivening developments.

Our image creation strategies are dictated by our state of mind and our state of mind can (and indeed must) change periodically as our expectations and desires for our work change. When Oestreich's glaze treatment changed, his forms changed as well. He felt that the forms he had been using just didn't work now that he was working with a soda glaze. When he took up soda firing with its bright nontraditional feel, Oestreich saw his forms becoming more angular and spiky. He sensed that this indicated that his work was not changing superficially but was undergoing a profound and global change. Even his interests and influences were changing. He found that while he retains his interest in the direct earthy forms and surfaces of traditional Japanese ceramics, he has become very interested in studying highly designed forms and surfaces. Art deco, with its geometric patterning and strong rhythmic cast, has become a passion for him. He has tried to integrate these approaches to imagery to mirror his vision of the world. We see in Oestreich's work the changes made over the course of a career by a potter who is acutely sensitive to shifts in the way he reacts to glazes, to forms, and to the union of the two.

Jeff Oestreich altering thrown forms.

Angelo di Petta

Angelo di Petta is a Canadian ceramist whose work is closer in spirit to European ceramics than to the ceramic work of North America. After undergraduate preparation at the Ontario College of Art, di Petta studied for three terms in the ancient ceramic institutions of the city of Faenza in Italy. Di Petta studied mold forming and complex image creation techniques, both specialties of the potters of Faenza. At this time, too, di Petta became familiar with avant garde Italian design exemplified by Italian tile design and by the work of contemporary Italian design groups.

Photo credit: Angelo di Petta.

Tubes, 4" x 5", 1995. Di Petta made these pieces from an earthenware clay body with an addition of sawdust. He pressed the clay inside a heavy cardboard tube and fired to cone 06 for the bisque fire. He then applied a cone 06 lead and chrome glaze and fired the piece to cone 06 for the final firing. Di Petta says he wanted these forms to represent the idea of a tube and the way a tube may become blocked or partially blocked.

Allegorical Landscape, *8" x 5" x 4", 1995. Di Petta built this piece by assembling slabs inside a hemispherical support form. Once he finished building the stoneware form, he covered it with a dark brown earthenware "skin." The earthenware clay cracked and blistered, creating a rich, highly textured surface. He made the black curly lines by cutting up a copper scrubbing pad and wedging bits of the copper into the clay. He fired the piece to cone 010, wet sanded it, and fired it to cone 02. He went on to multiple firings and applications of a soft blue and red terra sigillata. At this point the sigillatas pulled away, revealing the dark brown earthenware layer. He applied cone 06 and cone 010 glazes to complete the imagery.*

Di Petta uses commercially prepared plastic clay bodies and prepared casting slips. He feels these prepared mixtures are better than what he can make himself and they are very convenient. He forms his pieces using slipcast, press mold, hand-formed slab, and solid forming techniques.

Di Petta is interested in unusual ways to use traditional technologies. He often uses casting slip in unusual ways, brushing or pouring the slip on a plaster bat or in a bisque-fired form and working from these forms. His work is marked by an interest in repetitive elements whose character owes their origin to the character of the mold-forming process. This is not the only reason he is interested in mold forming. "When I first went to Italy to study in Faenza, I saw casting put to use and the thing I really liked about it was that you were working with many processes and many steps: model making, mold making, and casting and each one presents different challenges." He doesn't look upon slipcasting as an economical way to produce many identical pieces. He sees it as a way to make imagery in clay that he cannot make any other way. He likes the problem-solving

aspects of mold methods of forming. He enjoys the opportunity to create all kinds of interesting forms, repeated shapes, and cloned shapes.

He likes working with plaster, regarding it as a wonderful material in its own right. It can give him soft and clay-like imagery or imagery that is crisp, sharp, and stone-like. He likes the transformations that take place when he first works in plaster, then moves to the next step to cast the slip in the plaster mold. He feels that mold forming gives him the freedom to use clay in ways that other methods don't allow, ways that allow complex and unusual forms. He likes the fact that he doesn't have to deal only with the plastic character of clay. In mold forming he can do other things with clay. Methods that rely on the use of clay in its plastic form leave their mark and have their limits just as do other approaches to clay forming. They are so ubiquitous, however, that we often don't notice their profound impact. Di Petta is just as interested in the kinds of forms he can get when using clay in its slip form as he is in forms made from clay in its plastic state. When he does work with plastic clay, he likes to tinker with it and will often load it with a material that encourages texture and limits plasticity, such as sawdust. He experiments constantly with his forming methods, moving from solid forming to press forming to mold forming. Recently he has used the same form as the basis for a mold and as a finished, exhibited, art object. He says of this, "Lately I have carved into thick pieces, then bisque fired them and then used them as molds for further development of the piece. They are at once mold and molded."

Di Petta works with a great variety of surface finishes. In recent years he has often sanded his pieces to give them a smooth "beach stone" surface. He often leaves the clay unglazed and finishes such surfaces with a light coating of wax. Di Petta also uses slips and slip trailing strategies. While he only uses them when

Left: How Things Evolve, 16", 15", and 14" long, 1995/1998. These three parts constitute one piece. Di Petta made the first piece of this group in 1995 from a light earthenware clay body mixed in a pug mill. He assembled thick slabs to form the piece. He let them become leather hard, then carved them to create the specific shape he wanted. The piece is quite thick near its center (about 3/4") then tapers to a very thin edge. Because he created the shape by carving, this strategy is closer to a solid forming technique than to a classic slab forming one. He then fired the piece to bisque. Though it took only about an hour to make, a number of years passed before the piece was finished. It lay on his ware shelf for the next three years because he wasn't sure how he wanted to finish it. Finally, in 1998 di Petta decided he should make it part of a series of three pieces. He thought such a series would be interesting visually and that he could use it to talk about the way forms evolve. He worked out a carefully formulated sequence in which he created the second piece using the first piece as a mold. The second piece, in its turn, became a mold for the third. In this way he created "generations" of imagery.

He made the second piece of the group using a clay body he made from Redart, ball clay, and flint with the addition of a good deal of sawdust. This is a thick-walled piece with a very simple form; it took only a few minutes to make. He made the form by pressing clay into the inside surface of the first piece. Therefore, the outer form of the second piece replicates the shape of the inside surface of the first piece. This is an interesting variation on normal press mold forming techniques. He then carved out an asymmetric trench in the center of this form. Di Petta fired the piece to a low bisque (cone 010), then immersed it in water and sanded it with a waterproof emery cloth to give it a smooth "beach stone" surface.

The third piece is paper thin; di Petta painted layers of casting slips over the carved out central section of piece number two so the outer form of this last piece replicates the trench he carved on the inner part of the second piece. Because he didn't use a mold with sides to contain the casting slip, he couldn't use a simple poured slip strategy. Instead he brushed the slip over the second piece, applying one layer on top of another to build a piece of appropriate thickness. In his last step he applied the same slip with a slip trail applicator. In this way he simultaneously built up a thicker cross section and created the tangled linear patterns on the surface. It took about an hour to apply the number of layers he needed to complete the piece.

Di Petta used varied surface treatments for the pieces in this group. He applied cone 06 commercial glazes to the first piece and painted its underside with a black glaze so all surfaces were covered by glaze. Conversely, on the second piece he wanted the observer to be able to appreciate the red clay body with no covering of glaze or stain. He merely gave the fired clay body a very light coating of liquid wax. He finished the third and last piece with a commercially made, cone 06 transparent alkaline copper glaze. Where thin, it is a light blue and where it is thick, it is a darker blue. Di Petta fired this work to cone 06 in an oxidation atmosphere. He used a top-loading electric kiln of standard design. Di Petta fired the glazed forms on stilts.

Di Petta says of this group, "I like the idea that these pieces have an imagery that reminds me of the passage of time. I want to create the feeling that the piece can continue to evolve and encourage the viewer to imagine further evolutionary stages." He feels this group of pieces is especially representative of his work because he used those forming methods that are most important to him, hand forming, press molding, and slip forming. He was also very interested in creating highly worked surfaces in this piece. When he glazed the last piece, he drew a linear design with a slip trailing applicator over the surface. He emphasized these relief designs with a transparent blue glaze which becomes darker where it is thick.

he thinks it appropriate, he is very fond of glazes. When he works with glazes, he spends time and effort exploring ways to create unusual combinations of materials or unusual glaze applications. He is especially interested in the interactions between materials and between the multiple layers of the glazes he uses. Di Petta often brushes on cone 06 commercial glazes. He likes to "dope" these glazes with added materials to give them an unusual and unexpected character. He fires his pieces in a top-loading electric kiln of standard design. He fires to the low-fire temperature of cone 06 in an oxidation atmosphere. Because the immature clay bodies suitable to the low fire don't slump in the fire, di Petta doesn't need to worry about sagging and slumping. He enjoys the freedom to use flat surfaces and distended shapes that he couldn't use if he were firing his pieces to maturity.

Di Petta's imagery is oriented to the exploration of processes and ideas. Liking to play with ideas, he sets himself problems and then tries to solve them. He sees his pieces in a

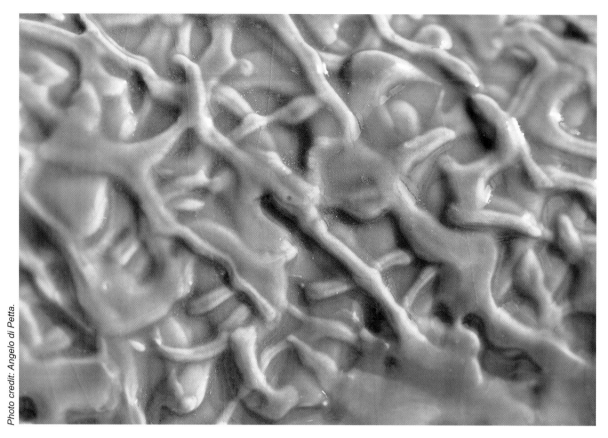

*Close-up detail of **How Things Evolve** showing the very tangled texture di Petta was able to create using a slip trailing strategy.*

three-fold way: as art objects, as a record of a process, and as the exploration of ideas through clay. He says, "I think that my pieces are about natural things, natural processes, natural occurrences. Time is important here. I use natural processes but speed them up so I can accomplish in an hour what in nature can take many years. For example, I use wet sanding. A rock on a tidal beach would come to look the same way naturally over a period of years but I speed up the process and furthermore, I am in charge of the shapes."

Di Petta was born in Italy and moved to Canada with his parents when he was eight years old. They settled in a suburb of Toronto. He had difficulty dealing with his new surroundings. Canada was strange to him. He had to learn a new language and fit into his new surroundings and his new school. He became a bit of a loner and in some ways he still is. "Because I was young it was much easier to adjust than if I had been older, but school sometimes seemed beside the point." In high school he began to take art courses and he liked them and did well in them. In grade 12 he realized that art might be an area he could study in college. He found a catalog describing the program at the Ontario College of Art in Toronto (for convenience it is usually referred to as the OCA). The program had great appeal for him. He was accepted and enrolled in 1968. Di Petta thought that environmental design or industrial design would be his main area of study in college. It was at the OCA in his introductory year that he took his first class in ceramics. At first he wasn't really impressed with clay. He says of this period that he asked himself, "What am I doing here?

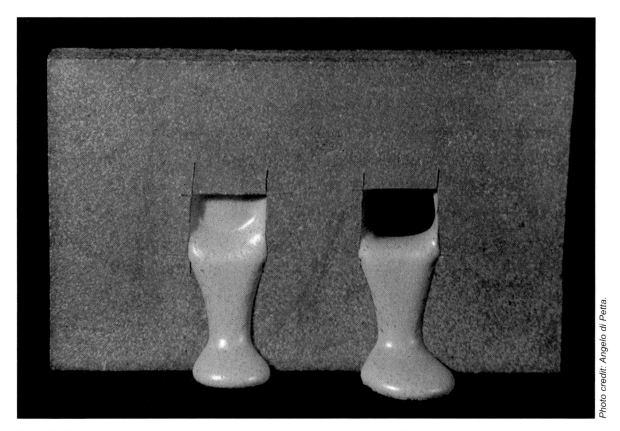

Flow Study (an older piece), 8" x 12", 1980. Here is a very early example of an image in which di Petta combined the technical with the aesthetic. He designed this piece so its materials would create the imagery during the firing. Di Petta began experimenting with this imagery after he accidentally over-fired a kiln full of low-fire ware made from a talc body. The pieces came from the kiln melted and distorted. He liked the look of the highly melted results and began to explore ways of using this effect. In this piece he worked to control and exploit the flowing imagery characteristic of over-fired talc bodies. He made quite a few of these pieces; each one was different because in each one, the inserts melted in a slightly different way. He made this piece by cutting square openings in a block of clay made from a high-fire stoneware body. He then inserted a white casting body (intended for low firing) in the openings. He laid a bed of silica sand on the kiln shelf to protect the shelf from the flowing earthenware, placed the piece on the kiln shelf, and fired it to cone 9 in a reduction atmosphere. The intense heat of the high fire melted the earthenware and its flow completed the piece.

Clay is a dirty unpredictable material. I want to be an industrial designer!" Then he took a course in metal work and liked it. He began to understand that he needed to be allowed a much freer sense of creativity than environmental or industrial design would allow. He didn't want to have to please clients and he didn't want just to design things, he needed to make them as well. At the end of his introductory year he chose to major in a program called "material art" which included metal, clay, and wood. While he liked metal, he began to appreciate the virtues of clay. In his third year he was strongly influenced by a visit he and his classmates made to a sewer pipe factory. The extruding process was fascinating and seemed to him to offer the promise of new ways to form ceramic work. He worked with this process intensively for several years. He also read about casting and though it was not taught at the OCA at that time, he found the idea of cast forming fascinating. By his fourth year at the OCA he was majoring in ceramics. He graduated from the Ontario College of Art in 1972.

Di Petta then applied to study in Faenza, Italy, at the *Istituto Statale d'Arte per la Ceramica*. Courses there are taught in Italian which wasn't an obstacle for di Petta whose family continued to speak Italian at home. In Faenza the students were taught a design-oriented approach to ceramics. They were taught to form their work using cast or press mold forming strategies and to fire at low temperatures in an oxidation atmosphere. Di Petta learned a great deal in Faenza and still remains in contact with many of his former teachers. When asked why he didn't study for a Master of Fine Arts degree in one of the well-known universities in the U.S., he answers, "I wasn't being pulled south, I was being pulled east; the Europeans seemed to think about ceramic materials and design in a way that was more appropriate to my needs." In 1973 he went to Faenza and stayed for one semester. He then went back to Toronto and worked in clay and started teaching part-time at the OCA. He also had an exhibition in a Toronto gallery, showing mostly freestanding sculptures made with thin, wafer-like forms. In all his work his approach was materials and process based and these concerns helped dictate his forms. In 1975 he was awarded a Canada Council grant, which he used to return to Italy to study in Faenza, this time for two terms. There was much to learn in Faenza and in this second period of study, di Petta set out to master these technologies and adopt them for his own work.

Di Petta returned to Canada in 1976 and took up teaching again at the OCA. Exploiting his experiences in Faenza he developed a course called Ceramic Design. The students worked with a wide variety of clay forming techniques including casting, pressing, extruding, and jiggering. They fired at the low temperatures that were emphasized in Faenza (the term faience, meaning low-fired highly decorated ware, is named after the city of Faenza). Di Petta worked with a great variety of cast forming methods and with unusual clay bodies such as melting bodies and colored clay bodies. He created complex and challenging design problems in clay. He explored ceramic faults with the idea of turning them into positive attributes. He made a good deal of experimental vessel work and received commissions to make large scale pieces for architectural settings. In these very large murals he applied press molded and extruded elements to pressed tiles. In the late 1980s he became chair of the program in applied art and design at the Ontario College of Art and carried out these duties for a time. In recent years he has had several solo shows and has taken part in many group exhibitions showing wall pieces and vessels. He has been concentrating on making objects that have some aspects of vessels and some of sculpture. He calls them "forms based on the world around him." Di Petta explores these forms with a free-ranging imagination and a strong sense of intellectual curiosity.

Angelo di Petta in his studio.

Barbara Tipton

Barbara Tipton is a ceramist and editor who lives in Calgary, Alberta. She is married to the ceramist John Chalke (see page 41). Though she is best known for her sculptural pieces, Tipton also creates functional pieces. Many of Tipton's pieces are marked with strong textures. She creates these textures by using a multiple layer glazing strategy and by firing her pieces many times.

Recovered II (Aegean), 7-1/2" x 8-1/2" x 2", multiple firings, 1998. Tipton's strategies allow her to integrate textures and color in her glazes. She has discovered that some glaze effects are only possible when she fires a piece many times. "To me this process is like painting in very slow motion." She refires until the piece has the rich surfaces she is looking for.

Tipton's husband, John Chalke, makes their clay bodies in the studio from dry materials. Tipton uses a number of different clay bodies, including cone 6 clay bodies for her functional work and low-fire clay bodies for her cone 05 sculptural work. She makes her sculptural pieces in the form of flattened, wall hanging teacups and teapots. Tipton makes these forms from wheel-thrown pieces that she alters and assembles. She starts by throwing a cylinder that has no base, then forms the top of the piece. Once she has taken the form off the wheel she flattens and stretches it. She lets the form become firm, adds a bottom, and makes the handle and spout. She says she tries not to put her hands on the outer surface of the piece because she wants the clay surfaces to be fresh.

After the bisque firing, Tipton creates the glaze surface. Typically she uses three or four different glazes. They react with each other to create strong color and texture. Tipton is concerned with surface and color variations, and the visual balance of her pieces. Her glaze recipes strongly influence the look of her pieces. She develops new recipes and retests old recipes a great deal and generally places a few test tiles in each firing. Additionally, she wants their color and surface quality to coincide with what she intuitively senses about the form. She often places contrasting or even conflicting surfaces on a single piece. Tipton also pays close attention to glaze application. Much of

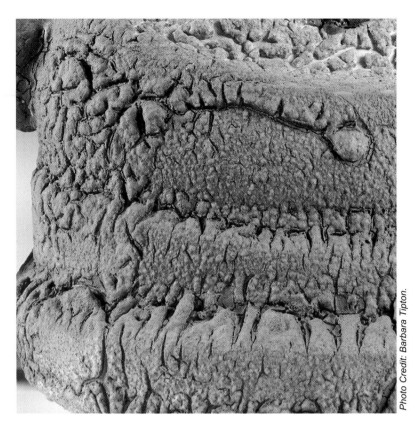

Photo Credit: Barbara Tipton.

Detail of **Red and Green**, 1995 (see page 244). This close-up clearly shows the complex textures of the crawling glazes.

her glaze work is dependent on layering and refiring strategies to encourage rich broken surfaces. When she switched to firing in the electric kiln she soon tossed out the axiom "never refire - remake instead." Now much of her glaze work is dependent on building layers through refiring and she creates her surfaces based on the results of the previous firing.

The thickness of an application affects the way Tipton's glazes shrink and crack. A glaze-fired piece puddled with slip and refired will develop a finer pattern of cracks where the coating is thin; more thickly coated areas may crack and crawl in large chunks. When the

slip is fired over a glaze it may peel away from the surface in some areas. She deals with this by applying more glaze - much like a glue - to fill those spaces. She then refires the piece. She has discovered that not only is refiring a way to build rich surfaces, but that some effects are only possible with three, four, or even more numerous firings. If she likes the form, once she starts glazing the piece she rarely feels the need to abandon it; she refires until she gets the look she wants. If, however, she takes the piece to a point where the form is obscured by overly thick glaze, she may then consider abandoning it.

When she began to fire her

Wild West Coffeepot, height 10", 1994. Tipton fired this piece to cone 6 in a soda kiln. She applied a slip trailed and brushed decoration using a fluid slip. She drew this imagery on the unfired clay, then fired the piece to bisque and applied a glaze on the inside of the piece. It is meant for use. Tipton enjoys making these pieces and enjoys the income from their sale. They are an important part of her work life. She feels that her wall forms refer to functional pottery and her functional pots give her ideas for her wall pieces.

sculptural pieces in the electric kiln, Tipton says she had to carry out "a total rethink about glaze." She came to think of glazes as not just a protective or decorative covering. For her, they were now an integral part of the piece. Firing in the electric kiln is quite different from firing in a fuel-burning kiln. She notes that with electric firing one almost always gets exactly what one has put into the work. This is a very demanding way to work but in return a whole world of surface choice is open to her. She loves the brilliant blue, red, and orange colors and the strong bubbled textures that can mark the surface of her pieces. These firings are in the oxidation atmosphere of an electric kiln at cone 05.

One of Tipton's most important decisions comes when she has to decide when a piece is finished. Many ceramists never refire. For them, the piece is finished when it comes from the glaze kiln. The decision is out of their hands - the results of the glaze firing are final and irrevocable. Because Tipton uses a work strategy that is highly oriented to refiring, she must decide when the piece is "done." She says she knows that she has finished the piece when she gets to the point where she can leave it alone. She makes this decision based on her feeling that the piece conveys a sense of unity of form and surface and a sense of visual balance.

Tipton's teapot and cup forms are images of the home and of domesticity. By placing the teapot image on the wall she is also talking about art (placing an object on the wall is the kind of thing artists do).

Tipton also makes pottery meant for use. She makes these pieces from a stoneware body and throws them on the potter's wheel. She applies slip trailed decoration and fires them to cone 6 in a soda vapor glaze kiln. She derives great pleasure (as well as useful income) from making this work. Pieces of this sort are important in another way as well. She feels that her sculptural wall forms refer to functional pottery and her functional pots give her ideas for her wall pieces.

Tipton first became involved with ceramics after she finished her undergraduate degree. She took her undergraduate degree at the University of Memphis in 1960 to 1964 and got a B.A. in drawing and painting. Their ceramics program was very small at that time and she took no ceramic courses there. After she graduated, she found a job working for a specialty magazine, a journal aimed at builders. This job wasn't very creative and missing this, she took a varied group of evening courses at the Memphis College of Art and Design. The ceramics program came to her notice at this time and looked very appealing. She took a chance on a course and fell in love with the medium. She took more ceramics classes and in 1967 went back to school full-time at the Memphis College of Art and Design, majoring in ceramics. She studied with Thorne Edwards and later with Peter Sohngen. She took a salt firing workshop and a course in glaze technology with Sohngen. She finished at Memphis with a B.F.A. in 1969. In 1972 she went to Ohio State for her M.F.A. There she studied with Michael Chipperfield and Margaret Fetzer. Another teacher who had a very great influence in her was Hoyt Sherman. Sherman was not a ceramist; he taught visual perception and painting. At Ohio State, faculty occasionally worked with graduate students in various art disciplines outside their field of expertise. As part of this program, Sherman came to her studio and talked with her about her work. She learned much from these thoughtful and wide-ranging conversations. At this time she was making pottery. She threw plates (some of which she altered), vases, cups, and saucers. She also made press-molded and slip-cast forms ornamented with decals. She experimented a great deal with a great variety of image creation strategies. These included salt glazing, photo transfer imagery, and lots of glaze experimentation at various temperatures and kiln atmospheres.

Tipton also embarked on a program of experimentation with stains. In the 1970s the world of studio ceramics embraced brilliant color. The Mason Stain Co., hoping to encourage this movement, donated a large selection of stains to the Ohio State University ceramics department. Many of these stains are at their best when fired in an oxidizing or neutral atmos-

Bronze Cup and Saucer with Blue Interior (an older piece), porcelain, 8" x 14" x 1", 1989. Tipton applied a glaze rich in manganese to create the bronze-like details. She fired this a number of times at cone 6 in an electric kiln. Tipton says the handle and the "steam" form were attached to the body of the cup with glaze and fired to permanently join them.

phere. During these experiments, Tipton intensively used an electric kiln. She finished her degree in 1975. During the 1977/78 school year, she held a visiting artist position at Dennison University in Ohio. In the fall of 1978 Tipton went to work for *Ceramics Monthly Magazine*. She began as a copy editor and became associate editor a few years later. She found the work at *Ceramics Monthly* to be extremely satisfying. She was reading many books and magazines and looking at slides of interesting and challenging pieces. She was constantly

thinking and writing about ceramics. She read of new surfaces, colors, textures, and exotic glaze recipes. For a time she carried out research on glazes made with an unusual material, zinc borate. She looks back to this period with great affection. The work-oriented atmosphere of the magazine strongly influenced her attitudes and ideas.

Tipton kept at her ceramic work as much as she could. She had a studio with an electric kiln and made work that had a strong reduction "look." She says at first the electric kiln represented an enormous obsta-

cle. She now thinks this was because she was attempting to replicate the look of the reduction-fired work she was familiar with. After a while she began to rely less on preconceptions and she had some success - shops asked for more pots with her electric fired glazes. She missed the surface variety provided by gas flame and atmospheric fluctuation, however. Rather than giving up on the electric kiln she began to devise ways of making it work for her. This led to drawing and painting on the work with colored slips, then adding ingredients to those slips to create even more

Red and Green, 7" x 13" x 4", 1995, multiple firings. This piece is a nonutilitarian form made in the image of a teapot. It is a wall piece and its back is flat so that it may easily be hung on the wall. Like much of Tipton's work, it is marked with strong textures she creates by using a multi-layer and multi-fire glazing strategy.

Tipton started this piece as a wide bottom cylinder with no base. As she threw the piece, she created a tapered form. She then pressed down and in at the top to turn it into a closed dome shape. She moved a chunk of scrap wood along the surface to create a stepped contour. She left the form on the bat for an hour or so, then used a parting wire to free the piece from the bat. She then cut the cylinder vertically into two segments of unequal size. She took the larger section and threw it on a canvas topped table to deform the cylinder and encourage stretching. When she was satisfied with the shape, she let it become firm. When the form became cheese hard, she added a slab bottom. Tipton also used the smaller segment of the cylinder. She cut it vertically in half to create two textured wall sections, which she curled in on themselves to form the handle and the spout.

After the bisque firing, Tipton was ready to create the glaze surface. She used three different glazes: a glaze containing chrome, which is green where thin and red where thick; a gray colored glaze with magnesium carbonate to encourage crawling; and a glaze saturated with copper. Tipton says that when the copper saturated glaze was applied over the magnesium carbonate, some of its copper leached out to make the striking alkaline blue color around the lid-like form. She rubbed some of the chrome containing glaze into the interstices in the surface of the piece. She used a thick application of the chrome containing glaze on the spout and the handle to create the brilliant orange red color. She used a thinner application of the same glaze to create the green color on the body of the teapot. Where she had left glaze in the interstices, the glaze is thick enough to be red in color. She first applied a light coating of the chrome containing glaze to create a highly textured surface and a green color, then applied the glaze loaded with magnesium carbonate on the shoulder of the form to create the fluffy, silver gray surface. Where the silver gray surface parts, it reveals the green color of the underlying surface. Tipton applied the chrome containing glaze by pouring it over the form. She applied the saturated copper glaze and the magnesium carbonate glaze by painting it on with a loaded brush.

variety in her surfaces. She began to refire as a normal part of her work. Soon she discovered that not only was refiring a way to build a richer surface, but that some effects were only possible with a third, fourth, or even more additional firings. She was achieving recognition for her ceramic work and her work at the magazine.

In 1983 she helped to organize a symposium of Canadian and American ceramists where she met the Canadian ceramist John Chalke. In 1985 she and Chalke married. In 1986 they moved to Calgary, where Chalke had a home and maintained a studio. She taught a good deal in Calgary from 1986 to 1993. In Canada the schools have an employment category called a "sessional position." Its

character is similar to the status termed "adjunct" in the U.S. Tipton had sessional appointments at both the University of Calgary and the Alberta College of Art. She taught both ceramics and more general art courses such as drawing and design. For a time she edited the Canadian ceramics magazine, *Contact*.

Her life revolves around thinking, writing, editing, and making ceramics. She makes a wide variety of ceramic work, including utilitarian and sculptural vessels and purely sculptural pieces.

Photo credit: John Chalke.

Barbara Tipton firing the soda kiln. This photograph is not a portrait in the usual sense of the word. Instead, it is an excellent documentation of a moment in the work life of the ceramist.

Richard Zakin

In recent years I have been making wall pieces and vessel forms with colored clay bodies. I started in this work with the wall pieces and I feel they are the most persuasive. I make them using a multiple layering process. I use my varied clay bodies to create a complex interwoven imagery. I like the wall piece format very much and treat it very much like a painting. I like imagery that is very cerebral and reflective. I have tried in these pieces to create special worlds, remote and removed from everyday concerns. For me, the wall piece is a very private format, one that encourages knotty, challenging thinking. I don't want these pieces to be *about something*, I want them to *be* something.

Wall Panel, cone 3, height 14", 1996. I created this piece in the summer of 1996. I treated this wall piece very much like a painting. I worked with color, texture, and the surface character of the various clay bodies I had at my disposal. I used a color palette based on gray, umber, and blue clay bodies. I used a multi-layer imagery. I began by painting a kiln shelf with a kiln wash made from ground soft brick and dolomite, then placed a sheet of newsprint over the prepared shelf. I started making this piece by forming an open clay grid. I placed five vertical clay coils and nine horizontal coils on the newsprint sheet. I used a shiny, silver gray clay body for these elements. I then applied a layer of a mat surfaced umber colored elements over the grid and applied fairly shiny, gray colored elements over that layer. I applied a layer of shiny light gray elements and a layer of mid-gray elements to the surface and finished with elements with shiny strong blue surfaces. I let the piece dry under plastic for a few days, then dried it under newspapers. I single fired the piece to cone 3 in an electric kiln.

Photo credit: T.C. Eckersley.

The wall piece format allows me to exploit all aspects of these colored bodies. These bodies have, for me, a unique and otherworldly quality and a special look not found anywhere else in ceramics or for that matter in any other art media. They embody both form and surface; as I place one element on another during the building process, I create relief imagery, introducing color, shiny or mat surfaces, and texture. Form and glaze are locked together in an indissoluble bond. When I use these bodies, the process of creation is a one-step process - form creation and surface creation take place with a satisfying simultaneity. Their color and glassy surfaces are part of their makeup and not added after the forming process is finished. They need no glaze. They are semi-translucent and their color seems to come from within. I value the unusual appearance of these clay bodies and the wall pieces I make from them. They testify to the reaction of materials to the energy of the fire. In exploring these formulations I have had to learn a great deal about my materials and processes. I found it helpful to write a special purpose computer program to track their reactions to the fire.

I use bodies of various melting and surface types in this work. I want to create surface contrast as well as color contrast. Most of the clay bodies I use are satin shiny in surface. I contrast these with clay bodies that are mat or highly melted. I

Photo credit: T.C. Eckersley.

*Detail of **Wall Panel**, cone 3, fired in an electric kiln, 1996. Notice the puffy character of the highly melted, low clay content clay bodies I used to make this piece. These glassy bodies expand in the fire. Notice, also, my use of clay bodies of different surface character, mat, satin, shiny, and highly melted. The color is very strong, these low clay content clay bodies take color very well. I used white, tan, brown, blue, orange, and yellow clay bodies. I made the shiny brown shards from broken glaze test tiles. I worked my colored clay bodies over, under, and around these shards. This knitted them into the composition, making this (at least in part) a ceramic collage.*

have also created very highly melted bodies which I have dubbed "super-melts." The supermelts have a very "puffy" appearance. Their very active melts boil and bubble during firing. These bodies have characteristics that make them well suited to the work I want to do. They are highly specialized and limited; because they slump in the fire I can't use them to make three-dimensional vessels or sculpture. What they can do they do very well and they are very effective as tile bodies. They are very difficult to use but that helps to keep me interested. Their recipes are simple. I make them with a limited group of ingredients: clays, talc, feldspar, and frit. To encourage the glassy quality I want, I keep the clay amount low, using high silica materials (feldspars, frits, and flint) and the strong melter, talc, in judicious amounts. They have a high percentage of alkaline fluxes which are also powerful melters. Unfortunately these fluxes compromise plasticity and make these bodies only marginally workable. I have been able to combine plastic with nonplastic clays to improve workability. These bodies are difficult to work with but they are very rewarding.

Sample tile body recipe

XMay 3.2, cone 3

Silica	14
Potash feldspar	30
Boron frit	4
Talc	18
Ball clay	34

This is an ivory colored body with a pleasing satin shiny surface and a glassy character. The clay amount in this recipe is 34% - lower than in most clay body recipes. Silica sources are ground silica (flint), feldspar, frit, talc, and ball clay. The feldspar, frit, and talc contain strong melters. With all this encouraging a glassy surface and strong melting, it is no wonder that this body is quite glassy. I have made other bodies that have more frit and less clay and some of those fall into the category of supermelts. They melt and slump a great deal.

Color is an important aspect of these clay bodies. I use either colored clays or prepared stains for this purpose. I use natural clay colors for the earth colors and the dark colors and commercially produced stains for the bright colors. Because these clay body formulations are glassy they take stain color very well (in a way that reminds me of glazes rather than clay bodies). I use brilliantly colored stains to develop a wide palette of body colors. With these I create green, blue, yellow, and unusual orange/pink colors.

In using these glassy clay bodies to make my wall pieces, I have come to know their character very well and can predict the way they are going to act in the fire. They are improved by

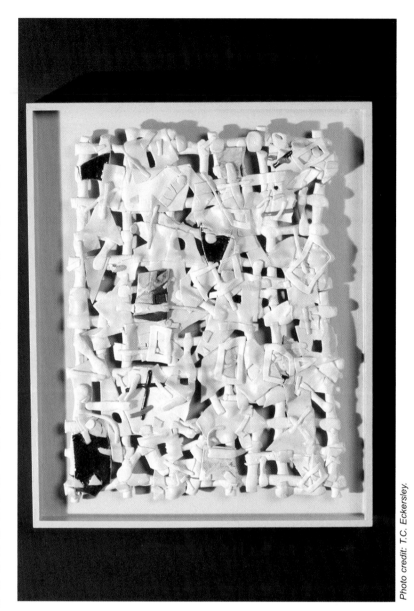

Photo credit: T.C. Eckersley.

Wall Panel, height 12", oxidation atmosphere, cone 3, 1996. I made this piece using dark colored clays and tried to emphasize the multi-layer character of the imagery. Within each layer I employed the same image elements, but used different imagery in each layer. I varied layers made from bodies with glassy surfaces with others that are mat and still others that are very highly melted and very shiny. I also contrasted a layer of one color with a layer of another. I continued until I had covered the surface with a dense interwoven pattern.

the fire. The shape of each element changes during the firing. Edges and surfaces are marked by a subtle swelling and take on a soft, rich, full character. Furthermore, form elements slump and drape over each other. This draping causes them to conform to form elements placed below them and partially reveal the outlines of these underlying shapes. I place a strong emphasis on process in the creation of my imagery. The advantage of this process orientation is that it has provided a consistent thread that it otherwise would have lacked. I need this because I periodically change the materials I use, the way I use them, and the forms I make with them.

I form my tile pieces on the kiln shelf. These very glassy bodies stick to shelves covered with normal kiln wash so I wash the kiln shelves using a mixture of 50 dolomite and 50 crushed soft brick. I then place a sheet of paper on the kiln shelf and build my tiles on it. I start with a base clay body and make coils to create a grid form. I use the same clay body to make planar elements which I add to the structure. I then use a second clay body to add more grid work and planar elements. The imagery gains complexity. I combine serpentine linear elements with rumpled planes and dark openings. So far I have used earth colored and gray colored clay bodies. I now add my brightest colored clays. I place these brightly colored elements so they look as if they are floating above the less brightly colored imagery they rest upon.

I have developed a work process in which I slowly build up the image in relief by placing one layer of clay elements on another. I start with an open grid base rather than a solid base. This lets me create openings in the surface of the piece.

These openings add interest. Each layer is made from the same clay and is composed of visual elements of a similar type. Within each layer I employ a group of elements related by a similar imagery. I then apply another layer of imagery. This is where I can create contrast because while I use a related imagery in a layer, I change my imagery from one layer to the next. I vary layers made from bodies with glassy surfaces with others that are mat and still others that are very highly melted and very shiny. I also deal with my colors in the same way, contrasting a layer of one color with a layer of another. I contrast soft and crisp imagery. I use clay bodies with different degrees of transparency or translucency. I continue until the surface is covered with a dense interwoven pattern.

When the piece is dry I move the tile on its kiln shelf from my work area to the kiln. I place the shelf inside the kiln and fire it. Because I don't glaze these pieces, I don't need to fire them first in a bisque fire. I fire this work directly to cone 3 in an electric kiln. After the firing I study the piece to decide if it is finished or if it needs another firing. If I think it needs more form or color variety I add new wet colored clay elements. When I fire the piece again, the new elements will fuse with the old and create an indissoluble bond.

In making imagery of this sort I am trying to make my own kind of realistic reflection of the world. It reflects not the surface appearance of the world but rather its processes. My pieces remind me of the patterns created by the growth of organisms - all sorts of organisms from plant life to human societies. Imagery of this sort is never sweet or emotional or hopeful. It tells no story but it has its own logic. With luck and skill it will be antic, complex, interwoven, shifting, multi-layered and it will have the look of an inevitable event.

After working with the wall piece format for a few years, I found myself wanting to use colored clays in vessel work as well. I worked hard to create colored bodies that allowed me to work in this format. I have developed a colored clay body recipe for vessels that satisfies me. I make the vessel pieces from a clay body similar to the wall piece clay bodies. It differs from the tile body in that it contains a higher percentage of clay. As a result, it does not slump as much, which I need for making vessels, and is less glassy, which I can live with. I am still trying to find a vessel form that works well with these colored clays and I hope to do that in the next few years.

Sample vessel colored clay body recipe

bd 2.9 low clay content clay body, cone 3

Soda feldspar	28
Talc	24
Ball clay	30
Kaolin	18
Clays	48
Silicates	52

Its color is light ivory and it has definite sheen. This is a

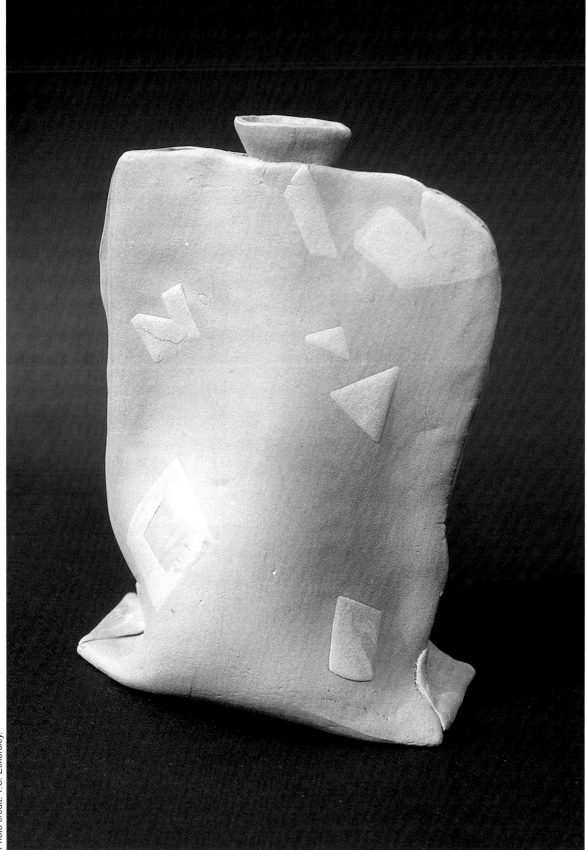

Left: Folded Vase, colored clay bodies, cone 3 firing in oxidation, height 7-1/2", 1996. This colored clay body is not as highly melted or as glassy as the tile bodies shown above. It still has a slight sheen, however, and it slumped a bit in the fire. I exploited the slumping to make a piece with a soft melted look. I made the piece by folding a slab, creating a foot area, and pinching the sides and forming a lip. I enjoy making forms using this impromptu method.

tough and durable clay body and considering its low clay content, it has fair workability. It is a light colored clay body and takes color quite well. I use standard hand-forming strategies to build my vessel forms with this clay body. It is limited in its workability so I must use care when working with it. Furthermore, it can slump in the fire. I must either choose forms that resist slumping or forms that exploit it.

Though I was always interested in art I never thought I would be a ceramist. I took as many art courses as I could in high school and decided I wanted to become an artist. At that time I thought I would spend my life working as a painter. I attended art school at Syracuse University from 1954 to 1958 with a major in painting and a minor in printmaking. I enjoyed my undergraduate years a great deal and remember many of the faculty with great fondness. I especially remember working with the perceptive teacher and painter, George Vander Sluis. He was very helpful to me. In the summer before my senior year I studied with Richard Pousette Dart at his studio in Rockland County, New York. He was a wonderful painter of the New York School who liked to work with multiple layers of abstract imagery. He would work on a painting for a year or so, let it dry for a year or

two, then apply another layer of paint. He might take five or six years to finish a painting. His paintings are marked by sgraffito and encrusted imagery. I graduated from Syracuse University in 1958 with a B.F.A. degree, then went on to the Brooklyn Museum School for the 1958/59 school year in a nondegree program in painting and printmaking, studying with the painter Reuben Tam. I spent the next few years in a New York City suburb, teaching part-time and making paintings.

I knew I had to decide whether I would teach or try to work as an artist. I had come to like teaching. I decided to try for the M.F.A. degree because that would allow me to specialize in art and to teach in college. I applied for graduate study to a number of places at various times. Most of these were painting programs but I was beginning to tire of painting courses and of purely two-dimensional work. I decided to apply to Alfred for ceramics. They were interested in my background, strong in art, wanting very much to learn about ceramics but free of any knowledge of the subject. They took a chance on me and I was admitted to the program. Alfred was a real revelation for me and I quickly became devoted to ceramics. I worked with Val Cushing, Robert Turner, Ted Randall, and Daniel Rhodes. I worked

very closely with, and assisted the sculptor William Parry. Parry was a particularly strong influence, he was a hand builder interested in unusual surfaces and clay bodies and I learned about them from him. He had a wonderful form sense and was very inventive. His lecturing style was personal and very moving. I admire him as a man and as a teacher and my connection with him remains strong. At Alfred I began to work with hand-forming methods of building. Most of our firings at Alfred were in the gas kiln and in a reduction atmosphere. Some of my work was sculptural and these pieces didn't work well when covered with the reduction glazes, so I decided to try the electric kiln. I thought it worked well with my sculptural pieces and began to work intensely with it. I graduated from Alfred with an M.F.A. degree in 1966. In January of 1967 I was hired to teach ceramics at the State University of New York at Oswego. I have taught at Oswego ever since.

A few years after I began teaching, I was in a group exhibition at the State University of New York at Binghamton. *Ceramics Monthly Magazine* prepared an article on the exhibition. The people at *Ceramics Monthly* asked a number of the participants to write about their work. I was one of this group. I was working with glazes fired in

Translucent Tile Panel *(an older piece), cone 6, low clay porcelain, 1983. I wanted this piece to be back lit so its translucent character is most fully revealed.*

an electric kiln at cone 6. I think they saw that this was going to be an area of interest to their readers because many of them did not have access to a fuel-burning kiln. The editors at *Ceramics Monthly* asked me to prepare some articles. I found I enjoyed writing these articles and have continued to write articles and books on ceramics. In 1981 I wrote my first book, *Electric Kiln Ceramics,* and have since written a general introduction to ceramic work, *Ceramics - Mastering the Craft,* a book on hand-formed ceramics, *Handformed Ceramics,* and a second edition of the electric kiln book. I have also given workshops and lectures and have traveled to many places in the U.S. and foreign countries to study ceramic work. I have a great interest in exploration which, if anything, has become stronger as I have gotten older. Over the years I have experimented with a wide variety of materials and work formats and work strategies. I have been fortunate enough to meet many of the artists who work in ceramics and this has become an important part of my life. These are spikey, exciting, and interesting people.

Once I had started writing about ceramics, it became a very important part of my work in the field. This was not the route I expected to take when I started out in clay. I suppose I ought not to be surprised, however, because I have always been very fond of books. Once I started writing I began to enjoy it a great deal and I now divide my time in ceramics fairly evenly between teaching, writing, and making. So my career has not worked out as I had imagined it when I was starting out. Now that I can get some feeling for its shape, however, it seems to me to be logical and I certainly find it satisfying.

Richard Zakin. I use this space as both office and studio. Though this mixed use can get in the way of my ceramic work, it is a great place for generating ideas and I see that as a central aspect of my work.

Barbara Frey

For a number of years *Barbara Frey* has made teapots with highly developed imagery. She feels the fusion of form and surface lie at the core of their character. She makes these pieces in groups or series. She has made her most recent teapots in the

Photo credit: Harrison Evans.

***Triage Teapot #13**, porcelain, cone 6 oxidation firing, 7-1/2" x 7-1/2" x 3-1/4", 1997. Frey creates her pieces using a cone 6 porcelain clay body. It is commercially prepared and is vacuum pugged to create a highly workable clay body. It builds well and is generally free of problems. Its color is off-white. In this piece Frey shows a stylized boat resting at an angle on a rock formation. Frey used a simple straightforward slab process to make the boat. She used paper templates as guides. She let the slabs approach the leather-hard state, then scored them and joined them with slip. She made sure all joins were completely sealed. Once she created the boat form, Frey started to create a complex patterned and layered imagery for its surface. She applied colored clay relief forms to create a rock-like imagery on parts of the surface. She wanted the brown colored relief imagery to remind the viewer of the layered imagery of rock strata. To create this textured relief she took a thin clay slab of colored clay and tore it into small fragments. She then applied these fragments, one next to another, to sections of the piece. After the upper part of the form was complete, Frey made the base in the form of a rock formation by carving a solid piece of leather-hard clay and hollowing it out.*

Frey draped plastic sheeting over the piece to dry it slowly. Part way through the drying process she reversed the plastic because water had gathered on its surface due to condensation. Frey first fired this piece to bisque at cone 08 to facilitate staining and glazing. She painted the rocks with a thin wash of stain to give it more color variation. She painted a white glaze in those areas with no relief imagery. She painted a blue, net-like pattern on top of the white glaze. She made this imagery using a diluted mixture of cobalt carbonate, Gerstley borate, and water applied with a fine brush. Frey wanted the viewer to be reminded of the blue and white net-like patterns in traditional Chinese and Japanese ceramics. She then fired the piece to cone 6 in an oxidation atmosphere in a top-loading electric kiln of a standard design. The firing was very straightforward with no soaking period.

form of boats. Frey emphasizes ideas and processes in this work. Her way of working is slow in tempo and her pieces are intimate and reflective in character. She encourages the viewer to slow down and appreciate this work in this same careful, intimate and reflective manner.

Frey creates her pieces using a cone 6 porcelain clay body. It is commercially prepared and is vacuum pugged and highly workable. It builds well and is generally free of problems. Its color is off-white. Frey uses slab-forming methods for much of her work. She also works with solid forming strategies to make some of the components and uses carved and sprigged relief imagery to enhance the surface of her pieces. Her imagery is complex and the carving process requires great care. It takes her about three days to carve one of her pieces. When it is dry Frey fires the piece to a cone 08 bisque. This facilitates staining and glazing. She finishes her pieces using stain washes in some sections and glazes in others. She then fires to cone 6 in an oxidation atmosphere. The firing is very straightforward with no soaking period.

In her daily life and in her teaching Frey is a very analytical person. She tries, however, not to be overly analytical when she is working. She feels this may dull her natural responses. She may look at the piece after she has finished it and try to understand where it comes from and where it may be going, but she doesn't specu-

Photo credit: Harrison Evans.

*Detail of **Triage Teapot #13**. This photograph allows close study of the images of rocks with their thin stain washes and the painted net-like patterns painted in cobalt blue on a white ground.*

late on these matters while she is making the piece. She does know that she likes to use archetypes (by this she means an emblematic form or image that all of us respond to in an almost instinctive way). She has used images of house forms and of Zen gardens in her work in the past. She uses boat imagery in her current work. She treats these as archetypical forms. Boats are very strong symbols with universal connotations. Frey's choice of the boat for her imagery, however, is based on more than this. She has a strong connection to boats. Frey's father taught biology at Indiana University at

Bloomington. He was a well-known figure in his specialty, paleo limnology, the study of the history of the development of freshwater life. These studies required him to take core samples from the bottom of lakes. As a result, he spent a good deal of his working life on or near water. As Frey was growing up, her father often asked her to join him on his expeditions. She spent memorable times with him on boats. They represent, for her, the time of her life when she came to an adult level of consciousness. Her favorite memory is of a trip to Iceland and two weeks spent helping him on a lake there. She was very close to him;

Triage Teapot #15, *porcelain, cone 6 oxidation firing, 7" x 7" x 4", 1997. This piece is of the same series as* **Triage Teapot #13**. *The overall idea is similar though it differs in details. Frey assembled the boat form from leather-hard slabs. She used colored clays to create a rock-like relief imagery on the surface of the piece. Frey carved grooves into the spaces between the rocks with a small loop tool and made the base in the form of a pile of rocks. She made the rocks using a solid forming process. She broke up a solid piece of dry clay with a hammer. This gave her a sharp edged stone-like imagery. She then rehumidified the dry clay "stones" by placing them in a plastic box and covering them with wet paper towels. Once they were wet again, she used them as building blocks and joined them together to make the rock pile which she used to form the base of the piece.*

Frey fired the piece to bisque at cone 08 to ready it for staining and glazing. She applied a thin wash of stain to the relief imagery to give it more color variation. She used prepared stains to color the base and the rock-like forms, mixing in a small amount of Gerstley borate to ensure that they would adhere to the clay. She used a variety of stains including browns, blacks, and greens and red iron oxide, brushing one on top of another. She wanted the layers to create a pleasing optical blend. She sponged off the stains on the top layers of the relief, leaving them in the textured areas of the design. Frey wanted these rock-like forms to remind the viewer of islands set in the ocean.

She then applied a green colored glaze over the grooved sections. When she fired the piece, the green glaze ran off the top edges of the carved imagery and settled in the grooves, darkening them and emphasizing the carving. She wanted this part of the surface to have the character of water.

now, after his death, she reflects her admiration for her father in her choice of the boat as a symbolic form.

Frey's teapots are at once teapots and boats. She pictures boats, bobbing up and down in the water. She wants to fuse these animated forms with the sober, formal vocabulary of the teapot. She is very fond of Yixing teapots; the Yixing potters made their pieces in the image of such objects as wooden stumps and vegetables in a simplified but very realistic way. We see this from the earliest Yixing pieces up until the present.

Finally there is the matter of her surface imagery. She uses both relief and painted imagery. She paints marks that she sees as a kind of nonliteral alphabet. She likes to use Chinese imagery, especially imagery that she saw on her trips to China. These motifs relate to Ching Dynasty (1699-1912) designs referring to clouds and to the elaborate architectural details she saw on buildings from that period. She talks about layers of knowing and conveys the image of peeling away one layer of meaning after another, arriving finally at a very deeply buried image. She also talks warmly of the scale of these pieces. These are not large pieces and they have an intimate scale. Teapots are "right" when made to this scale. They are small but she can pack a lot of visual information and a lot of references to feelings and ideas onto their surfaces.

Frey took ceramics for one

*Photo credit: Harrison Evans.*

*Detail of **Triage Teapot #15**. This photograph gives a good view of the way the glaze settled in the grooves of the carved surface, revealing the white color of the porcelain body.*

semester in high school in Bloomington, Indiana. She attended Hiram College in the fall of 1970 where she majored in French and in her sophomore year she studied in France. She completed her French major in that year. While in France, she also took a number of art history courses. She had two more years to take any courses she wanted and decided that she most wanted to take art courses. Upon her return from France she spent one more semester at Hiram studying art history. She took no studio courses at Hiram for she was waiting to take studio courses in a larger, more professionally oriented art department. She transferred to the Indiana University at Bloomington in January of 1973 and majored in

studio art. The next two years at Indiana were very exciting and she enjoyed them a great deal. She continued to take a great many art history courses to feed the rational side of her intelligence. She took ceramics and metals and eventually decided that ceramics was her medium. She remarks that she was interested in slab work with a strong concern for surfaces "right there from the beginning." Most of her work was in the sculpture format and its imagery was abstract. Her work was very eclectic. She tried a great variety of work strategies: salt fire, low fire with polychrome glazing, high-fire stoneware, raku, and cast-formed pieces. She worked with John Goodheart and Karl Martz. She learned important lessons from

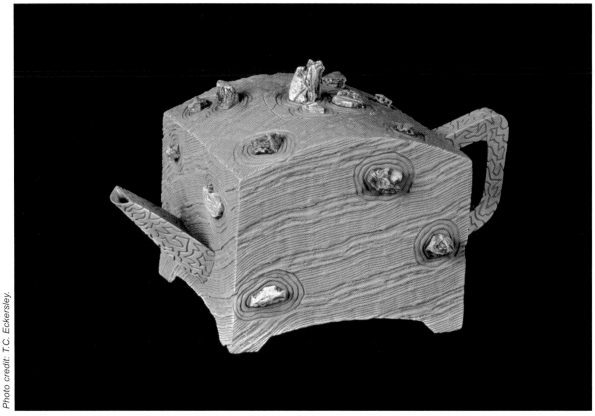

Round Trip Teapot #25 (an older piece), porcelain, cone 6 oxidation firing, 5" x 8-1/2" x 3-3/4", 1992. In this piece Frey used the imagery of a Zen Buddhist rock garden. These gardens, meant for contemplation, are composed of rocks set in a bed of gravel, raked in a sinuous pattern. The raked ridges symbolize water and the rocks are symbols for islands. In building upon this image Frey surrounded her rocks with a pattern of striated clay. She created the striated surface by rolling crinoid fossils (fossil aquatic animals) into the clay. She constructed this piece from colored porcelain. Frey made the rocks from a group of colored porcelain clays partially wedged together to create a marbleized effect.

Martz. She saw first hand the pattern of work and tightly focused exploration that he carried out on a day to day basis. His teaching style was nondirective but highly distilled, concentrated and intense. His attitudes represented 50 years of work and she was impressed by his knowledge of the field, his assurance and calm temperament.

In 1976 she finished her work at Indiana and applied to graduate schools. "When I applied, I had lots of breadth but perhaps less depth," she remembers. She was accepted in Syracuse University's graduate program, attending on a graduate fellowship - an academic award based on her undergraduate grades and her record of intellectual exploration. At Syracuse she worked with Henry Gernhardt, David MacDonald, and Margie Hughto. She began to work with porcelain and colored clay bodies and though she did glaze some pieces, she worked mostly with colored slips and colored clays. She made vases and wall pieces. She graduated from the program at Syracuse in 1978.

For the next two years Frey taught as a sabbatical replacement at the State University of New York at Oswego. She continued to create her ceramic work. At first she carried on with her work in porcelain, making open trays with paper-thin bases and walls, then she moved on to work with colored clay bodies and started a series of pieces whose form was that of a stylized house. She fired some of the later pieces in this series in the salt fire.

In 1980 Frey was hired by Texas A & M University in Commerce, Texas, teaching undergraduate and graduate students. For a time after her arrival she continued her work in the house series. She followed this with a group of geometric wall pieces in which she used very colorful low-fire slips. In 1987 she began making teapots. She says, "I was attracted to the teapot format because of its complexity as an assemblage of parts." This complexity meant there were many possibilities for variation. Furthermore, she liked the teapot format's status as a classic, widely admired ceramic form. She worked on a number of different series in her first years working with this form. Her first teapots featured strong abstract bas relief patterning done by throwing porcelain slabs on the wheel to create a spiral groove. She then cut and assembled these using hand-forming methods. The edges of these patterns intersected and where they came together they created a strong irregular pattern. She feels this series was very important in defining a number of concerns that are of long-standing interest to her. She moved on to pieces in which she used colored porcelain bodies. She gave each element in these pieces its own texture and color. She then created a group of teapots topped with depictions of classic Zen rock gardens. Most recently she has made teapots that resemble boats. The first

boat teapots had a kind of sly humor but most recently she has given them a more serious and expressive character. These pots are controlled but exploratory.

Travel has always been very important to Frey. When she was young, she traveled often and spent a number of years living abroad in Europe and Asia. She and her family lived for extended periods in London and the Philippines. When she was 16, she visited Kyoto, Japan, and its well-known Zen gardens, composed of raked gravel and rocks. These unique gardens made a powerful impression on her. Their imagery resurfaced many years later in her *Round Trip Teapots*. She spent her sophomore year in college in Paris. She continues her travels; in 1997 she traveled with a potter's group to one of the main ceramic centers in China, the city of Yixing. There the group worked in a ceramic factory where Yixing teapots are made. Frey learned a great deal and enjoyed meeting the workers in the factory and the atmosphere of intense participation she found in the group.

Frey's work has a complex multi-part character. She deals with disparate formal elements and with a complex carved, stained, and glazed imagery with all sorts of associations. Frey likes the complex multiplicity of elements of the teapot form. She enjoys juggling these varied parts and orchestrating them so they work in concert to produce intelligent and witty pieces.

Photo credit: T.C. Eckersley.

Barbara Frey in her studio.

Peter Pinnell

Peter Pinnell's work has its roots in functional pottery. He has stayed close to these roots in the sense that he continues to work with functional pottery forms. At one time he made his pieces in fairly large numbers in a production context. Now he creates one-of-a-kind pieces. This has given him the luxury of spending far more time on each piece and allows him to reveal the more intellectual side of his character in his work. This rational impulse is a powerful aspect of his personality and expresses itself in his work, both in his intellectual studies in the field of ceramics and in his explorations of form and imagery.

Teapot, height 5", 1998. Pinnell made this piece using a low-fire, terra cotta clay body. This is a thrown form with a hand-formed spout, handle, and lid. The lid opening is thrown, then altered. When the piece was cheese hard, Pinnell stamped imagery on the surface of the thrown form using a bisque-fired stamp. He then paddled the surface to refine the contour and partially obscure the stamped imagery.

When the piece was bone dry, Pinnell applied a terra sigillata using a wide Chinese brush. He polished his terra sigillata using first his fingers, then a plastic grocery bag. He then fired the piece to bisque. Pinnell finished the piece by applying a thin wash of a metal oxide mixture over the terra sigillata. This wash was composed of one part oxide and two parts Gerstley borate by volume. For this piece he used two oxide washes, the first based on red iron oxide and the second based on titanium dioxide. The two oxides, mimicking rutile, reacted to create the ocher color. Then he wiped the washes away, leaving the mixture only in the interstices. Pinnell fired the piece to cone 04 in an oxidation atmosphere, using a soaking firing before as well as after his kiln reached temperature. He did this by slowing the course of the firing as soon as he saw the cone beginning to fall and allowed the kiln to slowly arrive to temperature. He then continued the firing at low power for a time after the cone had fallen. This kind of firing promotes crystal growth on the surface of the glaze and encourages rich surfaces.

Pinnell's recent work has been strongly influenced by his trip to the pottery city of Yixing, China, in the fall of 1997. The ceramic ware of Yixing is made from a red clay body and fired to mid-fire temperatures in an oxidation atmosphere. This hand-formed ware is associated with tea and has been the staple of Yixing's pottery production since the late 17th century. Pinnell had an opportunity to work alongside some of the potters of Yixing and he learned a great deal from this experience. He was especially impressed with the forms and the forming methods employed by these potters and has adapted a number of these work strategies for his own work.

Pinnell uses a low-fire terra cotta clay body:

Red clay	40
Redart clay	25
Bonding clay	20
(a fire clay-like material) 50 mesh	
Ball clay	10
Wollastonite	5
Bentonite	1
Mica powder	10

(promotes melting, good workability, and good glaze fit)
1/4 cup barium carbonate per 100 pounds

Pinnell first mixes the wollastonite, bentonite, and barium in water before adding them to the body. He does this because the materials clump together if they are added to the body in the mixer. He adds the barium carbonate to avoid calcium scumming. He feels this amount of barium won't be harmful to either himself or the consumer. However, he notes that the barium is optional and understands that there are those who don't want to keep barium in their studio. To those who want to minimize scumming without barium, he suggests an alternative he learned

*Detail of **Teapot**. This very interesting photograph shows how Pinnell constructed the mouth and lid of this piece. He threw the opening for the lid, then added a small slab at the front of the opening. He threw the lid, altered its shape, and added the flange at the bottom. He likes the relationship between the round form of the teapot and its altered mouth and lid.*

Left: Ewer, wheel thrown, height 12", red clay, 1998. Pinnell first scraped the surface of this piece, then used a serrated knife to create the vertical lines on its surface. He spattered the surface with a slip to add visual and tactile texture. He rolled over the surface with a rubber roller (a brayer intended for use in linoleum printing) to give it a smooth and finished effect. He then applied a terra sigillata to the surface, polished the terra sigillata, then fired the piece to bisque. Next Pinnell applied a thin wash of a dark oxide stain over the surface of the piece and wiped the surface, leaving most of the mixture in the interstices. Pinnell fired this piece to cone 04 in an oxidation atmosphere. He used a soaking firing before as well as after his kiln reached temperature. Notice the shadowy mottled pattern on the surface. To obtain this effect Pinnell spattered slip over the surface of the piece and as the slip became firm, he rolled over the surface. This created a rough overhanging edge around each droplet. After he fired the piece to bisque, Pinnell applied a patina. The edges of the slip droplets held the patina. As a result, there's a dark outline of patina around each droplet of slip.

from the potters of Yixing: under all circumstances avoid wetting the overall surface of the piece. An overall application of water (or a watery mist) encourages the movement of calcium salts from the interior of the clay wall to its surface. Instead, keep the piece in a moisture laden closed chamber - a damp box. Pinnell made a damp box from an insulated picnic chest. He places a grate about 2" above the floor of the chest, adds water to a level below the grate, then places the ware on the grate. In this way he is able to keep the piece from drying while still assuring there is no direct contact with water.

Pinnell has a penchant for dividing the work processes into a great number of steps; each one offers the opportunity to shape and enrich the form and imagery. He forms his pieces using either wheel-thrown or slab-forming methods. At present Pinnell combines wheel forming with a good deal of hand-formed detail work. After taking the piece from the wheel, he often alters the surface using combs, knives, and stamps.

He does a great deal of slab-formed work, using templates as guides for shaping the slabs. In assembling pieces, he miters corners because he feels this kind of join is stronger and looks better than butt or overlap joins. He makes his forms with four feet. The Yixing potters work with four feet and their pots never tip over. Western potters often use three feet because a tripod form helps the potter avoid the rocking motion associated with four feet. Pinnell pays close attention to the feet as he builds them and fires the piece on a flat shelf to insure that the piece stands evenly.

When his pieces are leather hard, he scrapes and textures the surface with a bamboo spatula. Pinnell takes great pleasure in exploring unusual ceramic tools. He has assembled a group of hand-building tools that suit his needs, including toothed scrapers, textured and smooth rollers, and (perhaps most interesting) the mallet he uses for making strong slabs. Since his trip to China he has begun to hammer his clay slabs with this mallet (he copied the shape from mallets he saw at the Yixing potteries). Very few Western potters use this tool but he recommends it. He feels the hammer helps him make strong, very dense slabs that are very workable and resist cracking. Pinnell doesn't cover most of his pieces as they are drying. He knows he can dry pieces quickly if he seasons the clay and hammer forms the slabs before beginning the building process.

When the clay body is bone dry he applies terra sigillata. He polishes the terra sigillata using first his fingers, then a plastic grocery bag (he prefers the softer surfaced biodegradable bags). He then fires the piece to bisque. If he is using slip-trailed imagery on a piece, he makes a slip from his clay body (passing it through a 50-mesh sieve to create a smooth mixture). Surfaces are very important to Pinnell. He is looking for a complex and rich multi-layered imagery.

Pinnell glazes the interior of his pieces with a simple three material glaze recipe. He likes this glaze and says it is worry free.

Spodumene (ceramic grade)	50
Gerstley borate	30
Ground silica (flint)	20
Mason satin black (6600 black, a highly reliable black stain containing cobalt)	10

Teapot, *height 5", 1997. Pinnell's forms often refer to the forms of traditional pottery. In its form this piece refers to the teapots of Yixing. In its surfaces, however, Pinnell uses slip-trailed imagery and terra sigillata. These methods are not used in Yixing; we see Pinnell combining methods from many sources. Pinnell made this piece using a low-fire, terra cotta clay body. He first formed his slabs by throwing them at an angle against his work board. He then thinned and strengthened the slabs by hammering them with a clay mallet. Pinnell used paper templates as a guide to make his forms and mitered the corners. He didn't cover this piece as it was drying, choosing instead to let it dry quickly which he feels he can do because he seasons the clay before he builds with it. When the piece was leather hard Pinnell scraped and textured the surface using a bamboo spatula.*

When the body was bone dry, he applied a terra sigillata. He made a slip from his clay body and used it to apply slip-trailed imagery with a homemade slip-trailing tool made from a basketball needle mounted on a rubber pipette bulb. After drying the slip-trailed imagery Pinnell finished the piece by applying a thin wash of a metal oxide mixture over the terra sigillata and slip layers. This wash mixture was composed of one part dark colored oxide and two parts Gerstley borate by volume. After applying the wash he wiped the surface, leaving most of the mixture in the crevices of the textured imagery. As a result, there is a strong contrast between the slip-trailed imagery and the terra sigillata base. Pinnell fired this piece to cone 04 in an oxidation atmosphere. He used a soaking firing before as well as after his kiln reached temperature.

His application strategies are often very complex. He feels that earthenware surfaces tend to be very simple and cheery and he isn't interested in that look. He wants to combine richness, subtlety, and complexity in his surfaces. He wants a rich patina surface that will remind the viewer of aged, partially corroded vessels. He accomplishes this surface by using layers of slips, terra sigillata, and stains. He builds up his imagery to create the rich look he wants.

In his recent work Pinnell fires to cone 04 in an oxidation atmosphere. He carefully controls his firing and cooling. Not too many years ago, it was not common for ceramists to fire down, or soak, the electric kiln. The ceramist fired until the cone fell and shut off the current to the kiln (or used an automatic shutoff device). Then it was pointed out that electric kilns (most of which are quick cooling) needed a soak firing to encourage the formation of complex, rich looking surfaces. Pinnell is convinced of the necessity to soak the kiln. However, he has added an important refinement by soaking *before* as well as after his kiln reaches temperature. While many ceramists soak the kiln after the desired temperature is reached, only a few slow the course of the firing before the cone has fallen. Pinnell slows the rate of temperature rise as soon as he sees the cone beginning to fall and allows the kiln to slowly arrive to temperature. He feels this encourages extremely rich surfaces.

Pinnell has a deep understanding of ceramic history. His forms often refer to the forms of traditional pottery. Much of his recent work refers to the teapots of Yixing. While his surfaces don't mirror the simple but very rich unglazed surfaces of Yixing ware, his forms are very close to Yixing forms. His imagery also mirrors his interest in those aspects of the visual arts that we call "design." When he talks of his pieces, he talks of line, shape, form, process, and balance. All of these are associated with the term design. In the 1950s these principles held sway, in the 1960s and '70s they came to be seen as somewhat old-fashioned. In the 1980s till now they have come to be seen as hopelessly out of date. Are they coming back now? Pinnell's shows us that you can make work that looks quite contemporary and still value design.

During his high school and undergraduate college years Pinnell was not at all concerned with the visual arts; he was deeply involved with the study of music. He went to Columbia College in Missouri to study music in 1972 and received his B.A. degree in music in 1976. Though Pinnell became a ceramist rather than a professional musician, he still is strongly influenced by music and the attitudes of a musician. His experience as a thoughtful musician seems to have influenced his understanding of such things as form, rhythm, and the sense of order and of "rightness" that we feel when every aspect of the piece works

in harmony with all the other parts. His training in music had a strong intellectual and analytical cast. Pinnell absorbed this training with its assumptions about the way music (especially classical music) is shaped and the way it affects its listeners. Pinnell's interest in harmony and dissonance, in repetition and rhythm in the visual arts, is strongly influenced by his training in music.

Pinnell took a ceramic course in his final year at Columbia College and his response was immediate and intense and led him on the path to ceramics. He stayed on at Columbia for another two years, supporting himself by working as a security guard so he could continue his explorations of clay. This work (and most of the work he made for the next 20 years) was in the high fire. In 1978, starting all over again as an undergraduate, he attended the New York State College of Ceramics at Alfred. He studied there with Tom Spleth, Val Cushing, and Wayne Higby, most of the time working with high-fire porcelain. He became very involved with ceramic technology (he has been interested in this from the beginning of his work in ceramics). He graduated from Alfred with a B.F.A. in ceramics in 1980. From Alfred he went to the University of Colorado at Boulder where he studied with Betty Woodman, Tom Potter, Wayne Branham, and Ann Currier; he received his M.F.A. degree in 1982.

From 1983 to 1986 Pinnell was Artist in Residence at the

Covered Jar *(an older piece), height 9", 1988. Porcelain, cone 10 reduction. This is an example of Pinnell's work in high-fired porcelain. It is a thrown piece covered with a green glaze. Its color is derived from copper. Pinnell ably exploited the character of porcelain on the lid of this piece. He first threw concentric rings on the lid, then applied a glaze low in silica and low in clay, creating a low surface tension. This encouraged the glaze to run off any sharp edges and revealed the white color of the porcelain clay body. Pinnell made this piece while living in Kansas City toward the end of his time working in the high fire. At this time he made a good part of the family income through sales of his work.*

Octagon Center for the Arts in Ames, Iowa. He and his wife (a librarian) moved to Iowa City in 1986/87 so she could get her Master of Science degree in library science. During this period Pinnell was invited by Clarie Illian to work in her studio. In 1987 the Pinnells moved to Kansas City where Pinnell made his living as a studio potter and taught ceramic technology at the Kansas City Art Institute. He continued to work in the high fire. In 1992, after 16 years, he felt the need for change in his ceramic work and took up work in the low fire; this change was a very big challenge for Pinnell. In 1995 he joined the faculty at the University of Nebraska in Lincoln. Until he arrived in Nebraska, he was still forming his pieces on the potter's wheel (but often altering the shapes considerably). However, when he started teaching full-time he moved completely into hand forming. Most recently, however, he has been making many of his teapots partially on the wheel. He wants to explore forming and the subtle relationships between process and the character of the fired object. It was his work in hand forming

that led to his trip to Yixing in the fall of 1997. At Yixing he had the opportunity to make a detailed study of the pottery and the creation processes used by the ceramists there.

Pinnell's training in music as a branch of culture prepared him to see ceramics as a branch of culture with rich and lively traditions. When he moved from music to ceramics, he traded one set of creative tools for a completely different set of tools. He brought his value systems with him, however. His interest in ideas and facility in handling them has encouraged him to an intensive study of ceramic history and technology. His involvement with the arts has encouraged him to carry out these explorations in the service of the creation of artistically significant work.

Peter Pinnell.

Photo credit: Julie Pinnell.

Chapter 5: Concepts

Introduction

How do ceramic artists arrive at their work? It's possible to make up elaborate theories but I found the best way to find out was to ask. I developed a series of questions to ask each artist and they seemed to tell the truth as they saw it. I didn't feel they were trying to edit the process. They presented their progress as a sometimes difficult but always intensely interesting process. Each of these narratives is different because the ceramists in this book are very different from each other. They are alike, however, in that none have tried to prettify the process or to claim powers they don't have.

In the first part of this book I asked questions of a wide variety of clay artists. These were questions I thought were interesting and I hoped they would be of interest to readers as well. Some were related to the technical and material aspects of the field - the tangible aspects of ceramic creativity. Others were related to the life experiences, the ideas and beliefs of these ceramists - the intangible aspects of ceramic creativity.

In this second section I think it is appropriate to make some generalizations from the answers to these questions. To do this I will try to assemble some of the information from these individual narratives and make a few generalizations on the general condition of ceramics in North America at this time.

Technology & Invention

This is a time in which experimentation and innovation are given great weight. Ceramics is a very different field than it was 30 years ago. There is less surety but much more experimentation, innovation, and variety. Perhaps this is the reason it seems that the only common thread we see in contemporary ceramic work is one of innovation across a broad front of ceramic types.

Many of the ceramists in this book are fascinated with what they can do with ceramic materials and work methods. For these artists, innovation is not an end in itself, instead innovation helps them create personal and unusual work. These ceramists have undertaken technical explorations of such areas of ceramics as ceramic materials, clay bodies, slips, stains and glazes, and surface application strategies.

An example of an artist who has spent a great deal of time and energy creating unusual clay bodies is Louis Katz. Katz has borrowed from an old Japanese technique to load his clay surfaces with materials such as rice, that will burn out. His revival of this highly textured clay body type shows us how contemporary an ancient technique can look. Another example is Neil Forrest, who has developed a contemporary version of the Egyptian faience body to make surfaces and colors that have a very unusual look. He loves the very hard glassy surface, the low moisture absorption, the very high density, and the rich surface character of this body. Forrest has used this body to make wall pieces and vessels. Others among the artists in this book are looking for bodies that are very workable or have great fired strength. The clay bodies of John Neely are also worthy of comment. In one of his most interesting work strategies, Neely combines a rich, high iron clay body and unusual firing strategies to create a surface marked by bands of varied earth colors.

Forming methods, too, can be the subject of technical experiment. We see Angelo di Petta opting for training in Italy to learn from the thousand-year tradition of Faenza. Already interested in alternative forming methods, he experimented there with extruding, slipcasting, and press forming and has been following this path since.

Ceramists are constantly trying to find or develop new slip or glaze recipes. An unusual recipe can serve as the special signature of a particular clay artist. There are glaze recipes that work so well and have such an individual look that ceramists find it worth their while to look for them. Ron Roy has worked with glaze development for many years. His knowledge of glaze recipe

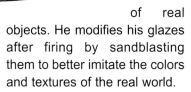

development is broad and deep. He works with a temmoku glaze whose color "breaks" from red where thin to black where it is thick. This effect emphasizes the carefully designed edges of his plate forms. In a very different approach, John Gill uses newly developed brilliant stain colors in his glazes. He arrives at colors that have not been available before for high firing. They expand on the accepted definition of ceramic color.

Many of the artists in this book are very interested in application strategies. For these artists, application strategies are as important or more important than the glaze recipe itself. They are a highly personal and a really creative part of ceramics. Both Barbara Tipton and John Chalke lay one layer of glaze over another. In doing this they create layers of incompatibilities and produce surfaces attesting to the bubbling and boiling that results from this kind of application. Eva Kwong's painterly application also results in a very personal imagery. She uses brush-applied, low-fire glazes to build up a patterned and shimmering glaze surface. Victor Spinski purchases many of his glazes. He wants his surfaces to look as close as possible to their original models. This means he must mirror, as closely as possible, both the color and texture

of real objects. He modifies his glazes after firing by sandblasting them to better imitate the colors and textures of the real world.

For some ceramists, experiments with clay, glaze, or glaze application can become one of the most important aspects of ceramic work. I have tried to show how all sorts of ceramic artists are inventive in their use of the technology. For these artists, the exploration of new imagery or new materials or new ways of creating form and imagery is very important. It is a source of energy and enthusiasm.

Work Strategies

A work strategy can be defined as a systematically organized group of actions chosen because they will create a desired result. The complexity of our medium demands and encourages great attention to work strategies. The ceramists in this book are very conscious of their work strategies. Over the years many have come to make their pieces using a complex work strategy, while others elect to stay with simple ones that work well for them.

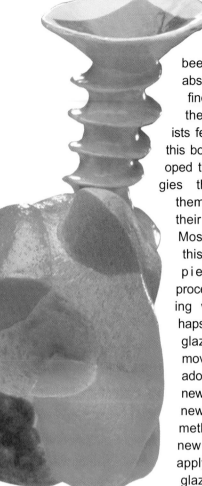

It has been very absorbing to find out how the ceramists featured in this book developed the strategies that help them create their pieces. Most often this was a piecemeal process, starting with perhaps a clay or glaze, then moving to the adoption of a new format, a new forming method, a new way of applying a glaze and finally, perhaps, a new or modified firing method. Typically, this process of development began during the artists' student years. Students will try a great many ways of working, taking up one type of work after another. Then at a certain point, the student will begin to settle on a particular work method and will begin to explore that work strategy in depth.

I have become very interested in the ways these artists discovered the work strategy that helped them break through to their own unique imagery. I wondered if any of them remembered a particular moment that was crucial in shaping a new approach to their work. When I first talked with the sculptor Victor Spinski about his development process, he had not thought about this for a very long time and I had to jog his memory. When I did, he was able to relive his creative moment. This was like finding a buried treasure. His retelling of this moment was very dramatic and exciting. Furthermore, what he is doing now is very obviously a deepening and refining of that casual action many years before. For other artists, the process was slow and regular, a process of building one part of the creative image on another. For most of these artists, the process continues and will never be complete.

Most of these ceramists continued this process after graduate school, improving their work strategies or even developing new work strategies. Neil Forrest is a good example of this. After finishing graduate school Forrest lived for a time in New York City. He needed studio space but couldn't find a space at a reasonable price, so he worked and fired in a tiny test kiln in his small New York apartment. This led to his adopting Egyptian faience because it lent itself to small forms that would fit in the kiln. He still works in this medium because it looks so rich and exotic. It also led eventually to the complex formal work he has developed with this clay body in mind. This process of development is ongoing and subject to change as the work evolves.

Some ceramists stay rigorously within a process for many years, repeating it until it reaches a level of surety and elegance. This is the pattern adopted by the sculptor Sylvia Netzer. Throughout her career she has worked with groupings of forms to create large segmented pieces. To make sure her work is constantly renewed, she varies her forms and her colors and surfaces. In this way her work strategy is the thread that binds the work together and the image elements are varied to create interest and variety. A completely different example is Roy Strassberg. Strassberg spent many years creating a group of colorful, antic, abstract sculptures. A few years ago he found that he had a great need to switch from this type of work to pieces in which he used a more subject-oriented imagery depicting the Holocaust. As his goals changed, he completely changed his work process.

Quite often artists told me that their work strategies had grown out of their reactions to imagery they had used in the past. Jeff Oestreich talked of his change from wood to soda firing in this way. He told me of his exposure to soda firing at Alfred and his discovery that he could use soda glazes to create bright colors and pooling glazes. These are individual examples but I heard similar narratives from many of these artists. As a group, they were restless and felt a spirit of urgency. They were not satisfied with what they had, and used that dissatisfaction as the engine that drove them to create better, more personal pieces.

Ceramic Form & Volume

To those who work with it, clay has a very special identity. It is a highly three-dimensional material that can be used to create highly three-dimensional objects. Clay lends itself to a fluent and direct expression in a manner similar to paint, but unlike paint, its expression is carried out in terms of objects with three-dimensionality as an important part of their attributes.

Even for those artists who work in the tile format, the form character of the medium makes a ceramic piece something other than a painting *on* clay or a painting *in* clay. Even when not used to build a three-dimensional form, its characteristic three-dimensionality gives it a strong identity as a physical object.

Most clay artists work with strongly three-dimensional objects. Form is the outer shape or contour of a three-dimensional object. Ceramic forms may be simple and direct - examples such as simple cylinders and spheres come to mind. Clay is highly workable, however, and lends itself to inventive and unexpected forms. Many ceramic forms are very complex, with shifting planes and irregular and shifting outlines that look different from every angle. For example, think of John Gill's complex forms, with their contours characterized by abrupt changes in direction.

Ceramists are especially concerned with volume. Volume is the size and capacity of the interior of a three-dimensional object. Jim Lawton says,

"Sculptors displace space, whereas potters capture it." Ceramists rarely work with solid clay forms, rather they make hollow forms by using clay walls to encompass and define a space. The ceramist starts a piece by creating a wall of clay on the potter's wheel or with coils, strips, or slabs of clay. The consequence is that ceramists are often very conscious of volume because they see form and volume as having very different attributes. For the ceramist, form is a shell or wall and volume is the space created and surrounded by that shell. The idea of volume requires much less of the ceramist's imagination than it does for artists who work with a solid material. It is much more difficult to picture the volume of a solid material than one that is hollow.

Form and volume are the core issues in the ceramist's work. This gives the work a generous spirit, a lively and complex character. Because form and volume are such important parts of ceramics, those trained in clay feel that successful work in the medium demands sensitivity to these attributes.

Form & Surface

When we ceramists speak of the character of the work, we are speaking of the character of the form and of the surface. Our material, clay, has dimension and form as its primary characteristic. Ceramists pay close attention to the form of their pieces. Clay forms, furthermore, can be finished with surfaces that enrich the appearance of the piece. These ceramic surfaces are one of the great resources of the ceramist.

Some of the ceramists featured in this book concentrate on the character of the form and ignore or minimize the impact of the surface. For these ceramists, the volumetric form possibilities of the medium are at its core and constitute the heart of the medium. They spend little time developing the surface. They want to focus on the character of the clay or the form and don't want to cover the clay with a distracting surface. Mary Barringer is a good example of a clay artist who wants to enhance rather than cover the surface of the piece. Her surfaces have texture as a result of the forming process. She may add a bit more as she finishes forming the piece. She enhances the natural color of the clay but is careful to reveal its natural character without covering it. Many of the other artists in this book set up a dialogue between form and surface. John Gill, Ron Roy, and Harris Deller are examples, I think, of ceramists who strive to achieve this dialogue.

Finally, there are those who pay a great deal of attention to ceramic surfaces. Some artists work with complex relief surfaces. Sandi Pierantozzi and Neal Patterson both work with a highly patterned relief. David MacDonald has developed an intricate relief imagery on the surface of his pieces. Other clay artists strive for surfaces enriched with complex painted imagery. These artists spend a great deal of time and energy developing their surfaces, for they are the source of much of the energy in their work. Andrea Gill and John Chalke make work that exemplifies this approach. Victor Spinski's rich surfaces mirror the real world. They evolved from the simple, splashed glaze effects he first used in his work in the 1970s. Over the years he has worked to perfect the color and texture of these surfaces. Still others pay most attention to the form but like to apply a decorative layer, a glaze to finish the piece in a pleasing way. Their surfaces function as a kind of patina that "finishes" the piece. Neil Patterson and Sandi Pierantozzi take this approach when glazing their highly patterned relief surfaces. Jeff Oestreich's surfaces evolved from simple reduction glazes to wood-fired surfaces to soda-fired surfaces, all the while picking up richness and complexity. Meanwhile, Roy Strassberg simplifies his surfaces and deprives them of the rich and appealing color they had in his earlier work. He traded this appeal for an atmosphere of stark emotional power.

Many of the artists I discuss here developed their form and surface imagery over a period of time. Barbara Frey is only one example of this. She has taken many years to develop the complex combination of colored clay and slip imagery she

uses in her pieces. Other artists in the book like to develop a new image type every few years. They thrive on the energy and variety this offers. For example, Ric Hirsch has moved his work over the past few years from a sculptural vessel form to a volumetric sculptural form. The form imagery has grown more complex and varied. There is much more contrast of sizes and textures than there was in his previous work and form now dominates its character. Another of these artists, James Lawton, saw his teapots as losing volume and their integrity as vessels. He realized he didn't want to abandon the vessel form and decided to return to an emphasis on the volumetric and vessel character of his pieces. In his most recent work he has combined the classical vessel form with a basket-like shell that produces even more complexity in the spatial character of his pieces.

Education

As I began to talk with the artists in this book, I came to realize just how important education was in shaping their work. Furthermore, it was obvious that for most of them as they were growing up, education seemed to be the most important thing in the world.

During their early explorations, some of these ceramists found that they needed to find a better program. They came to realize that they wanted to learn as much as they could about ceramics and that only in a few

places could they find the training of the highest intensity and thoroughness. They signed up for an intensive program straight from high school. Others were lucky and more or less fell into a fine school and found their way to a great ceramics program. A whole group of the artists I talked to, however, had to find their way to a good program over a period of years. If they realized as undergraduates that they needed to transfer to another school, they did. This was not always easy for them. They lost time, money, and credits. Those who took this route often place great value on the experience. They know how hard it is to find really good ceramic programs. Many others attended undergraduate programs that gave them a good foundation, then went on to the best graduate programs they could find. Those artists who were lucky enough to start out in very good programs or smart enough to realize that they should transfer to a good one, know now how fortunate they are. They know that the really good teachers and well-supported programs are rare.

Some of these artists studied ceramics in programs that they now think were poor. Sometimes this was because the mentor was just not interested. In other cases, the mentor had been interested but had burned out. Many of these artists studied in programs that were small and not well supported. Others never had a course of study specifically in ceramics. Some had a general studio background, others no art background to speak of at all. They had to pick up their knowledge of ceramics from workshops, the occasional course, and the short but intense programs of craft schools and summer workshops.

Some in this book describe their training as revolving very much around the personality and insights of a great teacher. They learned from this person's understanding of the medium and the field. Such programs derive their shape from the instincts of the professor. Planning is not a big part of such programs, but if the mentor is strong enough, the program will be strong. Others characterize their training as quite structured and formal. Programs of this sort generally offered a wide-ranging survey of the field in a disciplined and well thought out manner. The large complex programs in those departments that are seen as high powered are usually organized along these lines and don't leave much to chance. They encourage specialization and the professional's instinct to concentrate on those things that are most likely to enable the student to succeed. They have a number of faculty and the student gets to see more than one point of view. They are competitive and this is an excellent training ground for dealing with the strains of competition and lack of time that all clay artists face as they try to establish and maintain a career.

The really good programs

gave students the tools they needed. Students gained a great deal of discipline and a broad understanding of their field from their education. They learned intense work habits, learned how to use materials, how to make aesthetic judgments, and how to take chances and land on their feet. They learned to imagine themselves as successful. The clearest exposition of this is given by Richard Notkin in his description of his work under Robert Arneson in the ceramics studio at the University of California at Davis. Notkin says of his training there, "We simply worked. We worked very hard and we worked all the time, stopping only for sleep or occasional breaks. We were infected with the spirit of the work. Bob taught us to be artists, not students anymore."

All in all, the testimony of these artists would lead the observer to think that the system works and works quite well. Most of them think more highly of their graduate than their undergraduate education and feel that it was more intense and required a greater degree of maturity and commitment. Just about everyone in this book spoke a great deal about their education and its influence. It was a sometimes difficult and sometimes exhilarating rite of passage.

The Art Environment

Many of the ceramists I write about in this book are very sensitive to their artistic environment. This environment is created in many places and by a great number of people and institutions. Most important are galleries, museums, art departments in colleges and universities, craft institutions, ceramic supply houses, craft shops, magazines, conferences, and workshops.

Currents of thinking in what is called the "art world" have a great influence on ceramists. Mostly this is the world of art galleries in New York, Chicago, and Los Angeles. It is peopled by painters, sculptors, museum curators, gallery owners, and critics. Critical periodicals play an important role. Ceramists,

mixed feelings when she reread the material I had written about her. She talked of this and I realized that I found her reaction fascinating and that I had come to have some of the same feelings. I asked her to write some of her thoughts for the book.

In her note to me, Andrea wrote, "How I make my work is in total subjugation to some concept, some vision, about making. The process serves my needs, physically, emotionally, and conceptually. The process is a tool, and describing how it happens is of no practical use to anyone else because it was invented solely to serve a particular, even peculiar, set of questions that I have about the nature of art." She went on to say, "I worry that a descriptive explanation of the process misses the angst of years of thoughtful questioning that was required to actually make the work. It also misses the insane confidence that what is desired is actually of some importance. A simple description of process makes it all seem so plausible, so real. In fact, this description could be seen as a weird attempt at making some sense out of chaos.

"However, in thinking through why you would take the trouble to write this book, it occurred to me that it will serve a very useful purpose. I will actually enjoy reading how other people make their work, as I am a very nosy person and there is something of the voyeur in all these revelations. The biographical information will also be of interest as it can also be very revealing.

"As far as the technical descriptions are concerned, I think this book will also be important for anyone interested in late 20th century ceramics to know how the work was made. At this point, it seems that ceramics is very much defined by process: that the use of the materials is often central to the meaning of the work. So a detailed description of how work is made will be important in the future. Students searching for their own solutions might get some really helpful suggestions for solving specific problems. They will also see the conceptual connection between the invention in all its diversity of technique and the conceptual content of the work.

"I think artists sometimes are poor judges of the underlying reasons why they make what they make. I wonder if you disagreed with anyone on why they did what they did. But it is a record of why someone *thinks* they make what they make and that will be more interesting as time passes and the work settles into the context of our culture."

A final remark from myself [Richard Zakin]. I was surprised by the artists - they were forthcoming and good judges of why they made what they made. Yes, I sometimes had to delve beneath the expected answers to real ones. This didn't happen often and when it did the artists seemed to understand and conspired with me to come to the truth of things. Ceramists are very serious people and took this project seriously. Furthermore, I would like to think that these artists responded to the way I could talk with them and ask them these difficult questions. I certainly enjoyed their answers. This book has been a way for me to discover important things about ceramics and those who work with it. I have learned a great deal and have had a chance to talk seriously with a group of people I deeply respect. Finally, I feel that description is good and can tell us a lot. If the description is very good, we can infer what cannot be described on paper and we are free to come to our own conclusions.

Glossary

Absorb, absorption: to soak up (a liquid). For example, an immature clay body absorbs water.

Acid: compound usually having a sour taste and capable of neutralizing alkalis and reddening blue litmus paper. Acids are very important in ceramics. Silica, the central element in ceramic bodies and glazes, is an acidic material. Many clays are somewhat acidic and this encourages workability.

Additive process: characterized or produced by addition; for example the ceramist in an additive process adds or joins elements to the surface of a piece.

Aesthetic: pertaining to a sense of the beautiful or to the study of what is perceived of as beautiful.

Agate ware: clay bodies showing an irregularly striped pattern of varied colored bands.

Aggregate: any of various loose, particulate materials such as sand or fired clay. These are added to a clay body to make it stronger in the wet state and more workable. They also control shrinkage or warping.

Alkaline: the opposite of acid materials. Ceramists deal with many alkaline materials. Such compounds as sodium, potassium, and lithium are strong alkalies while calcium, magnesium and zinc are weaker alkalies. Alkalies encourage weak, flabby, unworkable clay bodies. If they are used, it is to create mature clay bodies at low temperatures. They encourage brilliant colored and highly textured glazes but also encourage running and crazing.

Alumina: one of the basic building blocks of clays and glazes. Clays, feldspars, and frits contain alumina. Alumina promotes plasticity and strength in clay bodies, and promotes durability and viscosity in glazes. Alumina is refractory (it discourages melting). Glazes with a moderate alumina content tend to be mat, opaque, nonrunning, and very durable. Glazes with a high alumina content may be dry surfaced.

Anthropomorphic: resembling or made to resemble a human form: an anthropomorphic carving.

Application: lay or spread on: to apply glaze to the ware.

Architectural: having the qualities of architecture; characteristic of architecture; structural; architectonic.

Arretine ware: red, polished pottery characteristic of the Roman Empire, so called because manufacture was at first concentrated at Arretium (modern Arezzo). The body was generally formed in a mold and was frequently decorated with raised designs. It was then painted with a red terra sigillata.

Articulated: having joints, composed of segments.

Artifact: handmade object from the past. The term often refers to an object found at an archaeological excavation.

Asymmetric: not identical on both sides of a central line.

Avant garde: advanced group distinguished by daring, unorthodox, and experimental approaches to creative work.

Bag wall: wall between the flame and the ware found in fuel-burning kilns.

Ball clay: fine particle plastic clay. These clays are used to improve workability in clay bodies and to encourage good suspension in glazes.

Barium: highly alkaline flux that encourages strong color and rich mat surfaces. Unfortunately it is somewhat toxic and should be used with great care. Symbol: Ba

Bas relief: complex art form that combines many features of the two-dimensional pictorial arts and the three-dimensional sculptural arts. Like a picture, a relief has a background that it rests upon; like a sculpture, three-dimensional forms are not merely pictured but are modeled.

Bentonite: clay-like material formed by the decomposition of volcanic ash. Because of its fine particle size, a small amount (2%) encourages plasticity in clay bodies.

B.F.A.: Bachelor of Fine Arts Degree. This is the degree granted undergraduates majoring in art in colleges and universities in the U.S., Canada, and Australia.

Bisque firing: preliminary firing of unglazed ware to prepare the work for glazing.

Blisters: bubbles and craters caused by formation of gases in the glaze during the fire. These can be avoided by allowing the gases to dissipate over a period of time by soaking the ware after the firing is complete (see soaking).

Blue and white decoration: method of ornamentation invented by the Chinese. The ceramist paints on the surface of white porcelain with a slip containing cobalt, then covers the imagery with a clear glaze.

Bone ash, calcium phosphate: used in some white clay bodies to encourage melting and translucency. Used in glazes to encourage bubbling, crawling, and crazing.

Borax: water-soluble compound of sodium, boron, and water. Sometimes used as a flux in glazes but its solubility in water limits its use. Also used for self-glazing clay bodies.

Boric oxide: has characteristics of both a weak acid and an alkali. It melts at a low temperature and is a strong flux. It is water-soluble and therefore of limited use in glazes.

Boron: an element. Materials containing boron encourage strong melting. Most boron containing materials are water-soluble and therefore of limited use in glazes. A natural material, Gerstley borate and fritted compounds of boron are not water soluble and have a widespread use.

Cadmium: colorant used to create red and orange colors. It is toxic and burns out in temperatures above cone 06. New stains have been developed in which the cadmium is shielded from the effects of heat and the materials in the glaze. These stains can withstand high temperatures.

Calcine: process of heating a material to drive off organic impurities and water or carbon (these are driven off as gases). Calcined materials are used to make recipes more stable and useful.

Calix: chalice.

Carbon trapping: buildup of carbon at the early stages of the firing that darkens and clouds glaze color. Though sometimes considered a glaze fault, many ceramists value its rich smoky effects and actively try to create it.

Cast forming: to form an object by pouring a clay slip into a mold and letting it harden. The result is a clay form that is a reproduction of the inner surface of the mold.

Casting slip: clay and water mixture with the addition of a small percentage of an alkaline deflocculant. A deflocculated clay slip needs less water to attain a liquid state. It will dry quickly in the mold without saturating the plaster.

Celadon: glaze often used on Chinese porcelains. It is a translucent, pale green glaze and has a satin mat surface. Celadon glazes contain calcium and iron and are fired in a reduction atmosphere.

Checkered bag wall: wall between the flame and the ware in a fuel-burning kiln in which bricks have been placed in such a way as to create openings so some flame can reach the ware and cause flashing.

Cheese hard: when a clay body dries to a point where it is still fairly moist and can be paddled and it will hold its new shape (see also leather hard).

Chinoiserie: style of ornamentation popular in 18th century Europe characterized by intricate patterns and the use of motifs associated with Chinese culture.

Chromium, chrome, chromium oxide: before firing this oxide is green in color. It makes rich green, orange, red, black, and pink colors. It is highly toxic and is often used in its stain form.

Clay body: compound of clay and nonclay materials chosen for their individual characteristics that, when combined, meet the specific requirements of the ceramist.

Clay to nonclay ratio: ratio of clay to nonclay materials in a clay body. This has a significant effect on the handling character of the clay body and the way it acts in the fire. Higher clay amounts encourage workability, lower ones encourage strong bonds between clay body and glaze and appealing body colors.

Cobalt: powerful colorant that yields blue colors. The two forms of cobalt widely available are cobalt oxide and cobalt carbonate. Both give a strong blue color.

Coil forming: "snakes" of clay built up in a spiral to form the wall of the piece.

Colloids: materials with a very fine particle size. Colloidal materials are useful to the ceramist because they encourage workability in clay bodies and good suspension in engobes and glazes. They may be added to the clay body during the mixing process.

Colorant: mineral or compound of minerals used to color ceramic materials.

The most common colorants are iron oxide, cobalt oxide or carbonate, copper carbonate, rutile (a compound of titanium and iron), and manganese dioxide.

Colored clay body: clay body that contains materials that yield color.

Cone, firing cone: narrow three-sided pyramids made from ceramic materials. Mimicking clay bodies and glazes, pyrometric cones react to the combination of time and temperature (often called heat work) by softening and bending. Ceramists use them to indicate the state of the clay bodies and glazes in the kiln.

Contour: outline of a figure or object; the edge or line that defines or bounds a shape or object.

Copper carbonate: useful colorant that yields green colors. The oxide is more powerful than the carbonate but the carbonate is less gritty and easier to use.

Copper oxide: useful colorant that yields green colors.

Crawling: glaze defect in which the glaze forms in separate droplets during firing rather than in a smooth durable surface. It is caused by dusty clay surfaces or by a very viscous glaze.

Crazing: crazing takes place when the glaze shrinks much more than the clay body. When this happens the brittle glaze reacts to the stress by cracking. These cracks create a web work of fine lines forming a geometric pattern.

Crocus martis: ferrous sulphate, a water-soluble form of iron oxide.

Cross draft kiln: fuel-burning kiln with the flue on the side opposite the source of heat. The flames travel through the ware and are then drawn up the chimney.

Cryolite: sodium, aluminum, fluoride. Its fluorine content encourages strong bubbling and boiling during the firing. Its out-gassing products are toxic during firing.

Damp box: moisture laden closed chamber. The ceramist places the piece in it to keep it from drying.

Damper: movable plate for regulating the flow of air in a fuel-burning kiln.

Decal: specially prepared paper bearing an image or design for transfer to the ceramic surface.

Defloccation: causes the platelets in a clay body to repel each other and make the clay more liquid and less plastic. Ceramists use deflocculation to create slips for use in the slipcast forming process.

Deflocculent: alkaline material that encourages clay particles to repel each other.

Delft ware: earthenware having an opaque white glaze with an overglaze decoration, usually in blue. Delft ware started as an imitation of blue and white ware from China but evolved into a product with its own identity.

Design: 1. artistic use of line, shape, form, color, and balance. 2. course that isolates line shape, form, color, and balance to allow students to study these aspects of art intensively.

Dipping: to plunge an object into a liquid so as to coat the object with the liquid. Many ceramists apply glazes by dipping the piece in the glaze.

Dolomite: calcium magnesium carbonate, a very common mineral useful in ceramic glazes. Dolomite, like all calcium/magnesium containing materials, is a weak flux till cone 8 and then a very powerful flux (and an encouragement to visual texture) at cone 8 and higher.

Egyptian Faience, Egyptian Paste: Egyptian paste bodies are a special sort of self-glazing clay body. They contain soluble fluxes and a water-soluble colorant (quite often one brilliant in color).

Electric kiln: kiln heated using coils made from a heat resistant metal alloy. An electric current is forced through the coils which radiate heat into the kiln chamber. The kiln chamber is made from insulating brick and the heat builds up in the kiln chamber.

Embedded imagery: imagery fixed in a surrounding mass. An example is an imagery made from a colored clay body embedded in another clay body.

Embellishment: to enhance or beautify by ornamentation; ceramic relief imagery is an example of embellishment or ornamentation.

Enamel: smooth, glassy low-fire glaze, usually opaque.

Engobe: Engobes have a clay content that varies from 25% to 50% of the recipe. The rest of the mix is nonclay materials.

Extruded: to force or press out; in ceramics extrusion is used to create clay forms of a specified cross section.

Extruder: machine used to force clay through a die to form the specified cross section.

Faenza: city in northern Italy and an important center for ceramics. It is especially known for majolica, tin-glazed earthenware produced from the late 14th century.

Feldspar: any of a group of minerals containing alumina and silica and lesser amounts of potassium, sodium, and calcium. Feldspars are important ingredients in clay bodies, slips, and glazes.

Filler: neutral material. Clay body fillers are nonplastic additions to the body generally used to increase strength and lower shrinkage. Their particle size varies from very coarse to very fine. Coarse fillers: see aggregate.

Fillet: coil of clay placed at the corner joining two ceramic form elements such as two slabs. The fillet strengthens the bonds between the two form elements, thus discouraging cracking at the join and giving it a more finished look.

Fire box: area in a fuel-burning kiln where combustion takes place.

Fire clay: coarse large-particle clay that contributes strength and workability. In itself it is only moderately plastic but it may significantly enhance plasticity by encouraging particle size differentiation. Fire clays tend to be buff, tan, or ocher in color due to a moderate iron content (1% to 3%) and titanium (1% to 3%).

Flashing: uneven color on the surface of ceramic ware created in the firing. There are many causes including direct flame, votalization, and a reduction atmosphere.

Flocculant: material that causes flocculation. Ceramic flocculants are usually weak acids

Flocculate/Flocculaton: to cause clay particle grouping by the addition of acidic materials to encourage plasticity.

Flocculent: acidic material that encourages tightly arranged clumping of clay particles. This can encourage plasticity.

Flocking: finely powdered cloth glued to ceramic surfaces after firing. It is used for producing a velvety surface on ceramic pieces.

Floriated, floriate: made of or decorated with floral ornamentation.

Fluting: evenly spaced vertical grooves or furrows created on the surface of the form.

Flux: material that causes melting. Examples are such materials as barium, calcium boron, sodium, potassium, and silicon.

Form: outer shape or contour of a three-dimensional object.

Frit: specially prepared compounds of powdered glass containing silica, alumina, and melters. While more expensive than many naturally occurring minerals that find use in ceramics, they are highly valued and used widely for their stabilizing character and strong melting powers. Sodium, calcium, and boron are the most common melting ingredients in frits.

Funk: ceramic movement of the 1960s and 1970s characterized by an interest in imagery from popular culture and marked by an ironic sense of humor and the use of visual/verbal puns.

Gerstley borate: fluxing material containing calcium, sodium, and boron.

Glassy: resembling glass, as in transparency or smoothness.

Glaze: glassy coating especially formulated to fit over a clay form. Glazes contain silica, alumina, and melter.

Globar: type of electric kiln with elements that are quite thick and can withstand firing temperatures up to cone 10. Unfortunately the elements are delicate and kilns of this sort are very expensive.

Greenware: unfired and still moist ceramic ware.

Grog: coarse-particled aggregate additions to clay bodies made from grains of fired clay. It discourages warping and encourages durability.

Ground silica (flint): a finely ground silica powder, free of impurities. This is an important source of silica in ceramic recipes (clay bodies, slips, engobes, and glazes).

Grout: fine particled mortar used to fill in the spaces between tiles or mosaics.

Harmony: consistent, orderly, or pleasing arrangement of parts; congruity.

High fire: firing temperatures from cone 8 to cone 12. Contemporary ceramists value the high fire for its muted earthy color range and wide variety of glaze textures.

Homosote: very thick cardboard material (usually 1/2" or more). Intended for the building trades, its durability and absorbency make it very useful to the ceramist.

Hydraulic pressing: creating forms such as plates and tiles using pressure. This pressure is created by using a hydraulic mechanism in a press designed for the process.

Impermeability: unpenetrable. In ceramics refers generally to the ability

of mature clay bodies to hold water without absorbing it or allowing it to flow through the body.

Impress: to produce a mark or image by pressing a stamp or tool into the surface of wet clay.

Inlay: process in which a clay or a slip is set into the surface of the piece to create an ornamental imagery.

Intangible: not tangible; incapable of being perceived by the sense of touch, an incorporeal or immaterial thing; impalpable.

Interstice: space between segments or parts. In the study of form: the space between one form and another. In glazing: any area that will catch glaze, a groove, crack, or the area where one form joins another forming a corner.

Iridescence: play of lustrous, changing colors looking very much like a film of oil in water. Iridescent surfaces in ceramics are members of a family of recipes called lusters.

Iron: common metallic element.

Iron - black iron oxide: FeO. Iron with one atom of oxygen. This is similar to red iron oxide but is darker in color.

Iron - red iron oxide: $Fe2O3$. Iron with two atoms of oxygen. Encourages brick red, tan, orange, brown, and soft green colors.

Iron chromate: blend of iron and chrome. Encourages black and gray colors (due to its chrome content, this is a toxic material).

Iron impurities: material that contains extraneous iron. A clay that contains iron impurities will darken the color of a clay body, for example, turning an otherwise white clay body light tan.

Kaolin: clay distinguished by its great purity and whiteness. Kaolins tend to be less easily worked than other clays but this difficulty is compensated for by their beauty and refined character.

Kiln: chamber used for holding and firing ceramic objects. Kilns allow control of the fire, the safe containment of pieces to be fired, and the attainment of high temperatures.

Kinetic: characterized by movement. Ceramic forming and glazing methods are kinetic activities. The movements that make up these activities influence the look of the resulting piece.

Kraft paper: strong unbleached brown paper appropriate for utilitarian tasks.

Kyanite: similar to grog, both are coarse aggregates. Kyanite, however, is more pure and free of color and melting impurities. It is made from small granules of aluminum silicate.

Leather hard: when a clay body dries to a point where it is still somewhat moist but can now hold its shape it is said to be leather hard (see also cheese hard).

Lime blowing (also spitting out and calcium popping): when a particle of lime or calcium is trapped inside the clay wall it will eventually absorb moisture, expand and push away a segment of the wall revealing the white colored speck at the heart of the break. It is most often looked upon as a fault in ceramics.

Lithium carbonate: material that encourages strong melting and rich visual textures. Unfortunately it can affect the brain and put the ceramist in danger. Spodumene, also a source of lithium, is preferred.

Low fire: firing temperatures up to cone 1. Contemporary ceramists value the low fire for its color and image possibilities.

Luster: state or quality of shining by reflecting light; a lustered surface can glitter or sparkle or can have a sheen or gloss.

Luster glazes: glaze recipes that produce metallic lusters. Virginia Scotchie's bronze luster glaze is an example of this kind of recipe.

Magnesite: source of magnesium carbonate, a mineral.

Magnesium: element of the alkaline earth group. Its chemical symbol is Mg. In ceramics the most important magnesium containing minerals are dolomite, talc, and magnesium carbonate; used to stabilize low- and mid-fire glazes and flux high-fire glazes. Talc is used a great deal in clay bodies where it acts as a flux.

Magnesium carbonate: commercial product that is very finely ground and encourages stability in low- and mid-fire glazes and melting in high-fire glazes. It also encourages good suspension in the glaze bucket.

Majolica: brilliantly colored glaze painting technique employing an opaque white glaze which serves as a ground for the application of colored stains. This technique was extensively used in European ceramics in the 15th and 16th centuries.

Majolica glaze: low-fire glaze type, the main ingredients of which are lead oxide (a strong melter) and tin oxide (an opacifier). These opaque white glazes are formulated to work well with applied color.

Manganese dioxide: strong colorant. In small percentages (1/4% to 1%) it encourages mauve colors. At larger percentages (up to 6%) it encourages dark gray and black colors.

Maquette: small three-dimensional model.

Mastic: paste-like cement used for gluing tiles or mosaics to a mounting board or a wall surface.

Maturity: arrival at a desired point in the firing. When applied to clay bodies, an optimum point at which warping and brittleness are kept to a minimum and the absorption rate is reasonably low: when applied to glazes, the point at which the glaze produces a desired effect. Generally glazes are called mature when they are fully melted in the fire and are glassy (though not necessarily shiny) in surface.

Melter: compound that causes melting, facilitating glaze formation. Melters include silicates, feldspars, and fluxes.

Metallic luster: thin iridescent metallic film produced on the surface of a ceramic glaze.

M.F.A.: Master of Fine Arts Degree. Training for advanced students of ceramics to prepare them for working in the ceramic field as an artist or an artist teacher (usually at the college level). Awarded in the U.S., Canada, and Australia.

Mica: feldspar-like material distinguished by a structure composed of numerous sheets that can be split apart. Ceramic suppliers sell a powdered mica. This can help clay bodies resist thermal shock and encourage melting and good workability.

Mid-fire: firing temperatures from cone 2 to cone 7. Contemporary ceramists value the mid-fire for its wide variety of color, durability, and economy.

Modular: construction in which modules play a significant role.

Modules: uniform structural elements.

Mold: hollow form or matrix for giving a particular shape to clay.

Mold forming: creation of ceramic forms by pressing moist clay or pouring liquid clay (casting slip) in the mold.

Molochite: porcelain grog

Molten: melted. A solid material is molten when heated to the point where it has melted and is in a liquid state.

Monochromatic: having one color. Monochromatic pottery has one color such as red, brown, gray, or white.

Multiple firing: firing a piece more than once. The term is generally understood to exclude bisque firing. Multiple firing strategies may be used to repair a fault or as part of a normal process of creating an imagery.

Muriatic acid: weak solution of hydrochloric acid used to clean grout from the surface of tiles and mosaics.

Narrative imagery: representation of stories, events, or feelings using clay, slip, or glaze imagery.

Nephaline syenite: feldspar high in sodium and alumina. A strongly melting addition to slips and glazes.

Nylon: short, very fine nylon fibers. When added to the clay body in amounts such as .5% it improves the strength and workability of the wet clay body.

One-of-a-kind/One off: a unique piece, not part of a group of pieces.

Opacifier: material that blocks the passage of light through the glaze, rendering the glaze opaque. Opacifiers encourage the formation of small bubbles or crystals that change the structure of the glaze and block the passage of light.

Oribe: type of Japanese ceramics. The term Oribe yaki ("Oribe ware") is used to describe a type of painted pottery influenced by the taste of the Japanese tea master Furuta Oribe (born 1544, died 1615).

Ornament: stamped, sprigged, carved (incised and excised), engraved, and cut (reticulated) imagery.

Oxidation: combination of an element with oxygen to create an oxide compound.

Oxidation firing: allowing ready access of oxygen to the firing chamber at all times. Most electric kilns are designed and constructed so that an oxidation atmosphere exists during the firing.

Panel: comparatively thin, flat form. In ceramics, a flat tile.

Paper pulp: mixture of water and organic materials that will become paper or cardboard when it dries.

Particle: very small piece. Dry clay or glaze materials are made up of granules or particles.

Particle size variation: varied particle sizes in a clay or clay body. A varied particle size encourages workability and strength.

Patina: metallic film occurring on the surface of the piece, produced during the firing.

Photo transfer imagery: process of converting a photographic image into a silkscreen or decal image that is then transferred to the surface of a ceramic piece.

Pinch forming: forming a piece by hollowing out a lump of clay. To do this the potter presses the thumbs into the clay, then presses the clay towards the fingers to thin the wall and increase the height of the piece.

Pinhole: very small bare spot in the glaze caused by a bubble forming in a glaze during the firing that doesn't heal. It is generally felt to be a glaze fault.

Plasticity: ability of wet clay to be formable and to hold its shape once the ceramist gives it form. It is one of the most important characteristics of clay.

Plasticizing agent: ingredient added to a clay body recipe to improve plasticity and workability. Plasticizers include organic materials such as yogurt and extremely fine particle materials such as colloids.

Porcelain: pure white clay body which is translucent where thin. Bodies are defined as porcelain if they contain no more than 50% clay (and that clay must be white in color); the other half must be composed of ground silica (flint) and feldspar. Porcelain, with its white color and hard glassy surface, can be very beautiful and it is highly valued.

Porcelain-like/Porcelainous: a recipe that does not satisfy the complete definition of porcelain but does have many of its characteristics.

Potash: potassium oxide.

Potassium: chemical element potassium is an alkali. It is a very important ingredient in feldspars.

Potter's wheel: wheel or disc designed to spin and hold a clay lump so it can be shaped by the potter's hands.

Press forming, press molding: creation of ceramic forms by pressing moist clay into a mold.

Process: series of progressive and interdependent steps by which a goal is attained. For example: to devise a process for creating a colored clay piece.

Production pottery: pottery designed to be readily produced in fairly large numbers and intended for sale at reasonable prices. Differences between each piece are small and the significance of each piece is as part of a group.

Pug mill: mill for grinding and mixing the ingredients of a clay body to a workable state.

Pyrometric cones: narrow three-sided pyramids. Mimicking clay bodies and glazes, pyrometric cones react to the combination of time and temperature (often called heat work). As time passes and the temperature increases, the cones soften and bend. The ceramist uses the deformation of the cone as an indication that the clay bodies are mature and the glazes are melted and glassy and that the firing is complete.

Pyrophyllite: mineral compound composed of alumina and silica. Pyrophyllite is used as filler in clay bodies. It discourages shrinkage and encourages durability.

Raku: quick firing and cooling method that originated in Japan. The original raku work consisted of a cream colored base glaze with brush-painted umber imagery. When adopted by potters in the U.S., the type was mutated in various ways, most notably to work with multi-hued, brilliant glaze color and metallic lusters.

Rebus: using pictures or symbols to represent a word or a phrase. The potter George Ohr used a rebus when he wrote on a clay coin, "I love you," then drew an image of a deer to suggest the phrase "I love you dear."

Recipe (the word "formula" is often used for this term): listing of the materials in a clay body, slip, or glaze.

Reduction cooling: creating a reduction atmosphere inside the firing chamber while the kiln is cooling (see striking).

Reduction firing: firing with a minimum amount of oxygen. In reduction firing, the potter interrupts the flow of adequate oxygen to the kiln's firing chamber at certain crucial periods during the firing. Reduction firing strongly influences the characteristic look of clay bodies and glazes.

Refire: fire a piece more than once. Generally done in the glaze fire to obtain a desired surface effect or imagery.

Refractory: resistant to heat.

Reoxidation: firing in an oxidation atmosphere after the kiln chamber has been fired in reduction. This modifies some of the effects of reduction and encourages color that combines the richness of reduction and the clarity of oxidation.

Rib (potter's rib): tool for smoothing the clay surface. It can be made from wood, rubber, metal, or plastic.

Rutile: colorant compound of iron and titanium. It encourages earthy orange colors.

Saggar: box made of refractory fired clay in which ceramic wares are enclosed and protected during the firing. Contemporary ceramists often fire pieces in saggars filled with organic materials. When they burn off during the firing, they leave rich markings on the surface of the piece.

Saggar clay: very fine particled ball clay used in clay bodies. It is highly plastic. It should not be used in amounts over 10% to 15% because it encourages shrinkage and cracking.

Salt firing: salt introduced into the firing chamber during the high temperature part of the firing. The salt is scattered throughout the kiln and over the surfaces of the work. The sodium in the salt unites with the silica in the clay to create a glazed "skin" on the surface of the pieces.

Salt kiln: kiln designed and dedicated to salt firing.

Sandblasting: blast of compressed air loaded with sand, used as an abrasive to soften glaze surfaces and give them a stony mat character.

Sawdust firing (also pit firing): in this kind of firing the ceramist places bisque-fired pieces in a heat proof container filled with sawdust. The sawdust is ignited and burns slowly for four hours or more. The effect of the uneven smoky fire is a mottled gray and black imagery. The pieces are usually finished with an application of wax.

Sawdust loading (of clay bodies): sawdust mixed in the clay body. The sawdust burns out, leaving a pattern of small pits scattered over the surface of the piece.

Scarab: a representation or image of a beetle. The ancient Egyptians used this symbol a great deal in their seals and amulets and on their pots.

Sculpture: figurative or abstract works of art in three dimensions, in relief or in the round.

Scumming: film of calcium that forms on the surface of the clay body or the glaze in low-fire work. It is generally felt to be a body or glaze fault.

Self-glazing bodies: bodies that contain water-soluble fluxes that migrate to the surface of the piece as it dries. The fluxes are deposited as a film over the surface of the piece. When the piece is fired, the film combines with the silica and alumina in the body to create a thin layer of glaze on the surface of the ware.

Shard: broken ceramic fragment.

Shivering: glaze patches forced away from the ware, leaving sections of unglazed body visible; most easily observed at the corners and edges of the piece. Shivering occurs when the body shrinks more than the glaze. It can be eliminated by increasing the shrinkage of the glaze or by decreasing the shrinkage of the clay body.

Sieve: tool with a meshed or perforated bottom used for separating coarse from fine particles in powders and liquids.

Silica: element that, along with alumina, is one of the building blocks of all clays and glazes. The sources of silica are powdered silica, feldspars, clays, and silicates (talc and wollastonite).

Silica powder (see also flint): ground silica is a finely ground silica powder, free of impurities. It is an important source of silica in ceramic recipes (clay bodies, slips, engobes, and glazes).

Single fire: going directly from the greenware state to the final firing, avoiding an intermediate bisque firing.

Slab: broad flat piece or slice of clay.

Slip: viscous mixture of clay and water. Slips are used in a number of ways, as a sort of "glue" to hold clay pieces together, as the raw material for slipcasting, and as a mixture of clay (or clays) and water, applied to the surface of the clay piece for decorative effect.

Slipcasting: to form an object by pouring a fluid clay slip in a mold and letting it harden.

Slip trailing: method that allows the ceramist to apply an ornamental raised line of slip on the surface of a ceramic piece. The ceramist fills a syringe with a thick slip and squeezes it to create a raised line.

Slumping: to deform and sag; typically clay forms slump during the height of the firing.

Slurry: thin mixture of clay with water, similar to a slip.

Soaking: firing strategy in which the ceramist maintains the temperature inside the firing chamber at a desired point (at maturity, or a few hundred degrees below maturity) for a period of time.

Soda firing: similar to salt firing but here the ceramist introduces soda (sodium carbonate) into the firing chamber during the latter part of the firing.

Sodium: an alkali and a very strong melter. It is one of the most important fluxes in ceramics.

Sodium bicarbonate: water-soluble compound of sodium and carbon, especially useful as a frit ingredient.

Sodium feldspar (also soda feldspar): this is an important feldspar type. Sodium feldspars are powerfully melting and very useful in the low and mid fire. They encourage brilliant color.

Sodium silicate: compound of sodium and silica. It is a strong melter and highly alkaline. It is often used as a deflocculant.

Soft paste porcelain: mid-fire porcelain. Traditionally, porcelain is fired to very high temperatures, 1260°C or higher (cones 9 to 12). Porcelain fired to a mid-fire temperature such as cone 6 must contain very strong melters, which make the body somewhat softer and less dense than porcelain, but it is still durable and beautiful.

Solid forming: method in which the ceramist forms the piece from a solid lump of clay. The ceramist will often go back and hollow out the form to avoid explosions.

Soluble: capable of being dissolved or liquefied.

Spodumene: lithium containing feldspar. It discourages expansion and contraction and encourages strong melts and visual textures. It should be used in tandem with other feldspars to avoid glaze fit problems.

Stains: calcined mixtures of kaolin and ceramic colorants. These colorants are modified by the addition of materials that affect their color. Stains are added to the glaze in varying amounts, usually 3% to 8%. While relatively expensive, they have certain advantages over naturally occurring colorants: their color range is wide and their action is predictable and reliable. They may, however, be adversely affected by other ingredients in the recipe and must be tested before use.

Stamping: to impress with a device made from a hard, nonstick material such as wood, plaster, or rubber.

Stoneware clay: term used in North America to designate a raw clay that matures at cones 8 to 9. It is plastic and workable. Its color is due to a moderate iron content (1% to 3%) and titanium (1% to 3%). Stoneware clays are valued for their blend of workability and strength.

Stoneware clay body: body that contains a high percentage of clay (mostly stoneware clay) and a low percentage of nonclay materials. Typical colors are buff, tan, orange, or brown. They have good particle size variation and are very workable and durable. They mature at cones 6 to 11.

Striking: maintaining a flame during cooling to cause reduction in the cooling phase. This encourages luster surfaces. This method was first used in the Middle East in the 9th century.

Strip coils: forming process where the artist rolls out strips of clay and assembles the form by adding one strip on another.

Strontium carbonate: compound similar to barium but much less toxic. In ceramics it is used as a flux that encourages mat surfaces and rich color.

Styrofoam: brand of expanded plastic made from polystyrene.

Subtractive forming: method for creating forms or imagery by carving away clay.

Symmetry: similarity of form on opposite sides of an object.

Syringe: device consisting of a tube with a narrow opening at one end and a piston or a rubber bulb at the other end. Ceramists use it for extruding a slip or glaze through the narrow opening.

Tactile: discernible to the sense of touch, capable of being touched or felt.

Talc: compound of calcium, magnesium, and silica. Its main use in ceramics is as a body flux. It is also used in glazes as a flux.

Talc body: a low- or mid-fire clay body that contains a significant amount of talc (usually 25% to 50%). Because of the slippery character of the talc, these clay bodies tend to be fairly workable though they are low in clay.

Tangible: capable of being touched; material or substantial. Palpable.

Technology: branch of knowledge that deals with the creation and use of technical means to aid in the creation of ceramic pieces.

Temmoku: glaze made from a dark colored, iron bearing clay slip. Both Daniel Rhodes and Nigel Wood propose an addition of wood ash. This would encourage the strong visual textures we see in these glazes.

Template: pattern used as a guide for cutting or forming. Templates are usually made from sheet metal, cardboard, or plastic.

Terra cotta clay: high iron clay. Due to their impurities, especially iron, these clays have a strong brick red color.

Terra cotta clays mature at a low temperature.

Terra sigillata: very fine particle slip. Made by separating the clay particles and retaining only the finest ones. Terra sigillatas are opaque, durable, and rich in color and surface.

Tessera: small tile-like element used along with other tesserae to create a mosaic. Tesserae are of concern to the ceramist because clay is a useful material for the creation of tesserae.

Thermal expansion: expansion caused by heat or temperature.

Thixotropic: property exhibited by some clays and clay bodies to soften and become jelly-like or even liquid when stirred or shaken.

Throwing (on the potter's wheel): forming ceramic pieces on a swiftly turning platform.

Tile: thin slab of fired clay, sometimes glazed. Some are purely ornamental, others are used to protect floors, walls, ceilings, and roofs.

Tin oxide: used in glazes as an opacifier generally in amounts of 2% to 3%.

Titanium: used in small amounts (up to 2%), this nontoxic material encourages visual texture and durability in glazes.

Tooth: texture. A strongly textured clay body is said to have tooth.

Top hat kiln: kiln that consists of a base and a top. The top can be raised and lowered over the base. The work is loaded on the base, then the ceramist lowers the kiln and fires the piece. This kind of kiln is quickly and easily loaded.

Treadle wheel: manually (pedal) powered wheel. The potter pushes rhythmically with the foot to turn the flywheel.

Trivet: tile or plate with short legs. In use it is placed under a hot platter or dish to protect a table.

Trompe l'oeil: (deceive the eye) way of working in two or three dimensions in which objects are rendered with extreme accuracy and fine detail. The emphasis is on illusion and mimicry of texture and color.

Utilitarian: emphasizing usefulness over beauty. Utilitarian ceramics are generally made for use at the table and in the kitchen, as plant containers and in architecture (especially in the form of tiles).

Viscosity: resistance to flow. In glazes a high viscosity glaze resists flow in the firing. A glaze that flows a great deal is said to have a low viscosity. Glazes with a low viscosity are marked by appealing glaze flow patterns but may flow onto the kiln shelf during the firing.

Vitreous: glassy. A material is defined as vitreous if it resembles glass in its hardness, glossiness, impermeability (ability to hold water), and/or transparency. Vitreous china is a hard, durable, water-impermeable material.

Volume: size and capacity of the interior of a three-dimensional object. The ceramist's methods almost always involve the creation of hollow, volumetric forms.

Volumetric: piece in which the form is marked by a strong consciousness of volume and takes its identity from its interior space - its volume.

Warp: to twist or distort. Ceramic pieces may twist or distort during drying or in the firing.

Water-soluble: capable of being dissolved or liquified in water.

Wax: solid substance similar to a fat or an oil. In ceramics, waxes are used to protect or beautify surfaces and to act as a resist material during glazing.

Wedging: kneading the clay body, forcing one part of a lump of clay into another. This forces much of the air out of the clay body and encourages a uniform moisture content.

Wedgwood ware: ceramic work made with colored clay bodies. Named after the English ceramists Josiah Wedgwood.

White body: clay body containing only white clay plus nonclay materials free of impurities.

White stoneware. comparatively workable, opaque white clay body. Like porcelain, it must contain only white or colorless clays and melters. Unlike porcelain, it may have a fairly high clay to nonclay ratio.

Whiting (calcium carbonate): a flux. Below cone 8 its melting power is fairly low. Above cone 8 it is a powerful melter. It is used in slips, engobes, and glazes. It promotes durability and, especially above cone 8, rich glaze surfaces.

Wollastonite: mineral in which calcium and silica are combined. It encourages resistance to warping in clay bodies.

Wood ash: ashes of burnt wood used because it encourages rich visual textures in glazes. The glaze melt has an uneven texture marked by runny and comparatively refractory areas in close proximity. Wood ashes are complex mixtures of coarse minerals, mostly fluxes, which melt unevenly in the glaze fire.

Wood firing: use of wood as a fuel in a ceramic firing. The wood ash and alternating reduction and oxidation atmosphere created during a wood firing creates rich effects on the surface of work fired in a wood fire.

Wood kiln: kiln designed for firing with wood. It requires a specially designed firebox which will accommodate the wood.

Workability: combination of durability and plasticity that defines the way the ceramist can work with a clay body. A clay body with good workability will be easily shaped and formed.

Wysiwyg: what you see is what you get. In ceramic parlance this means if it goes into the kiln with a particular look it will come from the fire with a similar look.

Yixing (or Yi hsing or I Hsing): ceramic center in China. It gives its name to a mid-fire ware, made with unglazed clay. Clay colors vary from tan, gray, red, brown, or black pieces. Yixing teapots are especially well known and admired.

Zinc oxide: most often used in small amounts (typically 2%) in ceramic glazes and is valued as a supplemental flux and glaze hardener. Zinc is of very low toxicity and can be used in glazes intended for use with food.

Zirconium opacifiers: group of compounds containing the element zirconium. This element encourages the formation of bubbles that interfere with the passage of light in glazes and make it opaque. Generally used in additions of 10% to 12%.

Index

Note: The letter c next to the page number indicates it is a caption.

abstract expressionism - 274
Africa and African culture
    MacDonald 77, 78c, 79c, 83
    Oestreich 226
    Patterson 121
aggregates added to clay bodies
    Chabot 217, 218c
    di Petta 232c, 233c, 234, 235
    Gill, John 14
    Huey 142c, 144c, 145c
    Mangus 195
    Neely 214
    Netzer 161c
    Patterson 121
    Pierantozzi 115
    Scotchie 181,183c
    Spinski 62
    Strassberg 22
    VisGirda 28
    Walker 202
Alberta College of Art
    Chalke 47
    Tipton 245
Alberta, University of
    Chalke 47
Alfred, New York State College of Ceramics
    Cochrane 93, 94
    Forrest 178
    Gill, Andrea 69, 76
    Gill, John 13, 17-19
    Higby 105, 111, 112
    Huey 143, 147, 275
    Lawton 157
    Neely 212, 213c
    Netzer 164
    Oestreich 231, 270
    Pinnell 265, 275
    Pitts 103
    Roy 131
    Schnabel 37
    Scotchie 185
    Zakin 251
American Crafts Museum
    Gill, Andrea 76
    Gill, John 17
    Higby 111
Anderson Ranch Art Center
    Patterson 125
    Pierantozzi 119
application strategies - 269
Arbuckle, Linda
    Schnabel 38
Archie Bray Foundation
    Gill, Andrea 76
    Gill, John 17
    Katz 52, 54
    Kwong 138
    Mangus 200
    Notkin 60
Arneson, Robert
    Gill, John 16

Notkin 56, 58-59, 273
    VisGirda 30-31
Arntz, Michael
    Hayakawa 190
Art Institute of Chicago
    Deller 89
    Lawton 157
    Pitts 103
Babu, Victor
    Gill, Andrea 74
    Gill, John 17
    Katz 52
    Notkin 57
Baldwin, Gordon
    Forrest 178
Banff Centre for the Arts
    Schnabel 40
Barringer, Mary - 141, 271
Bath Academy of Art
    Chalke 45
Bauer, Fred
    Higby 111
Bennington College
    Barringer 171
Bimidji State University
    Oestreich 229, 230
    VisGirda 31
bone ash
    Chalke 41c, 42, 44c, 46c
    Scotchie 183c
Bova, Joe
    Lawton 156
    Patterson 124
    Schnabel 38
Branham, Wayne
    Pinnell 265
Bringle, Cynthia
    Lawton 156
    Patterson 124
Brodie, Regis
    Chabot 222
Brooklyn Museum Art School
    Chabot 220
    Zakin 231
Brouillard, William
    Kwong 138
    Patterson 123
    Pitts 103
Brown, Ron
    Strassberg 24
Burns, Mark
    Hayakawa 192
Bush, Larry
    Pitts 103
Calgary, University of
    Chalke 45, 47
    Tipton 245
California State University
    Deller 88
    Hayakawa 192
    VisGirda 30-31
California, University of
    Hayakawa 190
    Notkin 58-59, 273
Callanwould
    Schnabel 37-38
Canada Council Grants
    Chalke 47
    di Petta 238
    Forrest 178
Cardew, Michael
    Oestreich 225, 230
Carey, Sheldon
    Neely 212

carved imagery
    Barringer 171
    Chabot 218c
    di Petta 235c
    Frey 255, 257c, 259
    Higby 106c, 107
    MacDonald 78, 79c, 80
    Mangus 196-97, 197c, 199c
    Spinski 62, 63c
Casson, Mick
    Patterson 125
casting - [slipcasting]
    di Petta 233, 234, 235c, 237, 237c, 238
    Gill, John 16
    Notkin 55, 55c, 57, 57c, 58c, 60
    Spinski 61, 63c, 67c
    Tipton 242
Centennial College
    Roy 131
ceramic science, influence on creativity
    Chalke 47
    di Petta 233-34, 237-38
    Mangus 200
    Neely 209, 211, 214-216
    Pinnell 265, 267
    Roy 131
    Tipton 242, 243
    VisGirda 30
    Zakin 247, 253
Ceramics Monthly Magazine
    Tipton 243
    Zakin 251-253
Chabot, Aurore - 208, 275
Chalke, John - 6, 269, 272
    Tipton 239, 240, 245
Chamberlin, Scott
    Pitts 103
Chicago, University of
    Notkin 57
Chihuly, Dale
    Higby 111
    Kwong 136
China and Chinese culture
*see also Yixing
    Chalke 44
    Cochrane 91c, 97
    Frey 254c, 257, 259
    Higby 106, 112
    Hirsch 10
    Kwong 135, 136
    MacDonald 81
    Neely 216c
    Notkin 60
    Pinnell 260c, 261, 263, 265, 267
    Walker 205c
Chipperfield, Michael
    Tipton 242
City College of New York
    Netzer 162, 165
Clairmont College
    VisGirda 31
clay bodies, experimental
    Forrest 173,173c, 175, 176
    Mangus 194-195, 200
    Neely 209-210, 210c, 214, 215-216
    Zakin 247, 247c, 248, 249-250, 253
clay body additions - 268-269
    Katz 49, 49c, 51c

clay body aging
    Chabot 218c
    Cochrane 92
clay body maturity
    Chalke 42
    di Petta 235
clay body plasticizing agents
    Forrest 174
    Higby 105c
clay body scumming
    Gill, Andrea 71
    Pinnell 261-263
    Schnabel 35
Clay Studio of Philadelphia
    Mangus 200
    Patterson 125
    Pierantozzi 118, 119
Cleveland Institute of Art
    Kwong 138
    Mangus 199, 200
    Patterson 123, 124
    Pitts 103
Cochrane, Bruce - 68
    Forrest 178
coil forming
    Barringer 166c, 167c, 166-167, 171
    Chabot 217, 218c
    Deller 84c, 85
    Gill, Andrea 72c
    Hayakawa 188
    Huey 143, 148c
    Kwong 134, 135c, 138
    Mangus 194, 199c
    Netzer 159, 159c, 161c
    Schnabel 34c, 35, 38
    Scotchie 181, 183c, 185
    Walker 202
    Zakin 246c, 249
Coles, Hobart
    Hirsch 10
Colorado, University of
    Chabot 223
    Gill, Andrea 76
    Gill, John 17
    Higby 108, 109
    Pinnell 265
Columbia College (Missouri)
    Pinnell 265
Columbia University
    Netzer 162, 164
computers (and ceramics)
    Roy 131
    Strassberg 21c, 25, 26
    Zakin 247
Contact
    Tipton 245
Coper, Hans
    Deller 89
    Hirsch 11c
Corcoran School of Art
    Gill, Andrea 74
Cornelius, Phillip
    VisGirda 31
Cornish School of Allied Arts
    Gill, John 14, 16
cracking
    Barringer 167
    Chabot 217, 218c
    Higby 105c, 106, 108
    Huey 143,144c, 145c
    Netzer 161c , 165
    Pierantozzi 115
    Pinnell 263

Roy 127, 127c, 129
Scotchie 180c, 181, 183c
Strassberg 21c, 22
Walker 202
Cranbrook Academy of Art
Deller 88
Forrest 178
Crumrine, Jim
Netzer 162
cryolite
Chalke 44c, 46c, 47
Scotchie 183c
Currier, Ann
Chabot 223
Forrest 178
Gill, John 19
Hayakawa 192
Pinnell 265
Pitts 103
Currier Gallery
Chabot 220
Cushing, Val
Cochrane 93
Gill, Andrea 76
Gill, John 17, 19
Higby 112
Neely 212
Netzer 164
Pinnell 265
Pitts 103
Zakin 251
damp box
Cochrane 92, 95c
Pinnell 263
Roy 127, 127c
Davis, Don
Scotchie 184
decals
Spinski 64, 67c
decoration/ornamentation
Chabot 218, 218c
Forrest 173c, 174c, 175,
178, 179
Frey 257
Gill, Andrea 69, 69c, 71, 73,
74, 75c, 76
MacDonald 78, 79c, 80, 83
Oestreich 229
deformation of clay forms
Barringer 167
Walker 202
Delaware, University of
Spinski 66
Deller, Harris - 68, 271
Dennison University
Tipton 243
Devore, Richard
Deller 88, 90
di Petta, Angelo - 208, 269
Dollhausen, Jack
VisGirda 31
Drake University
VisGirda 28
drying procedures
Chabot 218, 220
Cochrane 92, 95c
Frey 254c
Hayakawa 188
MacDonald 79c
Pinnell 263, 264c
Roy 127, 127c
Scotchie 181, 183c
VisGirda 28
Walker 201c, 202-203

education - 272-273
Edwards, Thorne
Gill, John 16
Tipton 242
Egyptian faience/paste
Forrest 173-176, 173c,174c,
175c, 176c, 178-179, 269,
270
Higby 111
Schnabel 37
Elsner, Larry
Neely 214
embedded imagery
Chabot 218, 218c, 220, 223,
223c, 224
Erickson, Robert
Notkin 57
Eton College
Forrest 178
European Ceramic Work Center
Scotchie 181, 186
extruded forms
di Petta 237, 238, 269
Hayakawa 188, 191c
Farmington Valley Art Center
Barringer 171
Farnam School of Art
Chalke 45
Ferguson, Ken
Gill, Andrea 74
Gill, John 17
Katz 52
Notkin 57
Fetzer, Margaret
Tipton 242
Filer, Pat
Mangus 200
Fina, Angela
Forrest 178
Lawton 156
Scotchie 184
firing - experimental
Chalke 42, 44, 47
di Petta 237c
Gill, John 14
Mangus 194, 195c, 196c,
197, 199c, 200
Neely 209, 209c, 210c, 210-
211, 212, 212c, 215-216
Pinnell 260c, 263c, 264c,
265, 267
floral imagery/flowers/gardens
Frey 258c, 259
Huey 142c, 143, 144c, 145
Kwong 136, 138
Patterson 124c
Pitts 99, 103, 104
Schnabel 38, 38c, 40
Walker 204c, 207c
Florida State University
Lawton 156
Florida, University of
Schnabel 37
Florida, University of South
Hayakawa 192
**forming methods, experimen-
tal**
di Petta 233-234, 235c, 237c,
238, 269
Frey 256c, 258-259
Hayakawa 187c,188, 191c
Higby 105c,106-108
Huey 144c
Oestreich 225c, 226, 227c,

229, 229c, 231
Pierantozzi 115, 115c, 119
Zakin 246-247, 246c, 248-249
Forrest, Neil -141, 269, 270
Frey, Barbara - 208, 272
Frimkess, Michael
Barringer 171
Frumkin, Allen
Notkin 59, 60
Fullbright Grant
Deller 89
Katz 54
Funk ceramics - 274
Deller 88, 89
Gill, John 16, 17
Hayakawa 190, 192, 193
Notkin 56
VisGirda 27
Walker 205
Furman, David
Spinski 65
Garrison Art and Craft Center
Chabot 222
Garth Clark Gallery
Lawton 156
Notkin 60
Georgia Southern College
Deller 89
Gernhardt, Henry
Frey 258
MacDonald 81, 83
Gill, Andrea - 68, 272, 275-276
Forrest 178
Gill, John 17
Pitts 103
Scotchie 185
Gill, John - iiic, 6, 269, 271
Forrest 178
Gill, Andrea 76
Pitts 103
Gillard, Joseph
MacDonald 80, 81
glaze application, experimental
Barringer 168-169
Chalke 41c, 42, 42c, 44, 44c,
47
Gill Andrea 69c, 72, 73
Gill, John 14, 18c
Hayakawa 190, 191c
Lawton 151c, 154
MacDonald 78, 79c
Mangus 195c,196c, 197,199c
Pinnell 263, 264c, 265
Roy 127c, 128c, 129c, 130-
131
Tipton 239, 239c, 240, 244c
Walker 201c, 203
glaze, crawling
Hayakawa 187c
Scotchie 181, 181c,
Tipton 240, 240c
Roy 130c
glaze, industrial
Roy 126, 131
Walker 203
glaze, low viscosity
Roy 127c, 129
glaze, metallic surfaces
Mangus 196c, 197
Patterson 121, 123c
Scotchie180c, 181, 181c,183c
VisGirda 28, 29c, 32c
glaze, multiple layers
Barringer 166c, 168-169, 172

Chalke 41c, 42, 44
di Petta 235
Hirsch 8, 9
Pinnell 263, 264c, 265
Tipton 239, 240, 244c
glaze recipes, experimental -
269
Chalke 41c, 42, 46c
Deller 89
di Petta 235
Mangus 196c, 197, 199c
Oestreich 226-227, 229,
230-231
Roy 127c, 128c, 129-131
Tipton 240, 242-243
Goodheart, John
Frey 257
Greek pottery
Lawton 156
Green, Ken
Hirsch 10
Greenwich House
Forrest 179
Netzer 162, 165
gritty slip
Chalke 47
Hirsch 8c, 9
Hamada, Shoji
Oestreich 230
Hampton University
MacDonald 80, 81
Handy, Arthur
Roy 131
Hardesty, Bill
Deller 88
Harper, William
Lawton 156
Hartsook, Jane
Netzer 162
Harvey, Roger
Gill, Andrea 74
Hayakawa, Joanne - 141
**Haystack Mountain School of
Crafts**
Chabot 222
Higby 112
Huey 147
Lawton 157
Schnabel 38
Helm, Robert
VisGirda 31
Hepburn, Tony
Forrest 178
Gill, John 19
Pitts 103
Schnabel 37
Scotchie 185
Higby, Wayne - 68, 275
Cochrane 93, 94
Forrest 178
Gill, Andrea 76
Gill, John 17, 19
Mangus 200
Neely 212
Pinnell 265
Pitts 103
Schnabel 37
Scotchie 185
Hindes, Chuck
Mangus 200
Hirsch, Ric - 6, 272
Holcomb, Jan
Walker 205
Honey, William Boyer

Gill, Andrea 74
Hotchkiss, Richard
  VisGirda 30, 31
Huey, Linda - iiic, 141, 275
Hughto, Margie
  Frey 258
  MacDonald 83
human form
  Barringer 170, 171
  Gill, Andrea 71c, 73,
  Hayakawa 188c, 190, 191c,
    193
  Lawton 155c
  Mangus 197, 197c
  Notkin 55c, 56, 58
  Pitts 104
  Strassberg 24c
  VisGirda 32c
Illian, Clarie
  Pinnell 267
Illinois Wesleyan University
  VisGirda 31, 33
Indiana University
  Frey 255, 257, 258
  Scotchie 186
  Spinski 65-66
innovation - 268-269
insects
  Forrest 173c, 174c, 178
  Kwong 135
  Mangus 197
Iowa, University of Northern
  Schnabel 38
Italy and Italian culture
  * see also Faenza, majolica
  Cochrane 96
  di Petta 232, 233, 236, 238
  Forrest 173c, 179
  Gill, Andrea 71, 71c, 74
  Hayakawa 193
  Mangus 196c, 197
  Walker 205c
Jacob, Howard
  Neely 211
Japan and Japanese culture
  *see also Oribe work
  Chalke 43
  Cochrane 93, 97
  Frey 254c, 259
  Gill, Andrea 73
  Hayakawa 192
  Hirsch 10-11
  Katz 52, 268
  Kwong 136
  Lawton 154
  MacDonald 81
  Neely 209, 212, 214c, 214-215
  Oestreich 230, 231
John Abbott College
  Cochrane 93
Johnson, Elma
  Scotchie 182
Jones, Ann
  Higby 109
Jones, Owen
  Gill, Andrea 74
Kaganoff, Sheldon
  Hayakawa 190
Kaneko, Jun
  Forrest 178
  Kwong 136
  Mangus 200
Kansas City Art Institute
  Gill, Andrea 74, 76

Gill, John 16-17
  Katz 52
  Notkin 57, 58, 59
  Pinnell 266c, 267
Kansas State University
  Spinski 65
Kansas, University of
  Neely 212
Karnes, Karen
  Chabot 222
Katz, Louis - 6, 268, 289
Kent State University
  Gill, Andrea 76
  Gill, John 18
  Mangus 200
kiln shelves
  di Petta 237c
  Huey 145c
  Forrest 175
  Netzer 159c
  Strassberg 22-23
  Zakin 246c, 249
Kohler Arts/Industry Program
  VisGirda 31
  Walker 207
Korea and Korean culture
  Deller 89
  Kwong 136
  Neely 214
  Pitts 99, 103
Kottler, Howard
  Hayakawa 190
  Higby 111
  Walker 204
Kwong, Eva - 68, 269
  Mangus 200
  Pitts 103
  VisGirda 31
Kwong, Hui Kwa
  Netzer 162
kyanite
  Lawton 151, 151c,
  Scotchie 181, 183c
landscape imagery
  Higby 107c, 108, 109c, 111,112
Lau, Bill
  MacDonald 81
  Netzer 162
Lavierdier, Bruno
  Netzer 162
Law, Mary
  Mangus 199
Lawton, Jim -141, 271, 272
Leach, Bernard
  Chalke 45
  Oestreich 225, 229
Levine, Marilyn
  Spinski 65
Levine, Phil
  Gill, John 14
lime blows
  Katz 49
Littell, Biz
  Mangus 200
livelihood and ceramics
  Barringer 171
  Chalke 47
  Gill, John 17-18
  Huey 146, 147
  Mangus 200
  Neely 211, 212
  Notkin 59-60
  Oestreich 229, 230
  Patterson 125

Pierantozzi 116, 119
  Roy 131
  Tipton 241c, 243
  Walker 205-207
Louisiana State University
  Lawton 156, 157
  Patterson 124, 125
  Schnabel 38
low fire clay bodies
  Chalke 42
  Gill, Andrea 69c, 73, 76
  Mangus 197
  Schnabel 38, 40
  Spinski, 61, 64
lusters
  Hayakawa 190, 191c
  Hirsch 10
  Mangus 194c, 196c, 197,199c
  Netzer 162
  Spinski 64
  VisGirda 27c, 28, 29c, 30c,
    31, 32c
Lyon, Bob
  Schnabel 38
MacDonald, David - vc, 68,
271-272
  Frey 258
MacKenzie, Warren
  Mangus 199
  Oestreich 229 -230
magnesium hydroxide
  Spinski 61
majolica
  Cochrane 94c, 96
  Gill, Andrea 71, 71c, 75c, 76
Mangus, Kirk -141
  Kwong 138
  Pitts 103
  VisGirda 31
Manhart, Tom
  Pitts 101
Manitius, Julia
  Cochrane 93
Mankato State University
  Strassberg 21, 24c, 25, 26
Marks, Graham
  Chabot 222
Marshall, Bill
  Oestreich 230
Martz, Karl
  Frey 257-258
  Spinski 65-66
Massachusetts College of Art
  Huey 145
Massachusetts, University of
  Gill, Andrea 76
  Lawton 157
  MacDonald 81
Mathews, John
  Spinski 65
McKinley, Don & Ruth
  Cochrane 94, 96
**Memphis College of Art and
Design**
  Tipton 242
Memphis State University
  Strassberg 24
Memphis, University of
  Tipton 242
Michigan, University of
  Higby 111
  Katz 52
  Lawton 157
  MacDonald 81

Strassberg 24
Millikin University
  VisGirda 31
Milnes, Bob
  Hayakawa 192
Minnesota, University of
  MacKenzie 229
Minoan (pots)
  Higby 109
mixed media
  Hayakawa 188, 188c, 189c
  Huey 143, 144c
  Netzer 163-164
  Notkin 55, 55c, 60
  VisGirda 27c, 32c
modular forms
  Netzer 161c, 164c, 165
molds, and mold forming
  Chabot 217, 218, 218c
  di Petta 232, 232c, 233,
    234, 235c, 238
  Forrest 174
  Frey 257
  Gill, Andrea 69c, 71, 72c, 75c
  Gill, John 16c
  Higby 105c, 111, 112
  Mangus 195, 196c
  Netzer 158c, 159, 160, 161c,
    164c
  Notkin 55, 55c, 56c, 57, 57c,
    58c, 60
  Patterson 123
  Spinski 62, 63c
  Tipton 242
molds, surface imagery
  Higby 105c, 106c, 107
  Mangus 195, 196c
  Pierantozzi 115, 119
molochite
  Deller 84c, 85, 86c, 87
  Pitts 98c
Montana State University
  Katz 52
Moravian Pottery
  Hayakawa 193
motifs
  Gill, Andrea 69c, 73, 74
Moty, Joyce
  Gill, John 16
multiple firings
  Chalke 41c, 44, 44c
  Spinski 61c, 62, 62c, 63c, 67c
  Tipton 239, 239c, 240, 241c,
    242, 244c, 245
  VisGirda 27c, 28, 31, 32c
**Museum of Contemporary
Crafts**
  Hirsch 11
**Museum of Natural History,
New York City**
  Chabot 222
Myers, Ron
  Patterson 125
**National Endowment for the
Arts**
  Gill, Andrea 76
  Gill, John 17
  Lawton 157
nature, forms from
  Barringer 170
  di Petta 236
  Forrest 174c, 178,
  Huey 142, 142c, 143, 144c,
    145, 147, 148c, 149

Kwong 135, 136
Schnabel 34, 38, 40
Nebraska, University of
Higby 111
Pinnell 267
Neely, John - 208, 269
Nelson, Glenn
Cochrane 93
Netzer, Sylvia - ivc, 141, 270, 274
Newman, Ruth
Walker 204
New York, State University of
Frey 258
Hirsch 10
Strassberg 24
Zakin 251
Nicholas, Donna
Chabot 222
North Carolina, University of
Scotchie 182
Notkin, Richard - 6, 273
Nova Scotia College of Art and Design
Cochrane 93, 94, 96
Forrest 179
Oestreich, Jeff - 208, 270, 272, 274, 275
Ohio State University
Tipton 242
Walker 207
Ohio University
Neely 212
Ohr, George
Mangus 194c
Ontario College of Art
di Petta 232, 236
Roy 131
organic materials (in ceramic recipes)
Huey 142c, 143, 145c
Katz 49, 49c, 51c, 53c
Oribe work
Chalke 43c
Lawton 154
Ostrom, Walter
Cochrane 93, 96
outdoor ceramics
Walker 207
paper pulp in clay
Spinski 62
Park Street Studio
Barringer 171
Parmalee, Cullen
Neely 211
Parry, William
Neely 212
Schnabel 37
Strassberg 24
Zakin 251
Pasadena City College
VisGirda 31
pattern
Barringer 168
Deller 87
Forrest 178
Neely 215
Patterson 271
Pierantozzi 115, 116c, 119, 271
Patterson, Neil - 68, 271, 272
Pierantozzi 119
Peed, Mike
Katz 52
Penland School of Crafts

Huey 147
Lawton 156, 157
Mangus 199
Patterson 121, 123c, 124
Pitts 103
Schnabel 38, 39c, 275
Scotchie 184
personal identity - 274-275
Peters Valley
Mangus 200
Pharris, Mark
Gill, Andrea 74
Pierantozzi, Sandi - cover art, 68, 271, 272
Patterson 125
pinch forming
Barringer 166c, 167, 167c
Chabot 217, 218c
Deller 89
Gill, John 15c
Hayakawa 188
Mangus 195, 195c, 196c
Pierantozzi 115, 115c
Pinnell, Peter - 208, 275
Pitts, Greg - 68, 275
plaster
di Petta 234
Pompili, Lucien
Gill, John 17
Pop Art - 274
Pope, Ric
Katz 52
porcelain
Cochrane 91c, 92, 97, 97c
Deller 84c, 85, 85c, 86c, 87, 87c
Frey 254c, 255, 256c, 257c, 258, 258c
Gill, John 17
Hayakawa 188, 191c
Higby 105c, 106c, 106-107, 108, 112, 275
Kwong 136, 137, 138
Mangus 200
Neely 210, 214, 214c,
Pitts 98c, 99c, 100, 103
Roy 127, 127c, 128c, 131
Walker 201c, 202, 204c, 206c
Poor, Henry Varnum
Gill, Andrea 74
Portnoy, Theo
Spinski 66
post fire assembly
Higby 105c
Netzer 161c,162-163, 164c
Schnabel 34c, 35, 37
Potter, Tom
Chabot 223
Pinnell 265
Pousette Dart, Richard
Zakin 251
Pratt Institute
Barringer 171
Chabot 220
Netzer 165
raku
Higby 107c, 109c, 111, 112
Hirsch 8, 8c, 9, 9c, 10, 11,11c
Lawton 155c, 156
Strassberg 24
Randall, Ted
Gill, Andrea 76
Gill, John 17
Higby 111-112

Zakin 251
Reeve, John
Chalke 45
Reitz, Don
Cochrane 93
Mangus 199
Strassberg 24
Rhode Island School of Design
Gill, Andrea 74
Gill, John 17
Higby 111
Huey 147
Kwong 135, 136, 138
Mangus 199, 200
Pitts 103
Walker 205
Rhodes, Daniel
Zakin 251
Rice, Jacqueline
Gill, Andrea 74
Gill, John 16, 17
Walker 205
Rie, Lucie
Oestreich 230
Rippon, Ruth
VisGirda 30
Rochester Community College
VisGirda 31
Rodaco Clay
Roy 131
Rosen, Stanley
Barringer 171
Roy, Ron - 68, 269, 271, 274
safety
Gill, Andrea 72
Hayakawa 191c
Oestreich 229
Pinnell 261, 263
Schnabel 35
Scotchie 183c
saggar firing
Neely 210c
Sakezumi, Katseyuki
Mangus 200
Salomon, Judith
Patterson 123
Pitts 103
salt firing
Cochrane 93, 94
Kwong 133c, 134, 138
Mangus 197, 197c
Neely 210, 211, 212
Salter, Pam
Neely 212
San Diego State University
Hayakawa 193
Walker 207
sandblasting - 269
Spinski 64
sanding
Barringer 169
Deller 85, 86c
di Petta 235c, 236
Sault College
Hirsch 10
Schnabel, JoAnn - 6, 275
School for American Crafts at the Rochester Institute of Technology
Hirsch 10
Schulman, Norman
Gill, John 17
Higby 111
Kwong 136

Mangus 200
science, images from
Kwong 133, 134-136, 140
Neely 209, 211, 214-216
Netzer 160-161
Scotchie, Virginia - iic, 141
Sederstorm, Robert
Hirsch 10
sgraffito and incising
Barringer 168
Deller 85, 86c
Kwong 133c, 134, 134c, 135c, 140
Shaw, Richard
Spinski 65
Sheridan College (School of Craft and Design)
Cochrane 94, 96, 97
Forrest 178
Sherman, Hoyt
Tipton 242
silicon carbide
Chalke 41c, 42
Kwong 138
Simon, Michael and Sandy
Lawton 156
size, questions of
Chabot 223
Notkin 56-57, 60
Walker 207
Skidmore College
Chabot 222
slab forming, experimental
Chabot 218, 218c, 223
Chalke 41c, 42
Gill, John 14
Huey 143, 144c
Netzer 162
slips
Barringer 166c, 168-169, 170c, 171
Frey 254, 258
Gill, Andrea 69c, 71-73, 76
Hirsch 8c, 9
Kwong 133c, 134, 134c, 135c, 138, 138c
Neely 212c
Pitts 99, 99c, 100, 101c
Spinski 61, 63c, 67c
Tipton 240, 241c, 242, 243
slip trailing
di Petta 234, 235c, 236c
Pinnell 263, 264c
slumping
Chabot 217, 218c
di Petta 235
Higby 107, 108
Zakin 247, 248, 251, 251c
Smithson, Robert
Kwong 136
Smithsonian Institution
Higby 111
soaking (during kiln firing)
Chalke 41c, 42
Frey 254c
Pinnell 260c, 263c, 264c, 265
soda firing
Chalke 47
Katz 50c, 51, 51c
Oestreich 226-227, 228, 231, 270, 272
Sohngen, Peter
Tipton 242
Soldner, Paul

Chabot 222
Higby 109,111
VisGirda 31
South Carolina, University of
Scotchie 180, 186
Southern Illinois University
Deller 89
Sperry, Robert
Hayakawa 190
Walker 204
Spinski, Victor - 6, 269, 270, 272
Spleth, Tom
Forrest 178
Pinnell 265
Pitts 103
St. John, Richard
Neely 211
Staffel, Rudi
Kwong 136
stains
Barringer 166c, 168,
Chabot 218, 218c
Forrest 175
Frey 254c, 255, 255c, 256c,
259
Gill Andrea 71, 71c, 72, 73
Gill, John 18c, 19
Schnabel 35
Tipton 242
Walker 203
Zakin 248
Staley, Chris
Walker 205
Staller, Jeff
Netzer 164
stamped imagery
Oestreich 226
Pierantozzi 115
Starkey, Peter
Patterson 125
stencils
Gill, Andrea 73, 75c
Stephenson, John
Higby 111
Katz 52
MacDonald 81
Strassberg, 24
Stewart, Bill
Strassberg 24
Strassberg, Roy - 6, 270, 272,
275
Stull, Robert -
MacDonald 78, 81
S'vres
Hayakawa 193
Syrause University
Frey 258
MacDonald 77, 78, 81, 83
Zakin 251
talc body
Chabot 218c
Chalke 42
Gill, Andrea 71, 72
Lawton 151
Schnabel 35
Spinski 61
Takeazu, Toshiko
Mangus 199
Tam, Reuben
Zakin 251
teapots and teapot forms
Deller 84c, 87, 89
Frey 254, 254c, 255c, 256c,
257, 257c, 258c, 259

Gill, John 14, 16
Lawton 152c, 153c, 154,
154c, 272
Neely 209c, 212, 212c
Notkin 56, 57c, 58c, 60
Pinnell 260c, 261c
Tipton 240, 241c, 242, 244c
templates
Pinnell 263, 264c,
Temple, Byron
Lawton 156
Mangus 199
Netzer 162
Tepper, Irv
Gill, John 16
terra sigillatta
Chabot 218c, 222, 223
Cochrane 92, 92c, 94c, 95c,
96, 96c
Gill, Andrea 72c
Hirsch 8c, 9, 11c
Huey 142c, 143, 145c
Lawton 151c, 152, 153c, 154
Patterson 123
Pierantozzi 116
Pinnell 260c, 263, 263c, 264c,
265
Pitts 99c
Roy 128c, 129c, 130, 130c
Strassberg 23
testing
Chalke 47
Forrest 178, 179
Gill, Andrea 72
Huey 143
Kwong 136, 137-138
Neely 209-211, 214
Roy 131
Tipton 240, 242
Texas A & M
Frey 259
Katz 54
Timmock, George
Katz 52
Tipton, Barbara - 208, 269
Chalke 41, 47
Tollefson, Howard
Deller 88
Tower, James
Chalke 45
trompe l'oeil
Spinski 61c, 65
Tulane University
Schnabel 38
Tulsa, University of
Pitts 101, 103
Turner, Robert
Cochrane 93
Forrest 178
Gill, John 17
Higby 112
Lawton 156
Neely 212
Pitts 101, 103
Zakin 251
Tweedy, Joan
Chabot 222
Tyler, Chris
Hirsch 10
Tyler School of Art
Kwong 136
Patterson 125
underglaze colors
Chabot 218, 218c

Huey 146, 146c
Neely 212
Netzer 160
Pitts 100, 101c
VisGirda 32c
Utah State University
Neely 214
utility, questions of
Deller 89
Forrest 175, 178, 179
Katz 52
Lawton 154-156
Mangus 200
Neely 209, 212, 214
Oestreich 225, 226c
Patterson 120, 121, 123
Pierantozzi 113, 116, 119
Roy 127, 127c, 129, 131, 132
Tipton 242, 244c, 245
Walker 204-206, 207
Van Briggle Pottery
Higby 108
Vander Sluis, George
Zakin 251
vessel form
Barringer 167c, 171
Chalke 47
Cochrane 93
Deller 84, 88, 89
Gill, Andrea 73, 74, 76
Katz 48, 52
Lawton 154
Patterson 121, 123
Pitts 98, 99, 103
Vietnam War
Chabot 220
Notkin 56-58
Spinski 66
VisGirda, Rimas - 6
Kwong 138
Voulkos, Peter - 274
Chalke 47
Hirsch 11
Walker, Jamie -141
wall pieces and tiles
Chabot 222c, 223
Deller 85
Forrest 173c, 174, 175, 179,
179c
Hayakawa 193
Higby 111c, 112
Huey 143, 148c, 149
Kwong 137, 137c
Tipton 240, 241c, 242, 244c
Zakin 246, 246c, 247, 247c,
248, 248c, 249, 252c
war and war imagery- *see
also Vietnam War* -
Notkin 56, 58, 59
Strassberg 22, 22c, 23c, 24,
25, 26, 270, 275
VisGirda 27c, 29
Warashina, Patti
Gill, John 16
Hayakawa 190
Walker 204, 207
Washington State University
Kwong 138
Mangus 200
VisGirda 31
Washington, University of
Hayakawa 190
Higby 111
Walker 204, 207

wax finishes
di Petta 234, 235c
Netzer 158c, 159c, 160, 161c,
162c,
VisGirda 28
wax resist
Oestreich 227, 227c
VisGirda 28, 30
Weiser, Kurt
Gill, Andrea 76
Katz 52
Notkin 60
West Virginia University
Scotchie 185-186
wheel forming, experimental
Katz 49-50
Mangus 195
Tipton 240, 242
VisGirda 28, 32c
Walker 201c, 202, 203, 204
Wichita State University
Neely 211
Wildenhain, Franz
Hirsch 10
William Traver Gallery
Walker 204c
Winocur, Bob
Kwong 136
wood ash
Cochrane 92, 95c, 96c
Neely 214
Oestreich 230
wood firing
Cochrane 92-93, 95c, 96, 97
Katz 48, 50c
Kwong 138
Mangus 195, 197, 199c
Neely 214
Oestreich 270
Patterson 121, 123c
Pitts 98c, 103
Woodman, Betty
Chabot 223
Gill, Andrea 76
Gill, John 17
Higby 109
Pinnell 265
work strategies - 269-270
Wyman, William
Huey 146
Yixing [Yi Hsing]
Frey 257, 259
Neely 210
Notkin 56, 60
Pinnell 261, 263, 264c, 265,
267
Young Americans exhibition -
see American Craft Museum
Zakin, Richard - ic, iv-v, 208,
276
Strassberg 24
Zeller, Joe
Neely 212, 214
Zimmerman, Arnold
Cochrane 93
VisGirda 31
Zirbes, Georgette
Katz 52